The Law of Love

Sel...

Know thou of a certainty that Love is the secret of God's holy Dispensation, the manifestation of the All-Merciful, the fountain of spiritual outpourings.

Love is heaven's kindly light, the Holy Spirit's eternal breath that vivifieth the human soul.

Love is the cause of God's revelation unto man, the vital bond inherent, in accordance with the divine creation, in the realities of things.

Love is the one means that ensureth true felicity both in this world and the next.

Love is the light that guideth in darkness, the living link that uniteth God with man, that assureth the progress of every illumined soul.

Love is the most great law that ruleth this mighty and heavenly cycle, the unique power that bindeth together the divers elements of this material world, the supreme magnetic force that directeth the movements of the spheres in the celestial realms.

Love revealeth with unfailing and limitless power the mysteries latent in the universe.

Love is the spirit of life unto the adorned body of mankind, the establisher of true civilization in this mortal world, and the shedder of imperishable glory upon every high-aiming race and nation.

'Abdu'l-Bahá[1]

Other works by same authors:

John S. Hatcher:
Ali's Dream: The Story of Bahá'u'lláh (1980)
*From the Auroral Darkness:
    The Life and Poetry of Robert E. Hayden* (1984)
The Purpose of Physical Reality: The Kingdom of Names (1987)
Conversations (1988)
A Sense of History: A Collection of Poems (1990)
The Arc of Ascent: The Purpose of Physical Reality II (1994)

William S. Hatcher:
Foundations of Mathematics (1968)
The Logical Foundations of Mathematics (1982)
The Bahá'í Faith: The Emerging Global Religion (1989)
Logic and Logos: Essays on Science, Religion, and Philosophy (1990)
'The Foundations of Mathematics', *Encyclopædia Britannica* (1997)

The Law of Love Enshrined
Selected Essays

by

John S. Hatcher and William S. Hatcher

> Within every blade of grass are enshrined
> the mysteries of an inscrutable Wisdom,
> and upon every rose-bush
> a myriad nightingales pour out,
> in blissful rapture, their melody.
> Its wondrous tulips unfold the mystery
> of the undying Fire in the Burning Bush,
> and its sweet savors of holiness
> breathe the perfume of the Messianic Spirit.
> *Bahá'u'lláh*[2]

GEORGE RONALD
OXFORD

George Ronald, Publisher
46 High Street, Kidlington, Oxford OX5 2DN

© John S. Hatcher and William S. Hatcher 1996
All Rights Reserved

*A Cataloguing in Publication Number
is available from the British Library*

ISBN 0-85398-405-0

Typesetting by ComputerCraft, Knoxville, Tennessee, USA
Printed at Redwood Books, Trowbridge, Wiltshire.

for Lucia and Judith

Contents

Acknowledgements	ix
Preface (John Hatcher)	xi
Prologue on Proving God *(William Hatcher)*	1
Causality, Composition and the Origin of Existence *(William Hatcher)*	19
A Scientific Proof of the Existence of God *(William Hatcher)*	43
The Doctrine of the 'Most Great Infallibility' in Relation to the 'Station of Distinction' *(John Hatcher)*	59
Unsealing the Choice Wine at the Family Reunion *(John Hatcher)*	101
The Kitáb-i-Aqdas: The Causality Principle in the World of Being *(William Hatcher)*	113
Some Thoughts on Gender Distinction in the Kitáb-i-Aqdas: The Bahá'í Principle of Complementarity *(John Hatcher)*	158
The Model of Penology in the Kitáb-i-Aqdas *(John Hatcher)*	173
The Concept of Spirituality *(William Hatcher)*	189
Bibliography	251
References and Notes	255

Acknowledgements

William Hatcher's article 'A Scientific Proof of the Existence of God' appeared in *The Journal of Bahá'í Studies* vol. 5, no. 4. John Hatcher's article 'Unsealing the Choice Wine at the Family Reunion' was presented at the Association for Bahá'í Studies Symposium on the Kitáb-i-Aqdas, McGill University, Montreal, Canada, 17 June 1993 and was subsequently published in *The Journal of Bahá'í Studies*, vol. 6, no. 3. William Hatcher's article 'The Kitáb-i-Aqdas: The Causality Principle in the World of Being' was first published in *Bahá'í World* 1993-4. A version of John Hatcher's article 'Some Thoughts on Gender Distinction in The Kitáb-i-Aqdas: The Bahá'í Principle of Complementarity' was presented at the Association for Bahá'í Studies 14th Annual Meeting, Irvine, California, 1989, and subsequently published in *The Journal of Bahá'í Studies* vol. 2, no. 3. John Hatcher's article 'The Model of Penology in The Kitáb-i-Aqdas' was presented at the Fifth Scripture Studies Colloquium, Wilmette, Illinois, 31 March 1995. William Hatcher's 'The Concept of Spirituality' first appeared in Bahá'í Studies 11 in 1982.

We wish to express our appreciation to LouHelen Bahá'í School for inviting us to teach courses there together during the summer of 1995. It was during this opportunity to work together that this project was conceived. Lastly, we want to express our gratitude to our parents, Albert and Helen Hatcher, for nurturing in us the love of truth in all its forms.

Preface

Bahá'u'lláh, the Prophet and Founder of the Bahá'í Faith, states in several places that the capacity to understand important truths, such as those 'mysteries' contained in the utterances of the Manifestations, is not dependent on traditional learning but on spiritual capacity and receptivity:

> The understanding of His words and the comprehension of the utterances of the Birds of Heaven are in no wise dependent upon human learning. They depend solely upon purity of heart, chastity of soul, and freedom of spirit. This is evidenced by those who, today, though without a single letter of the accepted standards of learning, are occupying the loftiest seats of knowledge; and the garden of their hearts is adorned, through the showers of divine grace, with the roses of wisdom and the tulips of understanding.[1]

It is in this same vein that Bahá'u'lláh exhorts His followers to seek understanding about scripture not from an authoritative body of scholars but from those who are 'initiated into the divine mysteries' and are 'illumined in heart':

> Inasmuch as it hath been clearly shown that only those who are initiated into the divine mysteries can comprehend the melodies uttered by the Bird of Heaven, it is therefore incumbent upon every one to seek enlightenment from the illumined in heart and from the Treasuries of divine mysteries regarding the intricacies of God's Faith and the abstruse allusions in the utterances of the Day-springs of Holiness. Thus will these mysteries be unravelled, not by the aid of acquired learning, but solely through the assistance of God and the outpourings of His grace.[2]

Of course, since there is no specific group of individuals designated by these appellations (other than 'Abdu'l-Bahá and the Guardian),[3] it is the task of each individual to decide who among us is 'initiated into the divine mysteries' or 'illumined in heart'. What is clear from these passages is that these individuals may not be those who are the most learned in any traditional sense – they will not necessarily be those who have the greatest academic achievement or who have become recognized as having scholarly capacity.

Considered out of context, such statements might be taken to imply that Bahá'u'lláh rejects ordinary learning and scholarship or that 'human learning' or 'acquired learning' are somehow detrimental to spiritual insight or understanding. Nothing could be farther from the truth. Bahá'u'lláh repeatedly praises traditional learning as an essential means for human advancement: 'Knowledge is as wings to man's life, and a ladder for his ascent. Its acquisition is incumbent upon everyone.'[4]

What Bahá'u'lláh seems to be observing in these passages is that traditional learning, when it becomes abused or misused, can become an equally powerful deterrent to human progress. It is in this context that Bahá'u'lláh cites the tradition that says, 'The most grievous of all veils is the veil of knowledge'.[5] It is in this same context that Bahá'u'lláh praises the rank of those scholars who have not become blinded by pride in their own learning and who have instead employed traditional learning as an aid to recognizing the truth:

> Great is the blessedness of that divine that hath not allowed knowledge to become a veil between him and the One Who is the Object of all knowledge, and who, when the Self-Subsisting appeared, hath turned with a beaming face towards Him. He, in truth, is numbered with the learned. The inmates of Paradise seek the blessing of his breath, and his lamp sheddeth its radiance over all who are in heaven and on earth. He, verily, is numbered with the inheritors of the Prophets.[6]

In another sense, Bahá'u'lláh's caveats about traditional learning allude to the question of how one can be considered truly learned if one's mental prowess fails to induce a reformed character or an enhanced perception of reality. For example, Bahá'u'lláh asks who is more learned, the one adjudged by academic standards to have scholarly acumen, or one who has a transformed character and who is capable of recognizing the advent of the Manifestation:

> Consider, how can he that faileth in the day of God's Revelation to attain unto the grace of the 'Divine Presence' and to recognize His Manifestation, be justly called learned, though he may have spent aeons in the pursuit of knowledge, and acquired all the limited and material learning of men? It is surely evident that he can in no wise be regarded as possessed of true knowledge. Whereas, the most unlettered of all men, if he be honored with this supreme distinction, he verily is accounted as one of those divinely-learned men whose knowledge is of God; for such a man hath attained the acme of knowledge, and hath reached the furthermost summit of learning.[7]

In still another sense Bahá'u'lláh's assessment of traditional sorts of learning and scholarship focuses on the fact that in the past the so-called learned ones (the ecclesiastical leaders and divines of previous dispensations) have often been the most staunchly closed-minded to the new revelation:

> Leaders of religion, in every age, have hindered their people from attaining the shores of eternal salvation, inasmuch as they held the reins of authority in their mighty grasp. Some for the lust of leadership, others through want of knowledge and understanding, have been the cause of the deprivation of the people.[8]

Consequently, Bahá'u'lláh exhorts the learned ones of this day not to be closed-minded, not to judge the validity of this revelation by standards they have devised to reinforce their own opinions. In short, Bahá'u'lláh exhorts the learned to evaluate the revelation by its own merit:

> O leaders of religion! Weigh not the Book of God with such standards and sciences as are current amongst you, for the Book

itself is the unerring balance established amongst men. In this most perfect balance whatsoever the peoples and kindreds of the earth possess must be weighed, while the measure of its weight should be tested according to its own standard, did ye but know it.[9]

In the most general sense, then, Bahá'u'lláh is simply admonishing His followers to be good scholars. He is certainly not asking them to become mindless fanatics nor to abandon traditional learning or scholarly training. Bahá'u'lláh does note that traditional learning is truly valuable when it produces an improvement in human society instead of degenerating into 'futile wrangling':[10]

> The knowledge of such sciences, however, should be acquired as can profit the peoples of the earth, and not those which begin with words and end with words.[11]

For the Bahá'í, therefore, scholarship is by no means a pernicious evil. Used well, scholarship is an invaluable tool for the systematic study of reality. What Bahá'u'lláh criticizes is *bad* scholarship – the abandonment of scientific method in favor of personal bias, hidden agendas or *ad hominem* attacks. Of course, Bahá'u'lláh was well aware that He was speaking to the inheritors of a tradition of bad scholarship, a history in which scholarship has been the weapon of choice in the ongoing war between science and religion. Bahá'u'lláh was also aware that, from the Bahá'í perspective, this wrangling was a needless furor created by the failure of scholars (whether secular or sacred) to appreciate the unity of creation.

Bahá'u'lláh observes that for the one endowed with true understanding, there need be no adversarial relationship between science and religion. After all, the purpose of all scholarship is to investigate reality and the Bahá'í writings explain that all reality is one organic expression of the Divine Will – material reality is but the outward expression of spiritual reality:

> The spiritual world is like unto the phenomenal world. They are the exact counterpart of each other. Whatever objects appear in

PREFACE

this world of existence are the outer pictures of the world of heaven.[12]

Because of this integrity, this organic relationship between the twin – the spiritual and the material – aspects of reality, it is inevitable that in time the true student of science will necessarily become a student of religion as well. Conversely, the true student of religion must needs acknowledge the essential relationship between spirituality and the expression of the unseen in material form.

Clearly this is the major theme of the revelation of Bahá'u'lláh, that the coming of age of humankind will be signaled by the expression of our essential spiritual unity as a human family in terms of a global community, a divine economy, a world commonwealth. It is only logical, therefore, that among the most worthwhile types of scholarship are those studies that demonstrate the essential unity underlying the apparent dual nature of reality.

The discussions in this volume are attempts to accomplish this – to demonstrate the organic unity of creation by examining some of the most fundamental questions deriving from the assertion that physical creation is a precise expression of the Divine Will, an emanation of God, an eloquent expression of divine love. The inspiration for these essays is Bahá'u'lláh's Most Holy Book, the Kitáb-i-Aqdas, which functions as the lynch pin between the two aspects of reality. By establishing the blueprint for the Bahá'í commonwealth – what Shoghi Effendi says should be regarded 'as far as this planetary life is concerned, as the furthermost limits in the organization of human society'[13] – the Kitáb-i-Aqdas represents the translation of eternal justice into the fabric of human society, a perfect enshrinement of the law of love.

John S. Hatcher

Prologue on Proving God

William S. Hatcher

The Question of God's Existence

Certainly there can be no more important or fundamental question for human beings than the existence and nature of God. But for too long now public discussion of God's existence has been relegated to a largely emotional and even political debate between ardent, sometimes fanatical 'believers' on one hand and skeptical, self-satisfied 'realists' on the other. Not infrequently, religious believers refuse to admit the relevance of logical and scientific methods to an understanding of God, seeking thereby to escape what they regard as the tyranny of a materialistic, even demonic, science. In rejecting the application of objective and rational criteria to the question of God's nature and existence, religious believers thus appropriate God to themselves, making of Him their own creation – largely a tool for various sociopolitical programs that, because they lack intrinsic integrity, must be ever more stridently advanced in the name of a transhuman almighty power.

At the same time, scientistic materialism, by aggressively ignoring (and even attempting to explain away) the overwhelming evidence for God's existence generated by science itself, has discredited its much-vaunted objectivity and thereby given rise to the increasingly widespread popular perception that science is just one among a rapidly proliferating pantheon of competing belief systems. This view divests science of its inherent power to inform and transform us by providing cogent and incisive insights into the subtle, inner structure of reality.

Thus it has become a received idea, on both sides of the 'God' debate, that 'belief in God' is a matter of 'pure faith' – meaning emotional conviction. On the one hand, those who believe most strongly in God generally attribute such conviction to their feeling of inner certainty of His presence in their lives. Rarely, if ever, does one encounter a believer in God who was converted to such belief by a rational proof of God's existence. The perception of most believers seems to be that such proofs are, at best, weak confirmations of their inner experience and, at worst, nothing more than word games played by philosophers. On the other hand, most atheists and agnostics claim to base their skepticism about God on reason and science – on what they perceive as a lack of rational proof of God's existence.

The Bahá'í Approach

'Abdu'l-Bahá leaves no doubt concerning the duty of Bahá'ís to gain a rational understanding of the question of God's existence:

> Day and night you must strive that you may attain to the significances of the heavenly Kingdom, perceive the signs of Divinity, acquire certainty of knowledge and realize that this world has a Creator, a Vivifier, a Provider, an Architect – knowing this through proofs and evidences and not through susceptibilities, nay, rather, through decisive arguments and real vision – that is to say, visualizing it as clearly as the outer eye beholds the sun. In this way may you behold the presence of God and attain to the knowledge of the holy, divine Manifestations.[1]

However, elsewhere 'Abdu'l-Bahá makes it clear that rational proofs of the existence of God, though necessary, are only part of an overall, integrated process of spiritual and intellectual development.

> If thou wishest the divine knowledge and recognition, purify thy heart from all beside God, be wholly attracted to the ideal, beloved One; search for and choose Him and apply thyself to rational and authoritative arguments. For arguments are a guide to the path and by this the heart will be turned unto the Sun of

Truth. And when the heart is turned unto the Sun, then the eye will be opened and will recognize the Sun through the Sun itself. Then man will be in no need of arguments (or proofs), for the Sun is altogether independent, and absolute independence is in need of nothing, and proofs are one of the things of which absolute independence has no need.[2]

These counsels of 'Abdu'l-Bahá are representative of the harmony between mind and heart that is found throughout the Bahá'í writings. They describe a process that begins with the purification of the heart, proceeds to rational and authoritative arguments, and then results in a heartfelt conviction coupled with an objective knowledge and perception of the truth.

Why, one might well ask, should one purify the heart *before* undertaking the search for rational arguments? Perhaps the answer lies in the observation that, for most people, rational arguments, even when clearly valid, do not easily prevail over strongly-held emotions. Do we not often find ourselves in the position of 'knowing' something intellectually yet unable to acquire an emotional or psychological *feeling* of conviction? We should then reflect that what we often mean by proof is not logical or rational evidence but rather persuasion or conviction. This confusion between (logical) proof and psychological conviction grows out of the history of conflict between religion and science, faith and reason.

Indeed, 'Abdu'l-Bahá's counsel to purify the heart before undertaking a study of rational arguments has strong resonance with Bahá'u'lláh's similar counsel to the 'true seeker':

> But, O my brother, when a true seeker determineth to take the step of search in the path leading to the knowledge of the Ancient of Days, he must, before all else, cleanse and purify his heart, which is the seat of the revelation of the inner mysteries of God, from the obscuring dust of all acquired knowledge, and the allusions of the embodiments of satanic fancy. He must purge his breast, which is the sanctuary of the abiding love of the Beloved, of every defilement, and sanctify his soul from all that pertaineth to water and clay, from all shadowy and ephemeral attachments.

He must so cleanse his heart that no remnant of either love or hate may linger therein, lest that love blindly incline him to error, or that hate repel him away from the truth.[3]

It seems clear that the 'loves', 'hates' and 'attachments' referred to by Bahá'u'lláh are the sort of subjective preferences we commonly designate as prejudices. Perhaps, however, we too easily associate 'prejudice' with such gross and obviously irrational judgments as racial and class prejudices, failing thereby to acknowledge more subtle and deeply-rooted instances of prejudice. What else but a prejudice against religious belief itself could account for the atheist's irrational claim that his or her disbelief in God is based on science, when science gives overwhelming proof of God's existence? And what else but irrational fear and suspicion of science could incline a believer in God to denigrate the use of rationality, when Bahá'u'lláh has said that the intellect is the greatest and highest power that God has given to humanity and that the very purpose of His having endowed us with rationality is that we may know Him:

> Know thou that, according to what thy Lord, the Lord of all men, hath decreed in His Book, the favors vouchsafed by Him unto mankind have been, and will ever remain, limitless in their range. First and foremost among these favors, which the Almighty hath conferred upon man, is the gift of understanding. His purpose in conferring such a gift is none other except to enable His creature to know and recognize the one true God – exalted be His glory. This gift giveth man the power to discern the truth in all things, leadeth him to that which is right, and helpeth him to discover the secrets of creation.[4]

Thus the understanding faculty that God has given us is marvelously flexible. It can be used for knowing God Himself but also for comprehending the basis of moral action and for discovering scientific truth. Indeed, 'Abdu'l-Bahá specifically identifies science with this greatest of all gifts of God to humanity:

> The outcome of this intellectual endowment is science, which is

especially characteristic of man. This scientific power investigates and apprehends created objects and the laws surrounding them. It is the discoverer of the hidden and mysterious secrets of the material universe and is peculiar to man alone. The most noble and praiseworthy accomplishment of man, therefore, is scientific knowledge . . .[5]

All blessings are divine in origin, but none can be compared with this power of intellectual investigation and research, which is an eternal gift producing fruits of unending delight. Man is ever partaking of these fruits. All other blessings are temporary; this is an everlasting possession . . . it is an eternal blessing and divine bestowal, the supreme gift of God to man . . . science or the attribute of scientific penetration is supernatural . . .[6]

When He instructs us to purify our hearts as a precondition to the effective application of our reason, 'Abdu'l-Bahá is telling us *how* to use the gift of intellect that God has given us. The truly rational person is the one who is capable of committing himself emotionally – indeed passionately – to whatever truth his mind has perceived. Perhaps, then, the prevailing views that belief in God is purely emotional and that 'scientific rationality' is devoid of legitimate emotion and passion are both equally distorted conceptions of how the intellect should be deployed in the pursuit of truth and of the proper relationship between mind and heart.

Rational Proof and Psychological Conviction

From the Bahá'í viewpoint, the entire discourse about the existence and nature of God could be profitably reformulated in the language of truth (the description of what *is*) rather than the language of belief (our subjective ideas about what is). Since God does in fact exist, and has whatever nature is inherent in His Godhood, our task is to know Him – not just believe in Him. If God did not exist, then no amount of belief on our part would bring Him into existence. And since He does exist, no amount of unbelief on our part will bring about His non-existence, any more than our disbelief in gravity or entropy would alter these features of reality.

The very fact that we usually speak of 'belief' instead of 'knowledge' in relation to God betrays the fact that, in spite of ourselves, we tend to think of God as a human subjective idea rather than an objectively-existing Being. Reality, truth – what *is* – has no fear of being tested. The more a truth is tested the more clearly it is distinguished from falsehood and illusion, and the more an untruth is tested the more evident its falsity. Perhaps the general resistance to applying the 'hard' methods of science to the question of God betrays an inner fear (susceptibility) that our private and limited conceptions of God will not withstand such scrutiny.

Of course, it is quite understandable why a confusion of belief and knowledge has come about. The conditions of human existence are such that our physical life on earth quickly becomes meaningless and unbearable if we remain unaware of God's existence; unawareness of God increases our suffering. This existential condition of life provides a strong, emotional motivation for wanting God to exist. But that motivation does not, in itself, constitute a logical reason for affirming that God does exist. Nor, contrary to the claim of some atheists, does it constitute a reason for affirming that God does not exist. Hence the separation of belief – 'I want desperately to know that God exists' – from knowledge – 'I have overwhelming evidence that God does in fact exist.'

The pervasive meaninglessness of life in the absence of personal knowledge of God's existence can be quite reasonably viewed as a deliberate strategy designed by God to provide us with a strong and pure motivation to seek Him. The strength and sincerity of this motivation is clearly the first step and the essential precondition to seeking and finding God, but this motivation, however sincere, does not in itself dictate the optimal *method* for prosecuting the search for God. However, as we have seen above, the Bahá'í writings do provide that method: first, the purification of the heart; second, the search for rational and authoritative arguments; third, the direct perception and experience of God.

If we have purified our hearts in preparation for examining proofs of God's existence, then we will have already come to terms with the fact that we have a strong need and desire to know that God exists. The consideration of rational proofs can thus proceed on rational grounds rather than on the basis of 'susceptibilities', i.e. the emotional response these proofs initially provoke within us.

Some Particular Proofs

Having considered certain of these methodological issues, let us now turn to an examination of some proofs of God's existence, specifically with reference to the two following essays of the present collection.

The first and most fundamental evidence that God exists is that there is something and not nothing. We know that there is something because we observe through our senses, and become aware through our consciousness, of the existence of various concrete objects.

How do we know that our perception of the world is not an illusion? Although it is logically possible that all our perceptions of reality are illusions, this is not the most probable, rational or plausible possibility. The intersubjective verification, persistence and consistency of our perceptions makes it highly unlikely that they are all illusory.

Skeptics may well point out instances in which our initial perceptions of some configurations turn out to have been illusions. But the *possibility* that any given perception may contain distortions or illusions does not logically imply that all or even most of our perceptions are significantly distorted. Indeed, the fact that most of us act spontaneously on the assumption that our perceptions of concrete reality are essentially correct and the results of these innumerable spontaneous acts tend to confirm the non-illusory character of our perceptions.

However, we can do much better than this, with a little help from that consummate rationalist René Descartes. Suppose I grant for the sake of argument that all my perceptions are illusions. Still, *I*, the holder of these illusions, must exist in order to be aware (as I am) of these illusory perceptions. Thus I exist and am conscious (aware) that I exist. Therefore something exists and indeed (my) self-awareness exists.

Let us put it another way. It is conceivable that something could exist without being aware that it exists. Indeed, this is more probably the case with animals or plants, which do not appear to have consciousness (in the sense of self-awareness). But it is clearly not possible to be aware of existence (to have consciousness) without existing.

Thus consciousness (self-awareness) is the most fundamental condition of our existence because everything else we claim to know about reality is mediated to us by our consciousness: consciousness is a primary experience of being (existence).

That things exist immediately raises the question of the origin of existence, and thus of God conceived as the ultimate source of being. In particular, all concrete entities that we can observe (or have observed) come forth from some other reality, i.e. they owe their existence to something other than themselves: you have come forth from your parents, who came forth from the human race, which came forth from the earth, which came forth from the solar system, etc. Thus none of these observable entities can be God, for each owes its existence to something else and cannot therefore be the origin of its own existence and therefore not the origin of all existence.

Therefore, God, if He exists, owes His existence only to Himself and not to anything else. We say that God is *uncaused*. (In terms used by the philosopher Leibniz, to be uncaused means to contain within oneself 'a sufficient reason' for one's existence.) Now, suppose there is no God and that every existing entity owes its existence to something else, from which it comes forth. Then how did the *process* of 'coming forth' begin? If there is no 'first, uncaused cause', no ultimate origin of existence, then how did anything ever come into existence in the first place? Such (in a slightly modified form) is Aristotle's famous argument for the existence of an uncaused cause, and it is with a consideration of Aristotle's proof that we begin the first of the following two essays.

Again, one could object that it is nonetheless logically possible that there be no uncaused cause. This observation is true as far as it goes but should not be allowed to obscure the fundamental fact that the burden of proof is now on the shoulders of those who would reject Aristotle's argument, for they must now justify why it is more rational (plausible) to suppose that everything in existence comes from something else without there being anything which exists in itself.

In other words, either there is an uncaused cause or there isn't. If we proceed rationally then we must opt for the most reasonable of these two alternatives. The existence of an uncaused cause explains how the process of entity-generation was accomplished. If we deny the existence of an uncaused cause then we must find some other explanation for the process of entity-generation. In the absence of a satisfactory alternative explanation, refusal to accept the existence of an uncaused cause is irrational and unscientific. The logical burden of finding such an alternative is on the shoulders of the skeptics.

Many philosophers and scientists would accept the validity of Aristotle's first-cause argument. Indeed, it is difficult to raise serious objections against what Aristotle's proof establishes (the existence of an uncaused cause). But quite serious objections can be raised about what his argument does not establish. For one thing, it does not prove the *uniqueness* of God, for nothing in Aristotle's argument excludes the possibility of there being more than one uncaused cause. Secondly, Aristotle's proof does not prove that any one uncaused cause is *universal*, i.e. the cause of everything in existence.

A universal cause A is both uncaused and unique. It is uncaused since, by universality, it is its own cause, i.e. it contains within itself the reason for its own existence. Moreover, again by universality, A is a cause of every other entity B, and thus no such B can be uncaused (and hence no such B is universal). Following Avicenna, we devise a more subtle proof that gives us both the existence of an uncaused cause and its universality (and thus its uniqueness).

The key to understanding Avicenna's proof is found in the observation that, until now, we have dealt only with the *fact* of existence and the relation of cause and effect (coming forth) between entities. We have said nothing about the nature of existence or about *how* entities come forth from each other. More particularly, let us notice that all observable (macro)entities are *composites*, i.e. they are not unified substances but rather are constituted by parts or *components*. A composite entity E comes into existence when all of its components exist and when these components are bound together in a certain configuration (whole) that constitutes E. Thus we introduce a second fundamental relationship, the relationship of part to whole.

We now have four logical possibilities for any entity: caused or uncaused, simple or composite. When once we will have analyzed the logical relationships among these categories of existence, we will construct a rational proof that there is a unique, uncaused, simple (noncomposite), universal cause G. Moreover, the existence of G follows from the fundamental, logical properties of causality and composition just as surely as $1 + 1 = 2$. If such an entity exists it is certainly God since God has these properties and G is unique: G = God.

Logical vs. Comprehensive Definitions

This last point needs further elaboration. Given the fact that we will have proved the existence of some entity G, what gives us the right to consider that entity to be God? How indeed can we define what we mean by God in a way that enables us to know when we have proved He exists?

The answer to these questions lies in the distinction between *logical* definitions and *comprehensive* definitions. A logical definition defines an entity by just one attribute of the entity, but an attribute that is sufficient to distinguish it from all other entities and thus determines it uniquely. A comprehensive definition, on the other hand, seeks to define the entity in the totality of its attributes. Thus a logical definition of the city of London would be that it is the capital city of the United Kingdom. Another logical definition would be that it is that city geographically situated at a certain latitude and longitude. Each of these definitions singles out London from all other entities in existence, yet neither defines London in all of its attributes. Moreover, the other attributes of London (e.g. its population or its class structure) are logically independent of the defining attribute: these other attributes cannot be deduced just from a knowledge of the defining attribute.

Many logical definitions of God are possible. For example, God is the uncaused cause, the universal cause, the ultimate origin of all existence, the creator of our particular universe, the creator of the human being, or the creator of human life on this planet.[7] Each of these definitions serves to determine or distinguish God from all other entities but none of them defines God in the totality of His attributes.

Bahá'u'lláh tells us that we humans will never be able to give a comprehensive definition of God and 'Abdu'l-Bahá goes further by saying that humans cannot hope to give adequate comprehensive definitions of even the simplest of physical systems. As it turns out, comprehensive definitions appear to be possible only for certain abstract, logical entities such as those involved in pure mathematics.[8]

Thus we recognize that God is beyond human definition or comprehension and that God has an infinity of attributes. Yet any attribute of God that is true only of God can serve as a logical definition of God. We have therefore proved that God exists whenever we have proved the existence of an entity G that has any particular defining attribute of God.[9]

This is what we accomplish in each of the following two essays. In the first we prove the existence of an entity G that is a universal uncaused cause. Since such an entity is unique and God (if He exists) *is* uncaused, we have therefore proved the existence of God. In the second essay we prove the existence of a force-entity F that has created the human being on this planet. Since the attribute 'creator of human life on this planet' applies only to God, if He exists, then F = God.

The Design Proof and its Variants

The modernized version of Avicenna's proof, which is found in the first essay to follow this prologue, shows that God's existence follows from the most basic logical properties of the two relations of causality and composition. By considering further properties of these relations we can derive still further proofs of the existence of God.

The classical *proof from design* argues that the existence of complex and highly structured composite systems is the greatest rational evidence for God because such highly structured systems are extremely improbable – the more highly structured the more improbable. In particular, the physical human being is the most complex and thus the most improbable of all known structures. The abundant existence of highly complex systems is strong evidence that some intelligent force has brought about this complexity because the probability of these systems coming into existence spontaneously is infinitesimal.

More formally, we can reason as follows: either highly complex systems have emerged spontaneously (by chance) or they have not. It is highly unreasonable to suppose that they have arisen spontaneously. Thus it is significantly more reasonable that some force is responsible for deliberately bringing about such highly ordered structures. This 'ordering force' F we call God. In particular, this ordering force has brought the human being into existence and thus satisfies a defining attribute of God. Hence F = God.

The proof from design is a powerful proof but in modern times there has arisen the following objection to it: perhaps these structures and the laws that govern them have always existed and thus never needed to be 'brought into being'. According to modern systems theory, the evolution of a system is governed by three things: first, the laws that determine the dynamics of the system (the way it evolves); second, the boundary conditions of the system, i.e. the type of energy input into the system that is necessary to maintain the laws; and third, the initial state of the system. If these laws have always existed, then they never had to be created, and if the system has always existed within the appropriate boundary conditions, then there is no reason why it could not have existed, at some past time, in a(n) (initial) state that would allow the laws of the system to produce the current, observed configuration.

The above objection to the design argument amounts to replacing God with 'inherent necessity': things are the way they are because there was never any real possibility of their being any other way. God, if He exists, was only necessary to set the whole process in motion, after which He is really irrelevant. This concept of God is known as Deism. The universal, uncaused cause of Avicenna's proof is quite compatible with a Deistic conception of God because the logic of the proof leads us to the existence of a unique, ultimate cause of all being but not to a God who intervenes continually in His creation.

However, as 'Abdu'l-Bahá may have been the first to notice, the same science of systems that has generated the objection to the classical proof from design has also generated an even more powerful argument in favor of a non-Deistic conception of God. The basic idea is as follows: we shift our focus from the design itself (the complex configuration produced by a system) to the *process* by which the design is produced. This process is known to be governed by certain laws of thermodynamics (heat and energy transfer), and a consideration of these laws in the process of biological evolution results in a modern scientific proof of the existence of God. In particular, the clearly random element involved in the process of evolution utterly refutes the 'inherent necessity' objection to the classical design argument. This argument based on evolution is the focus of the second of the two following essays.

The force of the scientific proof is so great because we are now dealing with an observable physical process that has occurred within a finite length of time: the emergence of higher, more complex life forms in the process of evolution. As we explore in some detail, this process can only be explained by the action of some force external to the process itself. Moreover, since this force is responsible for the process of evolution, it is also responsible for the product of evolution – the human being. This force of evolution thus satisfies one of the logical definitions of God: it is the creator of the human being on this planet. Hence this force is God and God exists.

The evolution-based argument thus establishes not only the existence of God but also provides at least one clear instance when God has intervened in (or interacted with) the ongoing processes of the world. Of course, we still do not know exactly *how* (by what mechanism) this intervention has taken place, only that it clearly has occurred. However, our knowledge of the process of evolution is continually increasing and it is not unreasonable to expect that we might one day understand the mechanism of this intervention. Some works of 'Abdu'l-Bahá, such as the Tablet of the Universe (as yet unpublished in English), give profound insights into processes of this sort.

We thus have a hierarchy of proofs of God based on a hierarchy of data. The most fundamental data is existence itself and the coming forth of entities from other entities (causality). This yields the existence of at least one uncaused cause. Then we have both causality (bare existence) and composition (the quality of existence or the nature of entities). This leads to a universal uncaused cause. Finally, we have design (or order) and the process by which order emerges from disorder. In the case of evolution, this leads to a creator of humankind who has intervened (by an as yet unknown mechanism) in the ongoing processes of the world.

Nor are these, by any means, the only proofs of God's existence.[10] Other data that give rise to rational proofs of God's existence are: the evolution of human society towards greater complexity and order; the Manifestations of God in history; the observable differences between human capacity and behavior, on one hand, and animal capacity and behavior on the other; the nature and origin of human consciousness.

All of this suggests that 'Abdu'l-Bahá counsels us to search out rational proofs of God's existence because these proofs lead us to the most profound understanding of how creation is structured and how it functions. Perhaps this is one reason why 'Abdu'l-Bahá exhorts us to seek out rational proof*s*, not just one convincing proof. Each particular proof begins with a consideration of certain data and then proceeds logically to God. These proofs are not just formal exercises in philosophical wordplay that we forget as soon as we are convinced that God really does exist. Each proof is the key to an understanding of a different aspect or attribute of God. Ultimately, the search for God and the search for truth are the same thing. In other words, to understand any phenomenon means to understand what it teaches us about God: 'No thing have I perceived, except that I perceived God within it, God before it, or God after it.'[11]

We have previously stressed the difference between rational proof and psychological conviction. However, we are now in a position to gain a somewhat clearer understanding of the relationship between the two. There are fundamentally two aspects to a rational proof: the data (or evidence) one uses and the logic of the proof itself. The more one understands about either aspect, the more convinced one is by the proof. Knowledge of logic is primarily abstract and conceptual, similar to mathematics. Knowledge of data is primarily empirical (factual).

A scientific proof of God's existence will be more convincing to someone who has a thorough understanding of the scientific data involved in the proof. The more abstract, philosophical proofs, such as Avicenna's, are more purely logical and will not tend to be very convincing to anyone unfamiliar with logic and philosophy.

The Nature of God

In the foregoing we have concentrated on the question of God's existence but have said rather less about His nature. The basic problem is the following:

With reference to, say, Avicenna's proof, we have established that God exists as the unique, uncaused cause (origin) of all existence. However, we conceive of God as a Being who created with a conscious purpose, design and intent. Could our origin of existence be just an impersonal principle or force?

To resolve the question of the nature of God, we appeal to a fundamental feature of the causality relation, namely, that a cause

C has to be at least as great as the effect E it produces – in the precise sense that C must have any positive capacity (as opposed to a limitation) of E to a degree that is equal or greater than E. (How else could C produce or bring forth E in the totality of its attributes?) Since man is a creation of God, and since man has intelligence, feelings and will, God must have these capacities to a degree that is at least as great as all men. But we observe that in men these capacities differ, without there being any limit as to their degree. That is, no matter how intelligent a person may be, it is possible for there to be an even more intelligent one. Or no matter how compassionate and kind a person may be, it is always possible for someone to be yet more kind and compassionate.

In other words, with respect to the *totality* of humanity, there is no limit to the degree in which these capacities can exist. Thus since God is the *unique* cause of *all* humanity, He must have each of these capacities to an unlimited degree. God is therefore all-knowing, all-loving and all-powerful. In fact, since God is the only uncaused Being, He is the only absolute existence. Hence God is absolutely intelligent, absolutely loving and absolutely powerful.

Of course, we cannot conceive with our own finite and limited minds exactly what it means to possess these various capacities to an absolute degree. We can only get an approximate idea by thinking of the most intelligent, the most kind and loving or the most righteous human being we can imagine. The saints and prophets of history provide us with examples of those who have developed or expressed these qualities to a high degree.

It might at first appear that our approach to the nature of God is anthropomorphic – that we are creating God in the image of man. But anthropomorphism means projecting all categories of human qualities onto God, both limitations and capacities. For example, we might think of God as being sometimes loving but also angry, jealous, spiteful, hateful, revengeful, etc. Or, again, we might think of God as being intelligent but also sometimes ignorant, neglectful or intellectually lazy.

Thus by attributing to God only positive qualities raised to an ultimate degree, we avoid anthropomorphism. But as a safeguard against inadvertently attributing human limitations to God, we must keep constantly in mind that God possesses these positive qualities to a degree that is utterly beyond our comprehension or imagination.

Of course, from the Bahá'í viewpoint, we know that the Manifestations of God are perfect reflections of the attributes of God and thus a focal point for our understanding of these attributes. And since our comprehension of the Manifestation is relative and progressive, we can understand that the implementation of 'Abdu'l-Bahá's counsel to seek out proofs of God's existence and nature is also progressive and cumulative, not a task that we fulfill once and for all only to forget about it when we are done. The present essays are an attempt to contribute to this ongoing process.

Causality, Composition and the Origin of Existence

William S. Hatcher

Introduction

The importance of the contributions to philosophy by the tenth-eleventh century Muslim thinker Avicenna (ibn Sina, 980-1037) has been generally recognized.[1] In particular, among religious-minded philosophers or those working within the framework of a distinct religious tradition, Avicenna appears to have been one of the first to conceive and prosecute the task of reconciling the 'truths of revelation' (in this case the Qur'án) with the truths of 'science' (i.e. the results of a rational-empirical investigation of reality, embodied in what was then called 'philosophy'). Indeed, Maimonides (1134-1204) and Thomas Aquinas (1225-74), building on Avicenna's work, attempted the same task for the Jewish and Christian traditions respectively, and each of the latter has been considered as representing the highest expression of philosophical thought within his tradition.

Given the strong similarities in the way that these three thinkers conceived of their task, and given also the many connections between and similarities among the three religious traditions they represented, it was naturally the case that they each dealt with many of the same basic questions and issues. Moreover, since each later thinker had access to the works of the preceding one(s), it would also be natural to suppose that there was a progression in the cogency and effectiveness with which each successive thinker dealt with a given issue. However, we will see that with respect to at least one major issue – rational proofs of the existence of God – such was not the case.

More specifically, we will be dealing with the so-called cosmological proof of God's existence, which goes back at least as far as Aristotle's well-known proof of the existence of an uncaused cause. We will see that Avicenna succeeded in giving a version of the cosmological proof that, with regard to Aristotle's, was new both in substance (the concepts and notions used) and in form (the method used). However, whereas Maimonides and Aquinas were partially successful in adopting the substance of Avicenna's proof, they were quite unsuccessful in adopting his novel method. This failure on their part was almost certainly due to the extreme sophistication of Avicenna's method. Indeed, in the course of his proof Avicenna uses notions of logic that were introduced into mathematics and philosophy only in the modern period (beginning with the latter half of the nineteenth century).

Let us begin with a consideration of Aristotle's original proof.

Aristotle's Proof

Rather than giving an exegesis of the original text, we will recast the proof in a more modern form that will enable us more easily to follow its various reformulations at the hands of later thinkers.

We posit the existence of a nonempty universe V of all entities. There is a binary relation of 'causality' between entities, symbolized by a single-bodied arrow $\rightarrow$. Thus, if a and b are entities, a $\rightarrow$ b is read 'a causes b' ('a is the cause of b') or 'b results from a' ('b is an effect of a'). An entity b is said to be (*other-*)*caused* if there is some entity a $\neq$ b such that a $\rightarrow$ b. An entity is said to be *uncaused* or *self-sufficient* if the relation a $\rightarrow$ a holds. We immediately assume the *causality principle*: Every entity a is either caused or uncaused and not both. Implicit in Aristotle's approach is also the *transitivity principle*, which we also assume, but only temporarily: If a $\rightarrow$ b $\rightarrow$ c, then a $\rightarrow$ c.

The causality and transitivity principles together imply that there are no circular causal chains among distinct entities, for let $a_1 \rightarrow a_2 \rightarrow \ldots a_n \rightarrow a_1$ be a circular causal chain C of length n. By the transitivity principle, each a_i in C causes every other a_j in C. In particular, then, $a_i \rightarrow a_i$ for every a_i in C. Thus every entity

a_i in C is uncaused which, by the causality principle, implies that no entity in C is caused. Hence, $a_1 = a_2 = \ldots a_n$. The importance of this result for Aristotle's proof will be seen presently.

In order to deduce the existence of an uncaused entity, Aristotle makes one further explicit assumption (the 'infinite regression principle'): An infinite regression of causes (i.e. an infinite descending causal chain) cannot exist. We now prove:

Aristotle's Theorem: There is an uncaused entity.

Proof. There is some entity a_1 (the universe V of all entities is nonempty). If a_1 is uncaused, then we are through. If not, then by the causality principle, a_1 is an effect of some other entity a_2. Thus, $a_2 \rightarrow a_1$ and $a_2 \neq a_1$. Now the entity a_2 is either caused or uncaused. If it is uncaused, then we are through. If not, then it is caused by some other entity a_3, which is different both from a_2 *and* a_1 (if $a_3 = a_1$ then we have a non-trivial circular causal chain, which is impossible as established above). More generally, if we have a causal chain $a_n \rightarrow a_{n-1} \rightarrow \ldots a_3 \rightarrow a_2 \rightarrow a_1$, with each a_i distinct, and if a_n is caused, then there is some $a_{n+1} \rightarrow a_n$ such that a_{n+1} is distinct not only from a_n but from all other a_i, since otherwise we would have a non-trivial circular causal chain. Thus if there is no uncaused entity in existence, we can extend the chain of a_i's without bound, leading thereby to an infinite descending causal chain. Since we hold such a configuration to be impossible, there must be some positive integer m for which a_m is uncaused and $a_m \rightarrow a_{m-1} \rightarrow \ldots a_3 \rightarrow a_2 \rightarrow a_1$. Thus a_m is an uncaused cause and, by transitivity, a cause of every entity in the chain.

The proof of Aristotle's theorem is called a *cosmological proof* (as opposed to a purely logical or ontological proof) because it involves an appeal to at least one empirical or factual truth (in this case the fact that at least one entity exists).

How successful is Aristotle's proof? On the positive side, there is no doubt that the argument is logically valid – that the conclusion follows logically from the hypotheses. Moreover, the causality and transitivity principles seem quite reasonable and are minimal in what they assume about the causality relation. The burden of the proof clearly rests on the infinite regression principle.

Assessing the validity of the infinite regression principle is difficult. On the one hand, we know from modern mathematics that there is nothing inherently contradictory about the existence of a discretely-ordered infinite set without a minimal element (which is just a precise definition of an infinite regression). The negative integers under the usual ordering constitute a model of such a system.

On the other hand, an infinite regression of *causes* is admittedly more difficult to imagine. Although the language Aristotle uses leaves little doubt that he considered any infinite regression to be impossible, he does attempt to justify the infinite regression principle on the basis of a very complete theory of causation.[2]

Aristotle's proof can also be criticized for what it does not prove. It does not prove the uniqueness of the uncaused cause, only its existence. It is perfectly compatible with the assumption that there can be any number of distinct uncaused causes, each generating a distinct causal chain. Nor has it proved that any uncaused cause is *universal*, i.e. that it is a cause of every other entity in existence. Finally, Aristotle's proof says nothing about the nature of God, only His existence. If, for example, we think of the First Cause as having consciousness and deliberateness of purpose, we will have to develop other arguments that go beyond the first-cause proof in some manner.

Avicenna's Proof

From Avicenna's writings on the subject[3] it is evident that he clearly perceived the various weaknesses in Aristotle's proof. Rather than trying to patch up these weaknesses in some *ad hoc* manner, Avicenna opts for an entirely new approach, one which does not even need the infinite regression principle.[4]

Again we have a non-empty universe V of entities and a causality relation a → b between entities. All of the above definitions related to causality are adopted wholesale. We also assume the causality principle (but not, as it turns out, the transitivity principle).

Avicenna's main innovation is to introduce a second relation (which we symbolize by ∈) between entities. The basic idea is that an entity may be a composite of other entities. Thus the relation a∈b between entities a and b is read 'a is a component of b'. An entity b is *simple* (non-composite) if it has no components. This means that for any entity a, a∈b never holds. If an entity b has at least one component, a∈b, then b is composite.

Thus with Avicenna's approach, entities can be classified according to two attributes, caused-uncaused and simple-composite, giving rise to four logical possibilities.[5] After recognizing this, Avicenna uses metaphysical arguments to exclude one of these four possibilities, namely, the case of uncaused composites. This gives rise to the following 'strong contingency principle', which we assume for the moment: no composite is uncaused or, equivalently, every composite is caused.[6]

One of the arguments Avicenna uses to justify the strong contingency principle runs as follows: an uncaused entity is self-sufficient, it owes its existence to itself alone. However, a composite exists by virtue of its components rather than by virtue of itself as a whole (entity), distinct from its parts. Therefore no composite can be self-sufficient, i.e. uncaused. Furthermore, reasons Avicenna, every observable, material entity (implicitly, *macro-entity*) has physical parts, i.e. is composite. Thus any simple entity must be incorporeal (non-physical) and invisible (non-observable). Finally, he argues, rather less convincingly, that there can be at most one uncaused entity, for at least one of two distinct uncaused entities would be composite, having both that by which they are similar (their each being uncaused) and that by which they differ. For the time being, we will simply assume the 'unicity principle': there is at most one uncaused entity.

In order to present Avicenna's argument in a logically coherent manner, we need one further principle, the 'potency principle': if a → b and c∈b, then a → c; every cause a of the composite phenomenon b is also a cause of every component c of b.[7] Although Avicenna does not identify this principle, he uses it in an explicit way that clearly shows he regarded it as inherent in the logic of the relationship between causality and composition. We are now ready to prove:

Avicenna's Theorem: There is exactly one universal, uncaused cause.

Proof. Let C be the collection of all caused entities in existence. As established above, every currently existing material entity is composite and therefore caused (by the strong contingency principle). Thus C is a (non-empty) composite. But, again by the strong contingency principle, every composite entity is caused. Hence C has some cause E → C, E ≠ C. The entity E is either caused or uncaused, by the causality principle. If E is caused, then E is a component of C, E∈C (since C is the collection of *all* caused entities). Thus by the potency principle, E → E, i.e. E is uncaused. This implication (E is caused implies E is uncaused) implies that E is uncaused. Thus E ≠ C is the unique uncaused entity (by the unicity principle). Moreover, E is a universal cause, i.e. E is a cause of every entity in existence. Indeed, let any entity a be given. By the causality principle, a is either caused or uncaused. If caused, a∈C, which implies by the potency principle that E → a. If a is uncaused, then a = E and thus E → a in this case also (since E → E). Hence E is a unique, uncaused (and thus non-composite) universal cause.

The language used by Avicenna in articulating his proof involved extensive use of the terms 'necessary existence' and 'possible existence'. However, as it turns out, Avicenna never invokes any principles of modal logic whatsoever.[8] If, in the texts of Avicenna, one were to substitute our 'uncaused' for Avicenna's 'necessarily existent' and our 'caused' for Avicenna's 'possibly existent', then one would obtain an exposition quite close to the one we have given above.[9] In particular, the various principles we have assumed were all used by Avicenna. However, as we shall later see, this purely linguistic matter proved to be a stumbling block to Avicenna's successors in their attempts to grasp the import of his proof.

CAUSALITY, COMPOSITION, AND THE ORIGIN OF EXISTENCE

Turning now to an analysis of the proof itself, notice that, like Aristotle's, it is a cosmological proof because appeal is made to the factual existence of material entities in order to justify the assertion that the collection C of all caused entities is a non-trivial composite. Notice also that, from the strictly logical point of view, the proof is more complex than Aristotle's. In fact, the proof is more complex than most proofs found in philosophical texts and is quite mathematical in tone and spirit. This undoubtedly reflects the fact that Avicenna was an accomplished mathematician.

Indeed, Avicenna's proof is highly precocious and breathtakingly modern. His use of the abstraction principle of set theory to obtain the abstract set C of all caused entities as a single composite entity anticipates by a thousand years the uses that Georg Cantor (1845-1918) made of this same principle. Nevertheless, as anyone even slightly familiar with modern set theory will immediately recognize, there is unfortunately a certain defect in the way Avicenna uses the abstraction principle. But our analysis of this very defect will allow us to reformulate Avicenna's proof (using a few techniques from modern class-set theory) in a way that not only removes the defect but also eliminates several of the hypotheses assumed in the original proof. Let us take a closer look at what is involved.

The problem begins with Avicenna's tacit assumption that the collection C of all caused entities constitutes an entity. On the philosophical side of things, it is quite clear that, even though all macro-physical objects are indeed composites, the converse is false, i.e. it is certainly not true that every collection of entities constitutes a composite *entity*. To be an entity a composite must have some internal coherence or structural unity. There is no problem with the *existence* of the collection C, only its status as an entity. Thus we must distinguish between those composites of entities that are themselves entities (like my body as presently constituted by the cells that presently make it up), and arbitrary aggregates, many of which will not be entities (e.g. the set consisting of my body as presently constituted, a single tree in the Amazon rain forest and an iceberg presently at the north pole).

On the logical side of the question, things are even worse. Suppose, for the sake of argument, that we grant entityship status to C. Now C is a composite entity and thus caused (by the strong contingency principle). But C is the collection of all caused entities, and C itself is such an entity. Thus C is a (proper) component of itself, C∈C, contradicting the well-foundedness principle of set-theory. The well-foundedness principle not only implies that no composite can be a component of itself, it also implies that there are no infinite or circular chains of componenthood (*membership*), $a_1 \ni a_2 \ni \ldots \ni a_n \ni \ldots$ or $a_1 \ni a_2 \ni \ldots \ni a_n \ni a_1$.[10] These are both principles with which Avicenna would have certainly agreed.[11]

Of course, there are consistent formal set theories in which the well-foundedness principle does not hold, but no one knows how to interpret these paradoxical systems so as to apply them meaningfully to collections of real objects (such as macro-physical entities).[12] To get a quick grasp of the paradoxical nature of self-membership, consider the following: it seems clear that we cannot actually form a collection of objects until every object to be included in the collection has been formed (e.g. my body at the present moment cannot exist *before* every cell that presently makes it up exists). Thus the collection C cannot exist until every caused entity exists. But if the collection C itself is a caused entity, then C cannot exist until C exists, until C exists . . . an infinite regression (or a circularity, depending on one's point of view). Considered in this manner, not only does Avicenna's argument not exclude an infinite regression, it in fact *depends on* the validity of an infinite regression!

Of course, in spite of all this, it is nonetheless true that if one adds to Avicenna's argument the explicit hypothesis that the collection C of all caused entities is an entity, then the argument is logically correct (the conclusion follows logically from the hypotheses). But the *ad hoc* and paradoxical nature of such an assumption destroys totally the usefulness of the proof. The hypothesis that God (a universal uncaused cause) exists is more reasonable than the entityship hypothesis for C, so we might as well just assume God exists and forget logic altogether.

It might occur to the reader that one way out of this dilemma would be to find some philosophically natural criterion of entityhood that would justify our declaration that C is an entity, removing thereby the *ad hoc* character of this declaration. In Avicenna's proof, the collection C turns out to be the collection of all entities in existence, except for God, and it is very difficult to conceive of a natural entityship criterion that would exclude most composites from entityhood while accepting C. Moreover, all the antinomies of modern set theory lie in wait for any over-liberal entityship criterion. (If, for example, we imprudently declare in one bold sweep that *all* collections of entities are entities, then we can deduce Russell's paradox by considering the composite entity W that is the collection of all entities X that are not components of themselves, $X \notin X$. The entity W is then both a component of itself and not a component of itself.) And, finally, whatever entityship criterion we chose, the self-membership paradox for C remains: the putative entity C would be a member of itself, $C \in C$, contrary to the well-foundedness principle of set theory.[13]

As it turns out, there is a natural way out of our dilemma. In a later section we will examine in detail how the application of a small, almost trivial fragment of modern class-set theory will restore Avicenna's argument in an even stronger form and on a more solid basis than the original. However, we want first to take a look at what Avicenna's successors did with his proof.

Maimonides

In his *Guide for the Perplexed*,[14] the renowned Jewish philosopher and theologian Maimonides devotes a section of his work to the question of proofs of the existence and nature of God.[15] He gives the following version of Avicenna's proof:

> There is no doubt that many things actually exist, as e.g. things perceived with the senses. Now there are only three cases conceivable, viz. either all these things are without beginning and without end, or all of them have beginning and end, or some are

with and some without beginning and end. The first of these three cases is altogether inadmissible, since we clearly perceive objects which come into existence and are subsequently destroyed. The second case is likewise inadmissible, for if everything had but a temporary existence all things might be destroyed, and that which is enunciated of a whole class of things as possible is necessarily actual. All things must therefore come to an end, and then nothing would ever be in existence, for there would not exist any being to produce anything. Consequently nothing whatever would exist [if all things were transient]; but as we see things existing, and find ourselves in existence, we conclude as follows: Since there are undoubtedly beings of a temporary existence, there must also be an eternal being that is not subject to destruction, and whose existence is real, not merely possible.[16]

At this point in his argument Maimonides has established the objective existence of at least one permanent (non-transient) entity. But even permanent entities can be caused. Thus, he continues, 'It has been further argued that the existence of this being is necessary, on account of itself alone or on account of some external force.'[17] He then argues that if the existence of the eternal being were dependent on some external source, then 'That force would then be the being that possesses absolute existence'.[18] Thus, 'It is . . . certain that there must be a being which has absolutely independent existence, and is the source of the existence of all things, whether transient or permanent . . . This is a proof the correctness of which is not doubted, disputed or rejected, except by those who have no knowledge of the method of proof.'[19]

Maimonides continues by addressing the question of composite versus simple entities, concluding that no uncaused entity can be composite: 'We further say that the existence of anything that has independent existence is not due to any cause . . . and that such a being does not include any plurality whatever . . . consequently it cannot be a body, nor a force residing in a body'.[20] Finally, he gives a metaphysical argument quite similar to Avicenna's to prove that there can be only one being (God) who has 'absolutely independent existence'.[21]

It should be noted that Maimonides gives only an oblique

reference to Avicenna (without mentioning the latter's name explicitly), stating that the proof 'is taken from the words of Aristotle, though he [Aristotle] gives it a different form'.[22] However, the terms used and the general tenor of the argument leave no doubt that Maimonides derived this proof from Avicenna's text. Indeed, this fact has been recognized by scholars for many years.[23]

Let us examine both the similarities and the differences between Maimonides' and Avicenna's arguments. To begin with, each author considers, in the course of his version of the proof, a certain class of entities. For Avicenna it is the class C of all caused entities, while for Maimonides it is the collection T of all transient beings. However, each author then proceeds somewhat differently.

Avicenna continues by invoking the strong (or weak) contingency principle to establish that the collection (composite) C of all caused entities must be caused by some entity E. But if no uncaused entity exists, then E must be caused and thus a component of C itself, $E \in C$. By the potency principle, this implies $E \to E$, i.e. that E is an uncaused entity, which is false. Thus an uncaused entity exists and is the cause of C.

Maimonides proceeds by invoking what we might call the 'transience principle': any collection of transient entities is transient. Thus the collection T of all transient entities is transient. Hence if only transient entities existed, nothing would now exist. But since we observe that many (transient) things do now exist, it follows, reasons Maimonides, that at least one eternal (permanent) entity exists.

Unfortunately, Maimonides is not through, because (as he acknowledges) the permanent entity whose existence he has established can nonetheless be caused (only by another permanent entity, of course). He therefore appeals (implicitly, but nonetheless clearly) to Aristotle's principle of infinite regression to conclude that there is some uncaused, permanent entity that 'is the source of the existence of all things, whether transient or permanent'.

There are a number of serious criticisms that must be leveled at Maimonides' proof. To begin with, in his own typology of beings, he fails to take into account all logical possibilities. He considers entities that have neither beginning nor end (the permanent) or those having both beginning and end (the transient). But it is clearly logically possible that there be entities that have an end but no beginning or that have a beginning and no end. Indeed, several major religions teach the doctrine of the 'special creation of souls', according to which each human being is endowed with a non-physical, non-composite soul or spirit that has a beginning (its creation by God) but no end (i.e. is immortal).[24] This failure significantly weakens Maimonides' argument before it even gets off the ground. In contrast, Avicenna deals explicitly with all logical possibilities in his typology, the caused and uncaused, simple and composite.

However, even if we accept Maimonides' dual classification of entities as either transient or permanent, there are serious difficulties with his transience principle: 'that which is enunciated of a whole class of things as possible is necessarily actual'. In arguing from the (local) transience of each individual (transient) entity to the global transience of the class T of transient entities, Maimonides clearly does not take into account the logical possibility that a system composed only of transient entities could exist eternally through a (presumably complex) network of interactions in which entities were constantly dying out and being born, but such that the total (simultaneous) extinction of all entities never occurs. In this case, every individual entity would be transient but the system (i.e. the 'whole class') would be eternal.

There is also the logical possibility that all things are transient and will eventually go out of existence but that this has not *yet* occurred. This possibility clearly refutes Maimonides' contention that 'nothing whatever would exist [if all things were transient]'.

Moreover, in affirming that total non-existence would be the inevitable result of a universe composed only of transient entities, Maimonides appears to contradict the generally accepted philosophical principle that even a relative existence cannot result in absolute or total non-existence. In modern science, this principle has been formulated as the law of conservation of mass-energy, which holds that the 'destruction' of a macro-physical entity is just the transformation of the mass-energy of that entity into some other form or forms, while the total mass-energy of the universe remains constant. Indeed, Maimonides cites the birth and subsequent death of macro-physical entities as his prototypical example of transience.

Thus Maimonides' transience principle is not just implausible but untenable. Again in contrast, Avicenna's contingency principle is highly plausible, especially in its weak form: if every entity of a class is caused, then the whole class is caused.

Finally, because he considers the class T of transient entities rather than the class C of caused entities, Maimonides must apply further argumentation to establish the existence of an uncaused entity, even after he has obtained the existence of a permanent entity. He thus must appeal to Aristotle's principle of infinite regression, an appeal which Avicenna's argument avoids entirely. Thus, in a certain sense, Maimonides' argument does not represent any real advance over Aristotle's argument.

To sum up: Whereas Avicenna's typology of beings treats explicitly all logical possibilities (caused, uncaused, simple, composite), Maimonides' does not. Whereas Avicenna argues that the unique cause of the composite of all caused entities is uncaused, Maimonides argues that there cannot be only transient entities in existence. Whereas Avicenna bases his argument on a highly plausible principle (the contingency principle), Maimonides argues weakly (in fact, falsely) that if only transient entities existed, then all entities would have now ceased to exist. Finally, whereas Avicenna's argument is complete in itself (modulo the problem about entityship conditions on classes), Maimonides' argument is not and necessitates an appeal to Aristotle's infinite regression principle, an appeal that is avoided by Avicenna.

Besides the question of the relative merit of the two arguments themselves, the most significant point is that Maimonides seems to have either misunderstood or misapplied Avicenna's method. For whereas the inference from the causality of individual entities to the causality of class of those entities is quite plausible, the reasoning from the transience of individual entities to the transience of the class of those entities is doubtful, as we have seen.

A defender of Maimonides might claim that Maimonides had in fact understood Avicenna's method, recognized the difficulty concerning the entityship condition for the class C, and sought to remedy it by substituting the ill-fated argument about transience. However, the much cruder errors in Maimonides' version of the argument, plus the fact that Maimonides never even mentions, much less analyzes, Avicenna's argument, are (in my view) more than sufficient grounds for rejecting this possibility.

Aquinas

Thomas Aquinas' version of Avicenna's argument is found in his famous work *Summa Theologiae*.[25] We quote the entire passage:

> The third way [of proving God exists] is based on what need not be and on what must be, and runs as follows. Some of the things we come across can be but need not be, for we find them springing up and dying away, thus sometimes in being and sometimes not. Now everything cannot be like this, for a thing that need not be, once was not; and if everything need not be, once upon a time there was nothing. But if that were true there would be nothing even now, because something that does not exist can only be brought into being by something already existing. So that if nothing was in being nothing could be brought into being, and nothing would be in being now, which contradicts observation. Not everything therefore is the sort of thing that need not be; there has got to be something that must be. Now a thing that must be, may or may not owe this necessity to something else. But just as we must stop somewhere in a series of causes, so also in the series of things which must be and owe this to other things. One is forced therefore to suppose something which must be, and owes this to no other thing than itself; indeed it itself is the cause that other things must be.[26]

Aquinas' proof can perhaps be viewed, to some extent, as a streamlined version of Maimonides' proof. In particular, Aquinas' proof has the same two-staged structure as Maimonides', first seeking to establish the existence of at least one necessary being and then appealing to Aristotle's infinite regression principle to prove that, among necessary beings, there is one that is necessary in itself. Of course, there is already a difference in that Aquinas speaks of necessary existence whereas Maimonides speaks of permanence. In its use of necessity, Aquinas' language is actually closer to Avicenna's than is Maimonides'. However, Aquinas' argument lacks any explicit remnant of Avicenna's method. Thus Avicenna goes to great length to establish the contingency principle and Maimonides explicitly states the transience principle, but Aquinas simply puts forth two assertions without any explicit justification. He affirms, first, that any non-necessary entity cannot have always existed and, second, that if there was a time when each currently existing entity did not exist, then there must have been a time when nothing existed.[27]

On the positive side of the balance, Aquinas definitely avoids the most dubious part of Maimonides' argument, i.e. the latter's assertion that a universe made up only of transient entities could terminate in total non-existence. Aquinas' contention is rather that a world made up only of non-necessary entities could never have come into existence in the first place. However, Aquinas gives no argument to exclude the logical possibility that the universe, even if made up only of non-necessary entities, has always existed. In this case, the universe never had to come into existence, it was always there – even if particular objects have, at different times, come into existence and then subsequently died out. In fact, such a view of the universe corresponds quite closely to that of contemporary scientific cosmology (as already mentioned above in our discussion of Maimonides' argument).

Aquinas' argument that any non-necessarily existing object must have, at some previous time, not existed is also open to serious question. The existence of a non-necessary entity A depends on certain conditions K. Aquinas appears to argue that if it is *possible* for the conditions K not to be met, then it *necessary* that, at some past time, they were not met. It is thus necessary that, at some past time, A did not exist. This logical inference from the possibility of non-existence to the necessity of non-existence is not justified by any generally accepted principle of modal logic.

Perhaps Aquinas is alluding to the Aristotelian principle that every potential must, sooner or later, be actualized. However, a possibility is not the same thing as a potential (especially with regard to questions of existence) and to identify the two in this context falls into the classic trap of treating existence as a predicate. Furthermore, even if we accept for the sake of argument the principle that a non-necessary entity must, at some time, not exist (i.e. realize its potential for non-existence), it is still logically possible that a given non-necessary entity A has always existed until now but will cease to exist in the future (when the conditions K for its existence will have been withdrawn).

Thus Maimonides insists that all transient entities must eventually go out of existence, whereas Aquinas insists that no non-necessary entity can have always existed. Each philosopher makes a 'one-way' non-existence argument but in opposite directions and each philosopher generalizes from the past or future non-existence of individual entities to the past or future non-existence of the entire universe of non-necessary (or transient) entities.

Thus even though avoiding the most serious defect of Maimonides' argument (i.e. Maimonides' claim that relative existence can terminate in total non-existence), Aquinas' argument nonetheless contains major lacunae in the form of *non sequitur* inferences from possible non-existence to necessary non-existence and from the prior non-existence of non-necessary individual entities to the prior non-existence of the system made up of such entities. Moreover, all vestige of Avicenna's method has disappeared from Aquinas' text. Indeed, in this connection let us recall that one of the major accomplishments of Avicenna's argument was to eliminate appeal to the Aristotelian infinite regression principle; but the two-stage structure of both Maimonides' and Aquinas' proofs require appeal to this principle.

It would appear that, from the thirteenth century onward, Aquinas' *Summa Theologiae* has been the major source for Avicenna's argument, at least for philosophers of the Western tradition. If this is indeed the case, it is perhaps due in part to a lack of knowledge of the Arabic language among Western philosophers, together with a presumption that Aquinas' form of the argument was faithful to the original.

For example, after explaining his principle of 'sufficient reason', according to which every existing entity must have a sufficient reason for its existence, Leibniz contends simply that 'contingent beings . . . can have their final or sufficient reason only in the necessary Being, which has the reason of its existence in itself'.[28] Elsewhere Leibniz also argues explicitly that the aggregate or collection of all contingent beings cannot have the reason for its own existence in itself.[29] This latter argument is, in fact, an explicit form of Avicenna's contingency principle, but I have no idea whether or not Leibniz was familiar with Avicenna's argument in its original form. In any case, the contingency principle is certainly natural enough to have been reformulated by other philosophers independently of Avicenna. The Leibnizian form of Avicenna's argument is the one used by the Jesuit philosopher F. C. Copleston in his broadcast debate with Bertrand Russell on the existence of God.[30]

Formalizing Avicenna's Proof

We left our discussion of Avicenna's proof without having resolved the dilemma over the entityship status of the collection of all caused entities. The solution we now propose is derived from two basic sources: modern class-set theory, first fully articulated by John von Neumann,[31] and modern physics, more particularly the theory of elementary particles. Specifically we will enlarge Avicenna's ontology to include not only (simple and composite) entities but also *phenomena*, i.e. classes or collections (systems) of entities that may not themselves be entities. Moreover, whereas Avicenna considered causality to be a relation between entities, we affirm that it is more properly (and naturally) viewed as a relation between phenomena. Finally, this enlarged ontology will necessitate a slight reformulation of the potency principle but will not involve the addition of any new principles. In fact, it will allow for the elimination of several principles whose assumption appeared necessary to Avicenna but which can be deduced from our hypotheses.

We thus have three distinct ontological categories: 1) simple (non-composite or atomic) entities; 2) composite entities; 3) composites (classes) that are not entities. In von Neumann class-set theory, these categories correspond respectively to individuals (*urelemente*), sets and proper classes. Composites generally are classes (whether entities or not). We use the term *phenomenon* inclusively for all three categories. Thus there are simple phenomena and composite phenomena, and among composite phenomena some constitute single entities while others do not.

In the physical universe as presently conceived, the three categories correspond respectively to elementary particles, physical substances (i.e. macro-physical objects) and collections of macro-physical objects (phenomena, systems or events). We conceive that causality '→' is a relation between phenomena (of all types). Thus any given phenomenon A, simple or composite, may (or may not) be the cause of another given phenomenon B.

Guided by these interpretations, informal as they are, we will proceed to formalize a suitable version of Avicenna's proof within a certain very small fragment of von Neumann class-set theory. The underlying logic of our proof is classical (non-modal) first-order logic with equality. Our language L has the following extra-logical primitive predicate symbols; one unary predicate symbol 'At' for 'is atomic', and two binary predicate symbols '∈' for 'is a component of', and '→' for 'causes' (or 'is a cause of'). There is one extra-logical constant symbol 'V' for 'the universe of all entities'. The terms, formulas and sentences of the language L are defined in the usual way, except that we use infix notation 'x∈y' and 'x → y' instead of the more formal '∈(x,y)' or '→(x,y)' for atomic formulas using '∈' and '→'. We use ¬, ∧, ∨, ⇒, ⇔, ∀, ∃, = for negation, conjunction, disjunction, conditional, biconditional, universal quantifier, existential quantifier and equality, respectively.

We use these data first to define two new unary predicate symbols 'Cl' for 'is a class' (or 'is a composite') and 'En' for 'is an entity', and one new binary predicate symbol '⊆' for 'is included in' (or 'is a subclass of').

CAUSALITY, COMPOSITION, AND THE ORIGIN OF EXISTENCE

D.1. Cl(x) for ¬At(x). A class (composite) x is anything that is not simple.

D.2. En(x) for x∈V. An entity is any component of the universe V of all entities.

D.3. x⊆y for (Cl(x)∧Cl(y)∧(∀z)(z∈x ⇒ z∈y)). x is a subphenomenon (subsystem) of y if x and y are composites and every component of x is also a component of y.

Notice that D.3 is the usual set-theoretic definition of inclusion between classes.

Next we axiomatize the precise fragment of set theory to be used in our proof.

S.1. At(x) ⇒ En(x). Every atom is an entity.

S.2. (∀x)(∀y)(x∈y ⇒ En(x)∧Cl(y)). Only entities are components and only classes have components.

S.3. ¬(x∈x). Nothing is a component of itself.

Notice that we need no 'collecting-up' operations, nor do we need the axiom of extensionality. Furthermore, there is no explicit existence assumption among our three axioms, nor will any of our philosophical principles directly postulate the existence of a phenomenon.

Of course, the rules of first-order logic imply the existence of at least one phenomenon. In particular, our extra-logical constant symbol V must be interpreted as designating some given phenomenon. Indeed, the above axioms and definitions imply that V is neither an atom nor an entity since, by S.3 and D.2, V is not an entity and thus, by S.1 and D.1, it is not an atom. We have thus proved our first theorem: Cl(V)∧¬En(V), i.e. V is a composite of entities that is not itself an entity. This is consistent with the intended interpretation of V as the universe (composite) of all entities in existence.

We now present the specifically philosophical assumptions upon which the proof is based, beginning with two further definitions of unary predicate symbols 'Un' for 'is uncaused' (or 'is self-sufficient') and 'Cn' for 'is caused' (or 'is contingent').

D.4. Un(a) for (∀x)(x → a ⇔ x = a). a is uncaused if a is a cause of a and the only cause of a.

D.5. Cn(a) for (¬(a → a)) ∧ (∃x)(x → a ∧ x ≠ a). a is caused if a is not uncaused and a is caused by some x different from a.

These are the same definitions of 'uncaused' and 'caused' as given informally above. Notice that Un(a) and Cn(a) are mutually exclusive (each implies the negation of the other).

And now for our philosophical assumptions.

P.1. (∀x)(Un(x) ∨ Cn(x)). Causality principle. Everything is either caused or uncaused.

P.2. (a → b) ⇒ (∀x)((x∈b∨x⊆b) ⇒ (a → x)). Potency principle. Any cause a of a phenomenon b is also a cause of every component and every subphenomenon of b.

P.3. (∀x)((Cl(x)∧(∀y)(y∈x⇒Cn(y)))⇒Cn(x)). (Weak) contingency principle. If every component of a composite is caused, then the composite is also caused.

P.2 appropriately generalizes the potency principle so that it applies to phenomena as well as to entities. It means that the notion of causality expressed by our axioms is that of 'total causality': for a to be a cause of b, a must be capable in and of itself of producing b.

Notice that we assume neither the transitivity principle nor Aristotle's infinite regression principle. Thus our axioms neither affirm nor deny the possibility of circular causal chains among distinct objects or of infinite regresses of causes. However, the logical axiom S.3 does exclude certain circularities of componenthood. We might sum all this up by saying that our axioms allow causality to be arbitrarily complex but put certain (minimal) limitations on the potential complexity of componenthood. It is very important to an understanding of our proof not to confuse the causality relationship '→' with the component relationship '∈'.

Our aim is to prove the proposition (∃x)(At(x)∧(∀y)(x → y)), which asserts the existence of an atomic entity that is the cause of everything in existence (and is thus self-sufficient). It will also follow that such an entity is unique. That such a strong existence assertion follows from our six assumptions (none of which are themselves existence assumptions) is certainly not immediately obvious. Moreover, we have already proved that the universal class V is not atomic and, in fact, not even an entity. That such a result does follow from these assumptions is an indication of the strength of the method Avicenna pioneered with his proof.

The desired result is the last in the following sequence of theorems. We will not give strictly formal proofs, but rather quasi-formal proofs using symbols from our language together with vernacular English terms.

T.1. $Cl(a) \Rightarrow Cn(a)$.

Proof. Assume the hypothesis $Cl(a)$ and suppose $\neg Cn(a)$. Then, by P.3, there exists some $y \in a$ for which $\neg Cn(y)$ holds. Thus, by P.1, $Un(y)$ holds and hence (by D.4) $y \to y$ also. But again by P.1 and D.4, $Un(a)$ and $a \to a$ hold. Now, applying P.2 with $b = a$ and $x = y$ yields $a \to y$. Then by D.4 applied to y, $a = y$. Hence, by substitution of equals, $a \in a$ holds, contradicting S.3. This contradiction establishes $\neg(\neg Cn(a))$, i.e. $Cn(a)$, and hence the implication $Cl(a) \Rightarrow Cn(a)$.

T.1 states that any composite phenomenon is caused. This is the strong contingency principle, assumed explicitly by Avicenna but which we have here deduced from the weak contingency principle P.3 and our other assumptions. In particular, T.1 definitely excludes the possibility that the universe V can be self-sufficient.

We have the following simple but useful corollary of T.1.

T.2. $Un(a) \Rightarrow At(a)$.

Proof. By D.4 and D.5, $Un(a)$ implies $\neg Cn(a)$ which, by T.1, implies $\neg Cl(a)$ which, by D.1, implies $At(a)$.

Thus any self-sufficient entity a must be atomic.

T.3. (a∈b∧Un(a)) ⇒ (a → b).

Proof. Assume the hypotheses a∈b and Un(a). By S.2, T.1 and D.5 there exists x → b, x ≠ b. Thus, by P.2 and a∈b, x → a. Hence, by Un(a) and D.4, x = a. Thus, by substitution of equals, a → b as claimed.

T.3 establishes that an uncaused entity is the cause of any composite of which it is a component.

T.4. (∀x)(∀y)((Un(x)∧Un(y)) ⇒ (x=y)).

Proof. Assuming Un(x) and Un(y), we infer immediately At(x) and At(y) by T.2 and thus En(x) and En(y) by S.1 and, finally, x∈V and y∈V by D.2. By T.3 applied to a = x and b = V, we then have x → V. By P.2, we thus have x → y which, by Un(y) and D.4, yields x = y as claimed.

T.4 establishes that there is at most one uncaused entity.

T.5. (∃x)(Un(x)∧x → V).

Proof. By P.1, D.4 and D.5, there is some x for which x → V holds. Such an x is either atomic or composite. Suppose x is composite, i.e. Cl(x) holds. Also, D.1, D.2, S.1 and S.3 imply that Cl(V) holds (as we have already mentioned informally above). Finally, by S.2, every component y of x is an entity. Applying D.3 to these data we thus have x ⊆ V. Now, by P.2, x → x holds. Thus, by P.1, D.4 and D.5, Un(x) holds and At(x) therefore holds by T.2. Thus, Cl(x), i.e. ¬At(x), implies At(x). Hence At(x) holds. But then, At(x) implies En(x), which implies x∈V which implies x → x by the potency principle. Thus, by P.1 and D.4, Un(x). The conclusion is now established.

We now know there is a unique, uncaused entity that is the cause of the universe V of all entities. Let us designate this entity by G. We then have:

T.6. $(\forall x)(G \to x)$.

Proof. Any x is either atomic or composite. If x is atomic, then it is an entity and hence a component of V. Thus, by T.5 and the potency principle, $G \to x$. If x is a composite, then $x \subseteq V$ by D.3 and $G \to x$ by the potency principle.

Thus God exists, is unique, and is the ultimate cause of every phenomenon in existence.

Let us stress here the very positive value of such a formalized proof as we have presented; it is that the logic of the proof is absolutely unassailable. Anyone who accepts the validity of logic itself, and who resists the conclusion, has only one option: he must refute one of the six axioms S.1-S.3 or P.1-P.3. Or, stated positively, for all who accept the validity of logic, debate about the existence of God can be reduced to debate about the validity of our six axioms. We might say that such a formal proof thereby 'localizes' the discussion of God's existence.

Philosophically, the burden of the proof rests primarily on the contingency principle P.3. For a discussion of the philosophical plausibility of the contingency principle in the context of this proof of God's existence, see my *Logic and Logos*, (which also discusses set-theoretical definitions and models of the causality relation).[32]

Conclusions

Our 'mathematization' of Avicenna's proof has produced a proof whose logical structure is certainly more complex than that of most proofs to be found in philosophical texts. Philosophers, especially metaphysicians of the pre-modern period, tended to multiply their philosophical assumptions rather than complexify the logic of their proofs.

What we have essentially done here is take the basic method pioneered by Avicenna and, using a few modern tools, push it to its limits. But all of the basic ideas were clearly present in Avicenna's original exposition. I therefore feel that it is legitimate to consider Avicenna as the 'spiritual father' of modern set theory in the same way, and to the same extent, that Leibniz is considered the spiritual father of modern logic.

A Scientific Proof of the Existence of God

William S. Hatcher

> If thou wishest the divine knowledge and recognition . . . apply thyself to rational and authoritative arguments. For arguments are a guide to the path and by this the heart will be turned unto the Sun of Truth. And when the heart is turned unto the Sun, then the eye will be opened and will recognize the Sun through the Sun itself. Then man will be in no need of arguments (or proofs), for the Sun is altogether independent, and absolute independence is in need of nothing, and proofs are one of the things of which absolute independence has no need.[1]

'Abdu'l-Bahá's counsel to the seeker after God seems to say at least two things: first, that rational arguments are useful and necessary starting points in the approach to God and, second, that the deepest and most adequate knowledge of God goes far beyond such arguments and is essentially transrational.

Interestingly, 'Abdu'l-Bahá stresses that the result of studying rational arguments will be to turn the *heart* towards God. This suggests that generating logical proofs of the existence of God is not an end in itself but rather a means of opening oneself to a deeper experience of the divine presence. Nevertheless, every major philosopher and every religious tradition have presented proofs of God's existence, and 'Abdu'l-Bahá Himself has presented a significant number of such proofs in His own writings. Most of the proofs given by 'Abdu'l-Bahá are variants of classical philosophical arguments, starting with Aristotle's well known argument for the existence of a primal cause.

However, in his Tablet written in 1921 to the Swiss scientist

Auguste Forel, 'Abdu'l-Bahá offers a distinctly modern proof of the existence of God, based on certain facts and principles associated with the phenomenon of biological evolution.[2] He argues that the cause of the composition (and decomposition) of living beings must be an unobservable, objectively existing, voluntary force (thus, a conscious force external to the process of evolution itself). Since this force has produced humanity, it must be greater than humans and is, therefore, a Being endowed with superhuman capacities.[3]

This particular argument may conceivably be original with 'Abdu'l-Bahá. Certainly it could not have been given in that form much before the early twentieth century because the scientific theory of evolution on which it is based was developed only in the nineteenth century. Moreover, most scientists who accepted the theory of evolution were philosophical materialists, holding that evolution made God irrelevant instead of proving God's existence. Though arguments similar to 'Abdu'l-Bahá's have appeared in the more recent literature on the philosophy of science,[4] I have yet to discover any that are earlier or even contemporaneous with 'Abdu'l-Bahá's Tablet to Auguste Forel.[5]

The argument based on evolution is not the only proof of God's existence given in the Tablet to Auguste Forel. However, the evolution-based argument is unique in the way it uses sophisticated scientific ideas, and its cogency and force are liable to be underestimated by anyone not familiar with certain fundamental principles of thermodynamics.[6] Thus, rather than undertaking a historical-critical approach to 'Abdu'l-Bahá's proof, we propose, in the present article, to give a thoroughly modern formulation of His argument, using scientific terms that were not necessarily current at the time 'Abdu'l-Bahá wrote. In taking this approach, we hope to convey something of the full strength of 'Abdu'l-Bahá's argument. Therefore, the remainder of this article will consist of an extended and careful reformulation of 'Abdu'l-Bahá's proof in contemporary scientific language.

A SCIENTIFIC PROOF OF THE EXISTENCE OF GOD

The Nature of Scientific Proof

Since our proof purports to be *scientific,* we need to begin by a brief discussion of the nature of science and of proof in science. This discussion is all the more important because there are so many commonly held misconceptions about the nature of scientific proof.

Science is composed of two fundamental aspects. One aspect is its concrete or observable dimension: we accumulate observations of some phenomenon and record these observations in the form of *observation statements.* This record constitutes our body of observed truths or *facts* about the given phenomenon.

The second aspect of science is its abstract or theoretical dimension. Having accumulated a certain number of observation statements about a phenomenon, we seek an explanation for these observations. We want to understand how the various facts about the phenomenon are related to each other. In other words, we seek to understand how or why the phenomenon occurs and how it operates. This quest leads us to formulate an hypothesis (or, if you will, a theory) that represents our mental conception of the underlying dynamic of the phenomenon. Such a theory is usually expressed in a language that uses *abstract* terms, i.e. terms referring to non-observable entities or forces (e.g. entities like electrons or forces like the strong nuclear force). Observation statements, in contrast, will use *concrete* terms, that is, terms referring to observable entities or configurations.

The way we test the truth of observation statements is by making further, more exacting, observations and measurements. However, because of the natural, intrinsic limitations of the human sensory apparatus and nervous system, we can never entirely eliminate errors from our observations of a given phenomenon, no matter how careful and exacting we may be. This is particularly true of phenomena that are extremely small (perhaps microscopic) or extremely remote (say, distant stars), but it is true in general, even of ordinarily accessible, everyday phenomena. Thus, the truth value of facts (observation statements) is always relative. The widely held belief that the facts of science are absolute or incontrovertible is therefore a misconception.

Testing the truth of the theoretical statements of science is a still more complicated process. We begin by deducing new observation statements as logical consequences of the theory; then we test these observation statements in the usual way. In other words, if our theory says that such-and-such a thing must happen, then we look to see if such-and-such a thing does in fact happen; if our theory says that snow is white, then we look to see if snow is, in fact, white. The new observation statements deduced from a theory are called *predictions* of the theory, and if they are confirmed by our experience, then we say the theory is *valid,* meaning 'validated or confirmed by observation'.

Thus, the truth value of a theoretical statement of science is also relative, for even if all current predictions of a theory are confirmed by observation, nothing excludes the possibility that in the future new predictions will prove false. There is also the possibility that newly conceived experiments will lead to the future falsification of current predictions, which, on the basis of current experience, appear justified.

With regard to the truth value of theories, we are therefore in a paradoxical, somewhat humorous situation. It is possible to prove almost absolutely that a theory is false because if some of the theory's predictions flagrantly contradict highly authenticated observations, then the theory cannot be true. It will have to be abandoned or else modified in some way. But no matter how many predictions of theory have been confirmed through observation, the possibility always remains of the theory's future falsification as a result either of novel predictions that contradict known evidence or novel evidence that contradicts known predictions.

Towards the beginning of this century it was thought possible to establish rules of so-called inductive logic that would allow us to pass from a set of particulars to a general conclusion with the same degree of precision that deductive logic allows us to pass from general principles to particular conclusions. However, it is now known that this is not possible, even in principle. A theorem of mathematical logic has established that, in general, there are an infinite number of mutually incompatible theories consistent with any given, finite set of facts. Since the finitude of human beings guarantees that there will always be only a finite set of facts for any given phenomenon, it follows that no set of observation statements ever determines a unique theory as an explanation for the phenomenon. As one logician has expressed it: theory is underdetermined by fact.[7]

Thus, fact gathering and theory making are, in some respects, mutually independent. Whereas fact gathering is a slow, gradual process, theory making involves a creative, discontinuous leap of the imagination. When gathering facts, we seek to know how things are. When conceiving a theory, we try to imagine how things might be.

It follows incontrovertibly from these considerations that none of the truths of science can ever be considered as proved absolutely. The notion of absolute proof is simply not part of science. The widespread belief that the essential characteristic of scientific truth is its absoluteness and exactness (in supposed contrast to the relativity and imprecision of truth in philosophy or religion) is a misconception. Though some people may deplore this relativity of scientific truth, it has a quite positive aspect because it makes truth seeking in science an enterprise that is dynamic and progressive rather than static and sterile. Moreover, the efficiency of scientific method has been powerfully confirmed by its success in generating an increasing number of highly validated theories resulting from its systematic application during the last several hundred years.

To summarize, a proposition may be said to be scientifically proved when we have rendered that proposition considerably more *plausible* (meaning *probably true)* than all known, logically possible alternatives. Thus to speak of a scientific proof of God's existence is to affirm that we can render the proposition that God exists considerably more plausible than any of the known alternatives (and, in particular, the alternative that God does not exist). In other words, we can know that God exists with the same degree of certainty that we know the strong nuclear force or electrons exist. Having dealt with these methodological issues, we now begin the proof proper.[8]

Visible and Invisible Reality

We first establish the principle of the objective existence of an *invisible world,* i.e. a portion of reality external to human subjectivity but inaccessible to human observation. In other words, there are forces and entities we cannot observe directly but which exist objectively, that is, independently of any human perception.

Let us start with a very simple example. Suppose we hold a small object like a pencil between our thumb and forefinger and then release it. We observe that it falls to the floor and we say that the force of gravity causes it to fall. But let us look again. Do we actually *see* any downward force acting upon the pencil, something pulling or pushing it? Clearly, not. We do not observe the force of gravity at all. Rather we deduce the existence of some unseen force (called gravity) acting upon unsupported objects in order to explain their otherwise inexplicable downward movement.

Now, let us look once again more carefully at the initial configuration of the pencil and ask the following question: at the moment the pencil is released, what are the logically (physically) possible directions it can take, *based strictly on what we can observe in the configuration*? The answer, clearly, is that any direction is logically possible. Nothing we can observe physically blocks the pencil from following any direction; nor can we observe anything that seems to favor one direction more than the others. Yet, what we do *in fact* observe is that one of the directions (downward) is privileged, for no matter how many times we repeat the simple experiment of releasing the pencil, it is the downward direction that is taken. Thus what we observe in fact is a persistent and significant deviation from randomness (chance).

In science, we say that the behavior of an observable phenomenon is *random* (due to chance) if all logical possibilities occur with equal relative frequency. In other words, if the behavior of an unsupported object like the just released pencil was in fact random, then we would expect that some of these other logical possibilities would actually occur from time to time. However, what we observe is not only that the various logical possibilities do not occur with the same relative frequency but also that one of these possibilities is uniquely privileged in being exclusively chosen. Thus what we actually observe is *a persistent, consistent, and significant deviation from randomness,* and it is this deviation from randomness (without any observable reason for such deviation) that leads us to appeal to the existence of an unobserved force as the *cause* of the observed non-random behavior.

This example concerning gravity illustrates a general principle of scientific method: Whenever we encounter an observable phenomenon that, for no observable reason, exhibits a persistent deviation from randomness, we feel logically justified in asserting that the observed non-random behavior is due to the action of some unobserved force or entity. Indeed, to do otherwise would be grossly illogical and unscientific. The existence of each of the four basic forces of current physics (gravity, the strong and the weak nuclear forces, and electromagnetic force) was deduced in this manner. So basic is this principle that all of science would collapse were it to be discarded.

However, let us note that we have not proved absolutely that gravity exists. It is logically possible (though, of course, highly implausible) that every observed instance of the operation of gravity, from the beginning of recorded history until the present moment, is nothing but an incredible coincidence. A skeptic (an 'agravitist') could say: 'I understand why you believe that gravity exists, but I prefer to believe that there is no such unseen force.' It is possible the skeptic might say that we will wake up tomorrow to find a world in total chaos and disorder, with unsupported objects flying in all directions, and we will then realize that all we have experienced for thousands of years has been just a series of very remarkable coincidences.

As we know from our discussion of scientific methodology above, we cannot refute such a skeptic in any absolute way. We can, of course, point out just how infinitesimal is the probability that he or she is right, but the skeptic is nonetheless free to choose to persist in an implausible belief. However, the skeptic cannot maintain anti-gravity skepticism while claiming to be scientific and rational in so doing. We have established that the existence of an unseen force of gravity is by far the most plausible of all known alternatives, and anyone who deliberately chooses a less plausible alternative is by definition unscientific and irrational. (Again, this is not the same as acknowledging that there are other logical possibilities, however implausible.)

Returning now to our example of the downward falling of unsupported objects, observe that we have shown much more than the simple existence of invisible or unobservable forces or entities. We have shown that observable effects can well have unobservable causes. We have shown that there are many instances of observable behavior that cannot be explained observably. In more philosophical language, we have shown that the visible world is not self-sufficient, that it does not contain a 'sufficient reason' for itself: the phenomena of visible reality are produced by (or arise from) invisible reality.

Let us illustrate this truth with a simple analogy. Imagine that we are standing on the shore of an immense ocean. The ocean and its hidden depths represent the immensity of invisible reality. Occasionally a fish jumps out of the ocean into the air and then returns to the ocean. The brief moment during which the fish is out of the water represents a phenomenon of visible reality.

This analogy expresses very well the view of physical reality that derives from modern physics (in particular from quantum theory): the perceived macro-objects of visible reality consist of billions upon billions of little energy packets called *elementary particles* in relative but temporary equilibrium states and in continual motion. These particles arise from invisible reality (pure energy) and, whenever their equilibrium states are destroyed, they return to invisible reality.

Random and Non-Random Phenomena in Science

In the foregoing discussion, we have established the following methodological principle of science: Whenever any phenomenon exhibits an observable, persistent, significant deviation from random behavior, without any observable cause, then we are justified in inferring the existence of an unseen force or entity as the cause of the phenomenon. We now need to go further and to ask whether there is any principle of science that can tell us what is probable and what is improbable. Probable configurations or phenomena are those that are most likely random; whereas, improbable configurations are more likely to result from the action of some invisible force (when, of course, there is no observable cause).

There is indeed such a principle. It is the second law of thermodynamics (the so-called entropy principle), first put forth by the French engineer Carnot (1796-1832) and the German physicist Clausius (1822-88). We will consider two statements or formulations of this law, one informal and heuristic, the second more precise and formal. However, both formulations are scientifically correct.

The first statement is: Disorder is probable and order is improbable. Or, with a bit more elaboration: Order, structure and complexity are improbable; while disorder, simplicity and uniformity are probable. On a common-sense level we can see why this is true: for order represents a few specific configurations, whereas any logically possible configuration represents disorder. Let us pursue this point a bit further.

Suppose we compare a pile of bricks and a well-built brick house. The pile of bricks represents disorder and the brick house represents order. If we want to transform a brick house into a pile of bricks, brick by brick, we can do this in any logically possible way. We can take any brick for the first brick, any brick for the second brick and so on. All possibilities lead to a pile of bricks. But if we want to transform a pile of bricks into a brick house, we cannot do this in any possible way. We cannot, for example, place any upper brick before we have placed a certain appropriate number of lower bricks. Thus transforming a brick house into a pile of bricks represents a process that leads from order to disorder, or from the improbable towards the probable. And transforming a pile of bricks into a well-built brick house represents a process that leads from disorder to order, i.e. from the probable towards the improbable.

Thus, if we built a brick house in the woods and left it to the forces of nature for fifty years, we would not be surprised to find that the house had degenerated into a pile of bricks. But if we left a pile of bricks under the same conditions for fifty years, we would be very surprised to find a well-built brick house in its place. The surprise we would feel in such a case represents our intuition of the truth of the second law of thermodynamics.[9]

Let us now give the second, more formal statement of the law. We begin with a few definitions. By a *physical system* we mean any physical entity (object) or any collection of such entities. The entities that make up a physical system are its components, and any collection of components of a system forms a *subsystem*. An *isolated* physical system is one that receives no energy from outside the system. We now state: in any isolated physical system, disorder will increase. Moreover, if the system remains isolated, then disorder in the system will increase until the state known as maximum entropy or total disorder is attained. This is a *stable state* of the system in that, once attained, no further change will occur unless energy is furnished to the system from the outside, in some appropriate manner. Informally stated: Any system degenerates towards disorder if 'left to itself'.

This formulation of the second law of thermodynamics leads naturally to the question of whether or not there are any truly isolated physical systems. As far as we know, there are no totally isolated systems (unless the whole physical universe is a closed system, which may or may not be the case). For example, most of the energy of the solar system comes from the sun but there is some radiation and energy input from outside the solar system. However, there are many relatively isolated systems, and in these systems the operation of the second law of thermodynamics has always been confirmed. Indeed, this law is one of the most universally verified and highly validated of all laws and principles of science.

One very important point should be stressed here. The second law of thermodynamics states that any isolated system will necessarily degenerate towards disorder but this does not exclude the possibility that non-isolated systems may also degenerate! To avoid degeneration towards disorder, it is not usually sufficient just to furnish raw energy to the system. Energy must be furnished in such a way, and in such a form, that the system can convert some of the energy into order (or use the energy to complexify its structure). How such a thing may happen will depend on the nature of the system itself (the relationships that exist between the components within the system), the way the system evolves, and the way it interacts with the outside.

Let us give two examples. The Brownian motion of air molecules in a closed room is assumed to be totally random. Suppose a bottle of a highly volatile perfume is unstoppered in this room. The initial configuration, with all the perfume in the bottle, represents order. Once the perfume is released and begins to volatilize, the Brownian motion of air molecules will rather quickly spread the perfume until it is uniformly distributed throughout the room. This is the natural degeneration towards disorder, wholly explainable by the random nature of Brownian motion. Suppose, now, that we modify the experiment by adding radiant heat from a source outside the room. The increased air temperature in the room will only increase the speed of the Brownian motion, thereby hastening the spread of the perfume (and thus the degeneration towards disorder of the system). In this case, the input of energy from outside the system will not result in any evolution towards order.

As a second example, consider the growth (complexification) of leaved plant systems on the earth. Such growth depends on the process of photosynthesis within the leaf subsystem of the plant. Photosynthesis uses direct sunlight as an outside energy source. If sunlight were eliminated entirely and replaced by another form of energy (say, heat), the growth of those plants would not occur. Thus the internal structure of a leaved plant allows it to utilize a certain form of outside energy (direct sunlight) to increase its complexity, thus to evolve towards greater order. But other forms of energy input may not result in growth and complexification (indeed, excessive or inappropriate energy input may well destroy the system).

Thus the observable world (visible reality) is composed of physical systems. Some are evolving from less probable to more probable states; some are (more or less) static or stable; and some are evolving from more probable to less probable states. Systems of the first type can be understood as the result of a random process. The stable systems are either in a state of maximum entropy or else maintained in a constant (or periodically fluctuating) state by means of continual inputs of energy from outside (e.g. the *dissipative systems* of Prigogine).[10] Those that exhibit evolution from more probable to less probable states cannot be the result of a random process. The cause of such a growth pattern can only be some observable input of energy (e.g. plant growth on earth that is fuelled by solar energy) or else some nonobservable (invisible) force. It is this latter case that we will now consider.[11]

God Exists

Let us now think of all the physical systems in the observable universe and ask which of these systems is the most complex, the most highly ordered, the most structured. The answer is clear and unequivocal: It is the human being, and in particular the human brain and central nervous system, which, beyond any possible doubt, constitute the most sophisticated set of behaving entities in the known universe (see, for example, the series of four volumes *The Neurosciences*). According to any standard of comparison, and with regard to any known physical system, natural or artificial, the physical human being is by far the most highly ordered and complex. In the following, unless otherwise noted, whenever we speak of the human being, we will mean the physical human being and not the human being in any metaphorical, cultural or spiritual sense.

We can already draw a first conclusion: Since the human being is the most highly ordered structure in the known observable universe, the human being is the most improbable of all physical systems and thus the least likely to have been produced by a random process. So, let us take a look at the process that did produce the human being – the process we call evolution.

First, we need to establish the facts (as far as we know them) of the process of evolution. The observables of the phenomenon of evolution are primarily the fossil record, found in the layers of sediment in various locations all over the earth. If there were contradictions or ambiguities in this record, we would have a major problem in interpreting these data. However, such is not the case. All these sedimentary layers show the same basic configuration, namely, that higher, more complex forms of life followed simpler, less complex forms. In other words, the process of evolution was a process of complexification, of moving from relative simplicity and disorder towards relative complexity and order. It was therefore a process of moving from more probable configurations towards less probable configurations.

Although we can easily become involved in intricate discussions about exactly how long the physical universe, the solar system or the earth have existed, or how long conditions for life existed on earth before life actually appeared, the basic pattern is unequivocally clear. The earth has existed for some billions of years (many expert opinions fix the age of the earth at about 4.5 billion years). The first, and most rudimentary, life forms are thought to have been blue-green algae, which may have appeared as early as two billion years ago. In any case, following the initial appearance of the algae, there was a long period (perhaps a billion years) during which they remained the only life forms. After the algae became abundant, other early forms of plant life appeared.

Through radioactive dating and other methods, it has been established with a high degree of certainty that the first crude forms of invertebrate animal life could not have appeared earlier than about 600 million years ago. Thus, the *process* of evolution, from one-celled animals to the emergence of the mature human being (about 50,000 years ago), took no longer than 600 million years, which, from the geological perspective, is a fairly short time-span. This shows that there was no time for anything like an 'unlimited' or 'open-ended' experimentation in evolution. Moreover, it is estimated that roughly a thousand species intervened between the appearance of one-celled organisms and the mature human being. In each case, the transition from one species to another was a process leading from a lower (and therefore more probable) to a higher (and thus less probable) configuration. Finally, the evidence from the fossil record consistently shows that evolution was not a smooth, gradual process. Rather, there were long periods of stasis and stability (the so-called plateaus), punctuated by much shorter periods of rapid change (towards complexification).

Thus evolution is clearly an example of a process that exhibits a significant, persistent deviation from randomness. Within a specified and limited time-frame, there was a persistent and recurrent movement from more probable to less probable configurations. It is therefore unscientific and irrational to attribute this process to chance. Indeed, just the transition from one species to the next could, if left to chance, take about as long as the lifespan of the earth itself, and to account for the whole evolutionary process we would have to multiply this figure by a thousand, yielding a figure much greater than the estimated lifespan of the entire universe (from the 'beginning' until the present).

In the light of these considerations, we have a scientific right – indeed we are compelled by the logic of scientific methodology – to conclude that the process of evolution is the result of the action of some unobservable force. In particular, we human beings are the 'end product' of evolution and thus owe our existence to this force. It seems reasonable to call this force 'God', but anyone uncomfortable with that name can simply call it 'the evolutionary force' (or, more precisely, 'the force that produced evolution and thus produced the human being'). Moreover, it is most reasonable to suppose that the force of evolution is different from all other forces that science has so far discovered or hypothesized, because according to our present knowledge, no other force could have produced the phenomenon of evolution.[12]

Now, just as in the case of gravity, a skeptic can refuse to accept the existence of the evolutionary force by choosing to believe that evolution was a random process, a series of highly unlikely coincidences; but in making such a choice the skeptic relinquishes any claim to be acting scientifically or rationally. From the point of view of scientific methodology, one must always choose the most likely among all known, logically possible alternatives. Although it is logically possible that evolution was a random process, it is clearly not the most likely possibility. Such a skeptic, especially a practicing scientist, needs to explain why he or she accepts and follows this basic principle of scientific methodology elsewhere but makes an exception in the case of evolution. If one has no trouble believing in gravity or the strong nuclear force, based on evidence of a kind similar to that for the evolutionary force, then why irrationally resist belief in the force of evolution?

We claim to have fulfilled our intention of giving a scientific proof of God's existence. We have shown, on the basis of an observable phenomenon (the coming into existence of the human being), that the existence of a nonobservable cause is the most reasonable of all known logical possibilities. However, one could well ask the following further question: to what extent are we justified in calling the motive force of evolution 'God'? Why do we not call gravity or the strong nuclear force 'God'? We deal with this issue in the following section.

The Nature of God

For the remainder of this discussion, let us accept as established the existence of an unseen force that is the cause of the process of evolution and thus of the human being, the end product of this process. It might seem at first that our identification of such a cause with God is rather arbitrary and gratuitous. However, a little reflection shows that this is not so.

To begin with, we know that this force is capable of producing a being having all of the subtlety and refinement that we humans are capable of exhibiting. We do not call gravity or the strong nuclear force 'God' because the effects these forces produce are not so marvelous as the effect produced by the evolutionary force. In the same spirit that has motivated our basic approach throughout this article, we can ask whether or not it is reasonable to suppose that a force capable of producing an effect such as the human being is at least as subtle as humans. This hypothesis seems as reasonable as (if not more reasonable than) any other logical possibility.

In fact, we know certainly that this force is capable of doing at least one thing that we could never do, namely the bringing into being of the human race. Indeed, the human race did not even exist during all of the time that this force was driving evolution forward. We are the result of the action of this force and we owe our existence to it. It has created us.

In our discussion of visible and invisible reality, we have already noted that, from the point of view of modern physics, invisible reality produces visible reality and, in fact, encompasses or surpasses visible reality. Thus, the invisible cause of evolution (and therefore of the human being) might also be plausibly supposed to encompass or surpass humans. In particular, we know from our own experience of ourselves that we have a conscious intellect and a free will. It is therefore not unreasonable that the force or entity which is the cause of our existence might also have such faculties as consciousness, intelligence and will – and most probably to a degree much superior to us. The only alternative is to believe that a blind, unconscious force, devoid of any intelligence, has somehow brought into being a creature who is endowed with conscious intelligence.

Indeed, if we know anything at all, we know that we have a conscious subjectivity because our knowledge of anything is mediated to us by this very subjectivity. Our subjectivity is thus the most basic condition of our existence. It is the inner space in which each of us lives, and we know that our subjectivity and our consciousness are the result of the action of this force. In this way, the knowledge of the nature of the force that has created us is most appropriately explored through a deeper knowledge of that which is most immediately accessible to us, i.e. our own inmost selves. It seems, therefore, that our knowledge of the existence and the nature of God is on the most solid foundation it could possibly be.[13]

The Doctrine of the 'Most Great Infallibility' in Relation to the 'Station of Distinction'

John S. Hatcher

> But the individual reality of the Manifestations of God is a holy reality, and for that reason it is sanctified and, in that which concerns its nature and quality, is distinguished from all other things. It is like the sun, which by its essential nature produces light and cannot be compared to the moon, just as the particles that compose the globe of the sun cannot be compared with those which compose the moon. The particles and organization of the former produce rays, but the particles of which the moon is composed do not produce rays but need to borrow light. So other human realities are those souls who, like the moon, take light from the sun; but that Holy Reality is luminous in Himself.[1]

It is clear from the Bahá'í writings that the Prophet or Manifestation is an intermediary between God and His creation, the means by which creation is brought into being through the revealed or creative word of God and the means by which all human advancement is accomplished. Bahá'í scripture asserts that this is possible because it is through the Manifestation that God guides humankind. The Bahá'í writings assert that this guidance is both explained and exemplified by the Prophet, who, in addition to conveying the infallible word, also possesses a stainless or sinless character.

What may not be so clear are a number of questions related to the station and condition of the Prophet. For example, the Bahá'í writings describe the Manifestation as *infallible*. Does this attribute apply to His observations about the material world (e.g. science and history) as well as to His explication of spiritual truth?

Similarly, are only those words He attributes to God infallible, or is everything the Manifestation does and says without error?

A related question concerns what 'Abdu'l-Bahá calls 'conferred infallibility'. When the Manifestation confers infallibility upon a successor, is He conferring authority only or do we infer that the authoritative utterances of these figures are literally without error? For example, when Muḥammad confers authority upon 'Alí and Bahá'u'lláh confers authority upon 'Abdu'l-Bahá, does this mean that everything these individuals say is true?

There are other important issues regarding the infallibility of the Prophet. When the Manifestation describes the point at which His ministry begins, He seems to indicate that He has undergone some sort of personal transformation, some change in His nature. Does this mean that before this point the Prophet is an ordinary human being and after this point He becomes a Manifestation?

Perhaps the most important question for our consideration concerns what Bahá'u'lláh describes as the dual stations of the Prophet – the 'station of distinction' and the 'station of essential unity'. Does Bahá'u'lláh mean to imply in this distinction the differentiation between the Prophet as a human being who is shaped by the society in which He appears versus the Prophet as an enlightened one who has suddenly become God's mouthpiece and thereby endowed with knowledge and infallibility?

The Word Made Flesh

According to Bahá'í scripture, the Manifestations are the crucial link between the unseen spiritual reality and the visible material world, between God and humankind. Their revealed utterance represents the voice, the authority, the power of God. Their appearances call creation into being and gradually fashion our planet from a molten seed spun off from stars into a womb from which is born and fostered what Bahá'u'lláh refers to as an 'ever-advancing civilization'.[2]

Similar to the Johannine concept of the revealed word as the effective expression of God's creative power,[3] the Bahá'í writings explain that it is solely through the advent of these specialized teachers that any human progress takes place:

> The enlightenment of the world of thought comes from these centers of light and sources of mysteries. Without the bounty of the splendor and the instructions of these Holy Beings the world of souls and thoughts would be opaque darkness. Without the irrefutable teachings of those sources of mysteries the human world would become the pasture of animal appetites and qualities, the existence of everything would be unreal, and there would be no true life. That is why it is said in the Gospel: 'In the beginning was the Word', meaning that it became the cause of all life.[4]

Bahá'u'lláh enunciates this concept in a variety of ways. For example, in one prayer Bahá'u'lláh observes in figurative language that the Manifestation is 'the Hidden Mystery, the Treasured Symbol, through Whom the letters B and E (Be) have been joined and knit together'.[5] Shoghi Effendi explains this allusion as follows:

> Shoghi Effendi, in letters written on his behalf, has explained the significance of the *'letters B and E'*. They constitute the word 'Be', which, he states, 'means the creative Power of God Who through His command causes all things to come into being' and 'the power of the Manifestation of God, His great spiritual creative force'.[6]

In another statement also meant to exalt the station occupied by the Prophets of God, Bahá'u'lláh in the *Kitáb-i-Íqán* states that the Manifestation serves as Godliness translated as best it can be into material form:

> Were any of the all-embracing Manifestations of God to declare: 'I am God!' He verily speaketh the truth, and no doubt attacheth thereto. For it hath been repeatedly demonstrated that through their Revelation, their attributes and names, the Revelation of God, His name and His attributes, are made manifest in the world.[7]

So it was that Christ answered Philip's question about the identity of the 'father' with the following response: 'Have I been with you so long, and yet you do not know me, Philip? He who has seen me has seen the Father; how can you say, "Show us the Father"?'[8] Bahá'u'lláh expresses the same idea about Himself in the *Súratu'l-Haykal* (The Surih of the Temple):

> Naught is seen in My temple but the Temple of God, and in My beauty but His Beauty, and in My being but His Being, and in My self but His Self, and in My movement but His Movement, and in My acquiescence but His Acquiescence, and in My pen but His Pen, the Mighty, the All-Praised. There hath not been in My soul but the Truth, and in Myself naught could be seen but God.[9]

Yet, in spite of these and various other passages attributing to the Prophets the motive force underlying all human progress and development – whether material, intellectual, social or spiritual – the Manifestations are careful to distinguish between their reality and the reality of God. The Prophets explain that their authority, their power, the very words they utter, and the actions they undertake derive solely from the divine Will. Christ states: 'For I have not spoken on my own authority; the Father who sent me has himself given me commandment what to say and what to speak.'[10] Muḥammad says, 'It is not for me to change it [the Qur'án] as mine own soul prompteth. I follow only what is revealed to me'.[11]. Bahá'u'lláh affirms:

> This thing is not from Me, but from One Who is Almighty and All-Knowing. And He bade Me lift up My voice between earth and heaven, and for this there befell Me what hath caused the tears of every man of understanding to flow.[12]

The Subtlety of Identity

The fact that the Prophets consistently distinguish between their station and the station of Godhead has not prevented significant controversy and confusion about this ontological differentiation. The issue of the nature of a Prophet caused in Christianity the most fundamental schism in the evolution of Christian theology, the problem of Christology (the study of the essential nature of Christ). The argument focused on whether Christ was a Prophet of God, and therefore divinely inspired, or God incarnate.

The matter was officially decided at the synod of Niceae in 325 AD where a vote determined that Christ was God incarnate, but some three hundred years later the Prophet Muḥammad soundly rebuked the Christian theologians for this erroneous doctrine. The distinction between God and the 'Apostles' of God is a major theme of the Qur'án – Muḥammad frequently discusses the historical continuity of God's grace as demonstrated through the succession of the Prophets. Muḥammad also emphasizes that Christ, though one of these unique beings and therefore an integral part of this expression of continuous divine revelation, was not God incarnate. In one explanation Muḥammad points out that it was logically inconceivable that the infinite God would have a physical son: 'Sole maker of the Heavens and of the Earth! how, when He hath no consort, should He have a son?'[13] In another surih Muḥammad makes the point that to attribute Godhead to a Prophet diminishes the concept of God and is the grossest sort of blasphemy: 'Jesus is no more than a servant whom we favored, and proposed as an instance of divine power to the children of Israel.'[14] Muḥammad makes the same observation about himself: 'Muhammad is no more than an apostle; other apostles have already passed away before him.'[15]

Of course, there is other clear evidence that the Prophets perceive themselves as servants of God: they pray to God for guidance and assistance. They repeatedly profess that all they do is through God's bidding and authority. Christ compares Himself to a vine which God has caused to bring forth fruit: 'I am the true vine, and my Father is the vinedresser. Every branch of mine that bears no fruit, he takes away, and every branch that does bear fruit he prunes, that it may bear more fruit.'[16] Bahá'u'lláh states that He is 'but a leaf which the winds of the will of thy Lord, the Almighty, the All-Praised, have stirred'.[17]

But what the early Christian thinkers sensed from Christ's words and from His essential reality was that this being was something more than an ordinary human, more than an inspired individual. In this light, the trinitarian doctrine was perhaps not so much an ignorant burst of blasphemy as it was a sincere attempt to give verbal expression to the reality of Christ, whom they knew to be possessed of complete Godliness as well as a power that was not of this world. Furthermore, the concept of mere 'prophethood' (the 'inspired individual', as they had come to understand such a concept from their own Judaic past) did not seem adequate to convey the power and majesty they recognized in Christ.

Perhaps for this reason Muḥammad repeatedly defines exactly what He means by the term 'Prophet' or 'Apostle'. Throughout the Qur'án He traces the historical evidence of God's divine guidance and states with unequivocal clarity that the Apostle is God's emissary and speaks as God commands, but He is a servant of God, not God incarnate. Yet, in no way does Muḥammad intend by this distinction to diminish the importance of the Prophets as the primary source of human advancement.

The Nature of the Manifestations

No doubt because of this history of confusion regarding the essential nature of the Prophets, Bahá'u'lláh makes the station of the Prophets a central theme of His major doctrinal work, the *Kitáb-i-Íqán*. 'Abdu'l-Bahá also speaks repeatedly on the nature of the Manifestations in numerous statements that appear in such collections of His talks as *Some Answered Questions*, *The Promulgation of Universal Peace* and *Paris Talks*. From these discussions we can derive a better understanding of this important doctrinal issue.

To begin with, it is clear that existence is ordered from highest to lowest, the highest form of existence being the essence of God, which is absolute, unchanging, pre-existent, non-composite and 'incomprehensible to the human mind'.[18] We can know the attributes of this essence as they are made apparent to us, but the essence itself will ever remain beyond our comprehension. Bahá'u'lláh notes that all the Prophets have alluded to God as singular and alone:

As to those sayings, attributed to the Prophets of old, such as, 'In the beginning was God; there was no creature to know Him', and 'The Lord was alone; with no one to adore Him', the meaning of these and similar sayings is clear and evident, and should at no time be misapprehended. To this same truth bear witness these words which He hath revealed: 'God was alone; there was none else besides Him. He will always remain what He hath ever been.'[19]

This concept of the uniqueness of God is the meaning of the oft repeated phrase in Qur'án that 'there is no God but God'. Likewise in the writings of the Báb we find 'Verily, verily, I am God, no God is there but Me; in truth all others except Me are My creatures',[20] just as we find throughout the writings of Bahá'u'lláh the phrase 'no God is there but Him'.

Knowing His worth, God brings into existence beings capable of knowing and worshiping Him. But because the Creator is eternal, this process of creating such beings must also be eternal. Consequently, we can discuss this process as being without beginning, or we can understand the particular expressions of that will (such as the expression of this process on our planet) as having a beginning.[21] It is from this perspective that we can comprehend the tradition that portrays God as a 'Hidden Treasure' and the creation of humankind as the process by which the attributes of that treasure become manifest in the world of creation:

> I testify that Thou wast a hidden Treasure wrapped within Thine immemorial Being and an impenetrable Mystery enshrined in Thine own Essence. Wishing to reveal Thyself, Thou didst call into being the Greater and the Lesser Worlds, and didst choose Man above all Thy creatures, and didst make Him a sign of both of these worlds, O Thou Who art our Lord, the Most Compassionate![22]

In other words, the process of creation begins with the Creator who wishes to manifest His attributes in the contingent world. However, this recognition means little unless it is freely understood and chosen. Therefore, in fashioning His creation, God has endowed a being (humankind) with the capacity to manifest the attributes of God as a means of understanding these attributes and as a sign of that recognition.[23] It is in this sense that human beings are made in the 'image' of God:

> Veiled in My immemorial being and in the ancient eternity of My essence, I knew My love for thee; therefore I created thee, have engraved on thee Mine image and revealed to thee My beauty.[24]

Of course, Bahá'u'lláh explains that while everything in creation reflects some of the attributes of God, only human beings are capable of manifesting or reflecting all the divine attributes:

> Upon the inmost reality of each and every created thing He hath shed the light of one of His names, and made it a recipient of the glory of one of His attributes. Upon the reality of man, however, He hath focused the radiance of all of His names and attributes, and made it a mirror of His own Self. Alone of all created things man hath been singled out for so great a favor, so enduring a bounty.[25]

This, then, is God's objective, to fashion a being capable of manifesting all of His attributes in the contingent world. So it is that from God emanates the will to create such a being, and this will 'Abdu'l-Bahá alludes to as 'the First Will', what is sometimes alluded to in the scriptures as the Holy Spirit:

> The first thing which emanated from God is that universal reality, which the ancient philosophers termed the 'First Mind', and which the people of Bahá call the 'First Will'.[26]

Of course, the 'First Will' must find expression in the contingent world before creation is effected, and the vehicle for that expression is the 'Word of God':

> Thou didst wish to make Thyself known unto men; therefore, Thou didst, through a word of Thy mouth, bring creation into being and fashion the universe.[27]

In the sense that this Word symbolizes the eternal expression of God's creative thought, this 'Word' is ineffable, but as that Word becomes expressed in the contingent world, it must needs find some means of conveyance. That intermediary is the Manifestation:

> And since there can be no tie of direct intercourse to bind the one true God with His creation, and no resemblance whatever can exist between the transient and the Eternal, the contingent and the Absolute, He hath ordained that in every age and dispensation a pure and stainless Soul be made manifest in the kingdoms of earth and heaven.[28]

Because the Manifestations are the means by which the eternal Word as expression of the divine Will is conveyed to the human reality, the Prophets are characterized as the Word of God incarnate, a poetic epithet that designates two capacities. On a more literal level it signifies the capacity of the Prophet to issue forth in human language divine guidance and education, since human progress is only 'latent' until, like a flame 'hidden within the candle'[29] the capacities are ignited by the divine educator, the Prophet. At the same time, the Manifestation is the Word made flesh – the Prophet perfectly manifests all the attributes of God. In short, if the Word represents the divine Will, and the divine Will expresses the attributes of God, then the Prophet is that Word and that Will translated into terms that human beings can best come to understand.

As a perfect soul, the Manifestation perfectly manifests the Holy Spirit as a perfect mirror might reflect the attributes of the sun's rays. The soul of the Manifestation is but an emanation from God, but unlike the human soul which potentially manifests the attributes of God, the soul of the Manifestation inherently manifests or incarnates all the attributes of God, though not the essence of God (by definition, nothing can). Stated another way, the soul of the Prophet is a complete expression of Godliness because the divine perfections of God are manifested in the appearance of the Prophet in the same way that 'the sun manifests all its glory in the mirror'.[30] This is what is meant in the first chapter of John, 'Abdu'l-Bahá observes, when it is stated: 'The Word was with God, and the Word was God'; namely, that, from the human perspective there is no effective difference between the two realities:

> If a pure, fine mirror faces the sun, the light and heat, the form and the image of the sun will be resplendent in it with such manifestation that if a beholder says of the sun, which is brilliant and visible in the mirror, 'This is the sun', it is true.[31]

'Abdu'l-Bahá does not mean to imply here that the soul of the Prophet is not also an emanation from God. He is careful to point out that when the attributes of God become manifest, the sun has not become divided into parts – the mirror is not a piece of the sun: 'the mirror is the mirror, and the sun is the sun. The One Sun, even if it appears in numerous mirrors, is one'.[32]

Infallibility as an Inherent Attribute of the Prophets

The essential distinction between the Prophet and ordinary human beings is not the quantity of attributes reflected. Unlike ordinary human beings, the Manifestation is inherently a fully actualized expression of the attributes of God. The human being can only strive to fulfill the capacity to reflect divine attributes, but since each attribute is capable of being infinitely more refined, such striving will never be perfectly accomplished for a single attribute, must less for the totality of attributes: 'for the human perfections are infinite. Thus, however learned a man may be, we can imagine one more learned.'[33] Even were it possible for an individual to achieve perfection, there would still remain an important difference between the perfected ordinary human being and the Manifestation – the Manifestations inherently possess that perfection from the beginning. Hence, this distinction between the Prophet and the ordinary human being is not a matter of degree but of an *essential* distinction.

To clarify more completely this difference, as well as the

additional distinction of the fact that the Prophet conveys divine guidance, 'Abdu'l-Bahá compares the 'individual reality' of the Prophets to the sun and the rest of humankind to the moon:

> But the individual reality of the Manifestations of God is a holy reality, and for that reason it is sanctified and, in that which concerns its nature and quality, is distinguished from all other things. It is like the sun, which by its essential nature produces light and cannot be compared to the moon, just as the particles that compose the globe of the sun cannot be compared with those which compose the moon. The particles and organization of the former produce rays, but the particles of which the moon is composed do not produce rays but need to borrow light. So other human realities are those souls who, like the moon, take light from the sun; but that Holy Reality is luminous in Himself.[34]

Shoghi Effendi likewise reflects on this theological or ontological doctrine when he discusses how the Manifestation, though not an incarnation of the Deity (not part of God's essence, which is indivisible), is a 'complete incarnation of the names and attributes of God'.[35]

This distinction between ordinary human beings and the Manifestation is extremely important as we consider the question of infallibility in relation to the Prophets. Simply stated, if infallibility is an essential attribute of Godliness, then it must likewise be an inseparable attribute of the Prophets who inherently manifest all the divine attributes. 'Abdu'l-Bahá makes this abundantly clear when He observes:

> Essential infallibility is peculiar to the supreme Manifestation, for it is His essential requirement, and an essential requirement cannot be separated from the thing itself. The rays are the essential necessity of the sun and are inseparable from it. Knowledge is an essential necessity of God and is inseparable from Him. Power is an essential necessity of God and is inseparable from Him. If it could be separated from Him, He would not be God. If the rays could be separated from the sun, it would not be the sun. Therefore, if one imagines separation of the Most Great

Infallibility from the supreme Manifestation, He would not be the supreme Manifestation, and He would lack the essential perfections.[36]

This description of what seems to be the unique station and powers of the Prophet leads us to a more subtle question regarding their nature. However completely human advancement depends upon the systematic appearance of these infallible beings, they are sometimes alluded to in the Bahá'í writings as human beings:

> ... of all men, the most accomplished, the most distinguished, and the most excellent are the Manifestations of the Sun of Truth. Nay, all else besides these Manifestations, live by the operation of their Will, and move and have their being through the outpourings of their grace.[37]

Of course, though they are alluded to here in some generic sense as 'man', (i.e. as a 'human being'), we observe again the unmistakably clear distinction between the Prophet as the source of human advancement, and ordinary human beings who 'live by operation of Their Will (the 'sun' as compared to the 'moon').

However, in spite of these essential distinctions between the Manifestation and the ordinary human being, Bahá'u'lláh takes great care to explain in *The Kitáb-i-Íqán* that one of the most important ways in which the appearance of each new Prophet imposes a Day of Judgment on those to whom they come is the fact that the Prophets are, to outward seeming, but ordinary human beings; consequently, they are initially recognized only by the pure in heart:

> For this reason, the divines of the age and those possessed of wealth, would scorn and scoff at these people. Even as He hath revealed concerning them that erred: 'Then said the chiefs of His people who believed not, "We see in Thee but a man like ourselves; and we see not any who have followed Thee except our meanest ones of hasty judgment, nor see we any excellence in you above ourselves: nay, we deem you liars."'[38]

In this same discussion, Bahá'u'lláh notes that one of the ways God tests the motive of those who seek the Promised Return is that each Manifestation appears in the guise of an unexpected persona:[39] Moses was a stutterer who was reputed to have murdered an Egyptian;[40] Christ was a lowly carpenter of questionable birth who ministered among prostitutes, illiterate fishermen, and tax collectors; Muḥammad was reputed to be illiterate; the Báb was a merchant; Bahá'u'lláh, though born into nobility, spent most of His life as an exiled prisoner.

Furthermore, since the earliest followers of the Prophet are often the outcasts, the meek, the lowly and the impoverished, the entrenched ecclesiastes from the previous dispensation are usually the most ferocious persecutors of the Prophet:

> They caviled at those holy Manifestations, and protested saying: 'None hath followed you except the abject amongst us, those who are worthy of no attention.' Their aim was to show that no one amongst the learned, the wealthy, and the renowned believed in them.[41]

The Two Stations of the Prophet

Because there comes a point in the lives of the Prophets at which they announce their station and proclaim Their mission, the question may still arise as to whether the Manifestations are essentially distinct from other human beings from the beginning, or a human being suddenly endowed or transformed. This may seem an unnecessary question in light of what we have already established (i.e. that the Prophet is inherently distinct from ordinary human beings). But given the fact that the Prophets themselves seem to describe a point of transformation in their lives, we would do well to consider what exactly occurs, because this is a terribly significant question, no less important or different in character in its own way from the question of Christology in Christian theology.

At the heart of this issue is Bahá'u'lláh's discussion about the dual nature of the Prophets. From some of His statements we might infer support for believing that the Prophets are ordinary human beings who undergo some profound and essential change. Bahá'u'lláh states that God has assigned unto the Manifestation a 'twofold nature':

> He hath, moreover, conferred upon Him a double station. The first station, which is related to His innermost reality, representeth Him as One Whose voice is the voice of God Himself. To this testifieth the tradition: 'Manifold and mysterious is My relationship with God. I am He, Himself, and He is I, Myself, except that I am that I am, and He is that He is.' And in like manner, the words: 'Arise, O Muḥammad, for lo, the Lover and the Beloved are joined together and made one in Thee.' He similarly saith: 'There is no distinction whatsoever between Thee and Them, except that They are Thy Servants.' The second station is the human station, exemplified by the following verses: 'I am but a man like you.' 'Say, praise be to my Lord! Am I more than a man, an apostle?'[42]

This passage might seem to indicate that the Prophet is an ordinary human being until transformed into a Prophet. If the Prophet is an ordinary human being whom God suddenly transforms and empowers, then His infallibility might be confined to that post-epiphany condition; whereas, if the Prophet is essentially different from birth, then all of His actions and powers (including infallibility) would be part of His nature from the beginning, in which case we need to decide what these points of ostensible change and dual stations really indicate.

A further study of Bahá'u'lláh's discussion of these stations helps to resolve any ambiguities about this question.[43] The first of these two stations Bahá'u'lláh designates as the station of 'essential unity':

> In this respect, if thou callest them all by one name, and dost ascribe to them the same attribute, thou hast not erred from the truth. Even as He hath revealed: 'No distinction do We make between any of His Messengers!' For they one and all summon the people of the earth to acknowledge the Unity of God, and

herald unto them the Kaw<u>th</u>ar of an infinite grace and bounty. They are all invested with the robe of Prophethood, and honored with the mantle of glory. Thus hath Muḥammad, the Point of the Qur'án, revealed: 'I am all the Prophets.' Likewise, He saith: 'I am the first Adam, Noah, Moses, and Jesus.'[44]

Bahá'u'lláh goes on to explain that to study the Prophets with a discerning eye is to realize that they are all part of one coordinated process, that the religion of God is one religion revealed in stages, and that the Word of God as an expression of the Will of God is pre-existent, eternal and changeless:

> It is clear and evident to thee that all the Prophets are the Temples of the Cause of God, Who have appeared clothed in divers attire. If thou wilt observe with discriminating eyes, thou wilt behold them all abiding in the same tabernacle, soaring in the same heaven, seated upon the same throne, uttering the same speech, and proclaiming the same Faith. Such is the unity of those Essences of being, those Luminaries of infinite and immeasurable splendor. Wherefore, should one of these Manifestations of Holiness proclaim saying: 'I am the return of all the Prophets,' He verily speaketh the truth.[45]

The second station Bahá'u'lláh designates 'the station of distinction'. Bahá'u'lláh states that this station 'pertaineth to the world of creation and to the limitations thereof':

> In this respect, each Manifestation of God hath a distinct individuality, a definitely prescribed mission, a predestined Revelation, and specially designated limitations. Each one of them is known by a different name, is characterized by a special attribute, fulfills a definite Mission, and is entrusted with a particular Revelation.[46]

Bahá'u'lláh observes that this necessity of adapting each revelation to a particular historical context is what causes the appearance of differences and 'limitations' among the teachings of the Prophets and among the religions that derive from these teachings:

It is because of this difference in their station and mission that the words and utterances flowing from these Well-springs of divine knowledge appear to diverge and differ.[47]

In other words, the 'limitations' are the conditions of history, not the inadequacy of the Prophet. Therefore Bahá'u'lláh emphasizes that this difference is in outward form only; the essential truth each conveys is fundamentally the same: 'Otherwise, in the eyes of them that are initiated into the mysteries of divine wisdom, all their utterances are in reality but the expressions of one Truth.'[48] Bahá'u'lláh notes that people have confused these two stations and thereby conclude that there is some distinction between or conflict among the various Prophets: 'As most of the people have failed to appreciate those stations to which We have referred, they therefore feel perplexed and dismayed at the varying utterances pronounced by Manifestations that are essentially one and the same.'[49]

Thus it seems clear from these passages and from the entirety of the *Kitáb-i-Íqán* that Bahá'u'lláh is not distinguishing between the human condition and the divine condition of the Manifestations when He employs terms designating this 'twofold nature' and 'double station'. He is instead making an important distinction between the changeless truth of the unseen world that underlies phenomenal reality and the need to translate that truth into terms appropriate for the particular historical circumstances and human capacities extant at the time and place in which the Prophet appears. This is, in effect, the abiding rationale for having divine guidance conveyed through a human personality living among us – we need to be able to identity with these other worldly teachers in order to relate our condition to the divine reality.

Both stations and both conditions are equally true and valid descriptions of the reality of the Prophet. On the one hand, it is 'Through their appearance the Revelation of God is made manifest, and by their countenance the Beauty of God is revealed'.[50] And yet, each also manifests 'absolute servitude, utter destitution and complete self-effacement. Even as He saith: "I am the servant of God. I am but a man like you."'[51]

Bahá'u'lláh concludes this discussion by implying that, in reality, these stations are not distinct realities of the Prophet, not a change in essence, but two distinct perspectives of the same appearance: 'Thus it is that whatsoever be their utterance, whether it pertain to the realm of Divinity, Lordship, Prophethood, Messengership, Guardianship, Apostleship or Servitude, all is true, beyond the shadow of a doubt.'[52]

The Meaning of the Point of Transformation

If the Prophet is essentially distinct from birth and if the dual stations do not allude to a human condition, in what sense is the Prophet a human being and what does He really mean when He says 'I am but a man like you'? Even more to the point, the Manifestations themselves describe a point of crucial change in their lives, what seems to be a type of epiphany or transformation in their station or status or being. Is this point of transformation their sudden awareness of their mission?

The language with which they describe this event seems to imply a sudden awareness that they have been anointed, that they are now distinct from others. Do they not portray a sudden infusion of knowledge, insight, inspiration and, we might presume, an infallibility associated with these conditions? Do they not announce that they have now submitted their will to the Will of God, that they have now become an instrument of the divine Will, and that they are now the mouthpiece through which God is speaking to humankind?

It is true that what *seems* to be happening is a transformation in the essential nature of the Prophet but a closer study reveals something else. True, the Manifestations describe a point at which something dramatic happens to them: Moses hears the voice of God emerge from the burning bush; Buddha becomes 'enlightened' sitting under the banyan tree; Christ experiences the descent of the holy spirit in the form of a dove as He is being baptized; while He is meditating in a cave, Muḥammad sees a vision of the Angel Gabriel; in Karbilá the Báb has a vision of the martyred Imám Ḥusayn; and Bahá'u'lláh sees the veiled maiden while He is imprisoned in the Síyáh-Chál. Before these experiences, we know relatively little about the lives of these figures. They function more or less as ordinary citizens. They may be distinguished by spiritual character and good deeds but prior to this experience few recognize them as having authority, nor do the Prophets themselves openly proclaim that they have authority or any special status. Furthermore, some of the Prophets describe this experience to others as unexpected and astounding.

The most complete description of such an experience is Bahá'u'lláh's own verbal portrait: 'I felt as if something flowed from the crown of My head over My breast, even as a mighty torrent that precipitateth itself upon the earth from the summit of a lofty mountain. Every limb of My body would, as a result, be set afire.'[53] In addition to portraying the mystical aspects of this experience, Bahá'u'lláh seems to describe a process of being transformed from one status to another:

> O King! I was but a man like others, asleep upon My couch, when lo, the breezes of the All-Glorious were wafted over Me, and taught Me the knowledge of all that hath been. This thing is not from Me, but from One Who is Almighty and All-Knowing. And He bade Me lift up My voice between earth and heaven, and for this there befell Me what hath caused the tears of every man of understanding to flow. The learning current amongst men I studied not; their schools I entered not. Ask of the city wherein I dwelt, that thou mayest be well assured that I am not of them who speak falsely. This is but a leaf which the winds of the will of thy Lord, the Almighty, the All-Praised, have stirred.[54]

Because Bahá'u'lláh in this epistle to the Sháh says that the 'breezes of the All-Glorious' taught Him 'the knowledge of all that hath been', we might understandably assume that this signifies a sudden infusion of omniscience from which derives His infallibility. Indeed, we might well assume that His infallibility is unique to those moments when this process of revelation is occurring. Such a conclusion might seem to be confirmed by the various written descriptions of how Bahá'u'lláh orally dictated His revealed work. Unlike human artists who must labor over their work, often taking a manuscript through many drafts and revisions, Bahá'u'lláh made no revisions and dictated without hesitation or pause.

Adib Taherzadeh describes this process in some detail in his study *The Revelation of Bahá'u'lláh*. He notes that the words of revelation 'poured forth' without revision or change and with such rapidity that 'His amanuensis was often incapable of recording them'.[55] The amanuensis, usually Mírzá Áqá Ján, would record this dictation in a hurried shorthand, and the illegible script would then be transcribed by the amanuensis, whereupon Bahá'u'lláh would review the finished work, correct any mistakes the amanuensis had made, then approve the copy.

The idea that the Prophet is in these instances functioning as a conduit for the word of God, not as creative artist in His own right, might seem confirmed by Bahá'u'lláh's own frank enunciation of His complete subservience to the Will of God:

> I have no will but Thy will, O my Lord, and cherish no desire except Thy desire. From my pen floweth only the summons which Thine own exalted pen hath voiced, and my tongue uttereth naught save what the Most Great Spirit hath itself proclaimed in the kingdom of Thine eternity. I am stirred by nothing else except the winds of Thy will, and breathe no word except the words which, by Thy leave and Thine inspiration, I am led to pronounce.[56]

However, there are various other passages in the Bahá'í writings which seem to indicate that Bahá'u'lláh as an individual personality has some active part to play in this creative process by which the divine Will is translated into human speech. For example, Shoghi Effendi states that the revelation of the Kitáb-i-Aqdas 'may well be regarded as the brightest emanation of the *mind* of Bahá'u'lláh' (emphasis added).[57] In characterizing the *Hidden Words*, Shoghi Effendi observes, 'They are jewel-like thoughts cast out of the *mind* of the Manifestation of God to admonish and counsel men' (emphasis added).[58] And yet again in discussing the final works produced by Bahá'u'lláh, Shoghi Effendi employs the same description:

> These Tablets – mighty and final effusions of His indefatigable pen – must rank among the choicest fruits which His *mind* has yielded, and mark the consummation of His forty-year-long ministry. (emphasis added)[59]

Shoghi Effendi seems to bestow on Bahá'u'lláh a more wide-ranging accolade when he praises the capacity of the Prophet to shape human history through 'His Will' by implementing 'His design for the children of men':

> Not ours, the living witnesses of the all-subduing potency of His Faith, to question, for a moment, and however dark the misery that enshrouds the world, the ability of Bahá'u'lláh to forge, with the hammer of His Will, and through the fire of tribulation, upon the anvil of this travailing age, and in the particular shape His *mind* has envisioned, these scattered and mutually destructive fragments into which a perverse world has fallen, into one single unit, solid and indivisible, able to execute His design for the children of men. (emphasis added)[60]

What is Really going on Here?

This perplexity about whose art this is (God's or the Prophet's) seems to lead us back to this concept of transformation. As we have already noted, whether operating in the station of essential unity (the eternal Word made flesh) or in the station of distinction (shaping the Word to befit historical context), the Manifestation is functioning as the precise expression of the First Will. If the Prophet has a creative part to play in this, it is an artistic process quite beyond a process we can understand with any exactitude. For if the Prophet fashions the inspiration into human language, He does so instantaneously, perfectly, with the tools of infallibility and flawless divine guidance. For all intents and purposes, the artistry of the Prophet is, at least from our perspective, naught but God's artistry.

What is more, our inability to distinguish between the power of Prophets and the power of God working through them is apparent even in the accounts from their childhood. Various anecdotes from the early life of the Prophets depict them as already exhibiting an other-worldly knowledge and an immaculate character. For example, there is the biblical account of Christ at the age of twelve. After going with His parents to Jerusalem to celebrate the feast of the Passover, He becomes separated from them, whereupon they return to Jerusalem and find Him conversing with the scholarly teachers: 'And he said unto them, How is it that ye sought me? wist ye not that I must be about my Father's business? And they understood not the saying which he spake unto them.'[61]

Several anecdotes from the early life of the Báb and of Bahá'u'lláh reflect this same precociousness of beings who possess extraordinary knowledge and who are all too aware of the fact that they are born into this world with a divine mission. Historian Hasan Balyuzi in his biography of the Báb relates several such episodes. In one of the more revealing of these, Balyuzi describes an episode in which the Báb seems to compare Himself with Christ:

> Hájí Mírzá Habíbu'lláh also tells us that, apart from teaching boys, Shaykh 'Ábid had a regular class for theological students. On one occasion some of these students posed a question which after a long period of discussion remained unresolved. Shaykh 'Ábid told them that he would consult some authoritative works that same night and on the morrow present them with the solution. Just then the Báb, who had been listening, spoke and with sound reasoning propounded the answer which they sought. They were wonder-struck, for they had no recollection of discussing that particular subject within earshot of the Báb, who might then have looked up references in books and memorized them to repeat parrot-wise. Shaykh 'Ábid asked Him where He had gained that knowledge. The boy replied smilingly with a couplet from Háfiz:
>
>> Should the grace of the Holy Spirit once again deign to assist,
>> Others will also do what Christ could perform.[62]

There are many other documented anecdotes from the lives of the Báb and Bahá'u'lláh that demonstrate both their innate wisdom and knowledge as well as their consciousness of their specialized purpose. It is sufficient here to note two incidents which clearly indicate that, prior to the dramatic point when His ministry begins, the Manifestation is conscious that He has a spiritual purpose and is well aware of the specific nature of that purpose.

Some time before the Báb declared His mission to Mullá Ḥusayn (on the eve of 23 May 1844), the Báb had been in Karbilá where, on more than one occasion, Siyyid Káẓim clearly indicated his reverence for the special station of the Báb whenever he was in the Báb's presence. Less inferential is an account in *The Dawn-Breakers* of Shaykh Ḥasan-i-Zunúzí regarding his encounter with Bahá'u'lláh in 1851, two years prior to Bahá'u'lláh's vision in the Síyáh-Chál. At the time, the Shaykh was an old man 'bowed with age' and was visiting the shrine of the Imám Ḥusayn. A few years earlier, in 1848, the Báb had told him to proceed to Karbilá because he would be 'destined to behold, with your own eyes, the beauteous countenance of the promised Ḥusayn'. The Báb went on to give the Shaykh a touching assignment when that event occurred:

> As you gaze upon that radiant face, do also remember Me. Convey to Him the expression of My loving devotion . . . I have entrusted you with a great mission. Beware lest your heart grow faint, lest you forget the glory with which I have invested you.[63]

Three years later as the old Bábí passed the gate of the inner courtyard of the shrine, his 'eyes, for the first time, fell upon Bahá'u'lláh':

> What shall I recount regarding the countenance which I beheld! The beauty of that face, those exquisite features which no pen or brush dare describe, His penetrating glance, His kindly face, the majesty of His bearing, the sweetness of His smile, the luxuriance of His jet-black flowing locks, left an indelible impression upon my soul. I was then an old man, bowed with age. How lovingly He advanced towards me! He took me by the hand and, in a tone

which at once betrayed power and beauty, addressed me in these words: 'This very day I have purposed to make you known as a Bábí throughout Karbilá.' Still holding my hand in His, He continued to converse with me. He walked with me all along the market-street, and in the end He said: 'Praise be to God that you have remained in Karbilá, and have beheld with your own eyes the countenance of the promised Ḥusayn.' I recalled instantly the promise which had been given me by the Báb. His words, which I had regarded as referring to a remote future, I had not shared with anyone. These words of Bahá'u'lláh moved me to the depths of my being. I felt impelled to proclaim to a heedless people, at that very moment and with all my soul and power, the advent of the promised Ḥusayn. He bade me, however, repress my feelings and conceal my emotions. 'Not yet,' He breathed into my ears; 'the appointed Hour is approaching. It has not yet struck. Rest assured and be patient.' From that moment all my sorrows vanished. My soul was flooded with joy.[64]

Of course, one might well argue that these anecdotes hardly constitute statements of theological doctrine. But there is other significant evidence in the authoritative writings of the Bahá'í Faith that explicitly proclaims that these individual do not become Manifestations – that they are from birth distinct from ordinary human beings.

We have already noted 'Abdu'l-Bahá's statement that infallibility and other divine attributes are inherent powers of the Prophet, but in another passage 'Abdu'l-Bahá notes that the Manifestations are aware of their station from early childhood: 'Verily, from the beginning that Holy Reality is conscious of the secret of existence, and from the age of childhood signs of greatness appear and are visible in Him. Therefore, how can it be that with all these bounties and perfections He should have no consciousness?'[65] Here 'Abdu'l-Bahá not only observes that they are aware of their stations; he also notes that They possess an infallible wisdom (a consciousness of the 'secret of existence') from the beginning.

In this same discussion, 'Abdu'l-Bahá explains that the epiphany the Prophets experience at the beginning of their ministries does *not*, therefore, signify a change in their spiritual essence or

Their spiritual station, both of which are Theirs from the beginning of Their lives: 'Then it is evident and clear that Christ did not reach to the station of Messiahship and its perfections at the time of baptism, when the Holy Spirit descended upon Him in the likeness of a dove.'[66] Bahá'u'lláh confirms this conclusion when He observes the following regarding God's designation of Prophethood:

> Whomsoever He ordaineth as a Prophet, he, verily, hath been a Prophet from the beginning that hath no beginning, and will thus remain until the end that hath no end, inasmuch as this is an act of God. And whosoever is made a Viceregent by Him, shall be a Viceregent in all the worlds, for this is an act of God.[67]

Another helpful insight into the essential distinction between the Prophets and ordinary human beings is given by Shoghi Effendi when he explains a fundamental and profound ontological difference: 'The soul or spirit of the individual comes into being with the conception of his physical body. The Prophets, unlike us, are pre-existent. The Soul of Christ existed in the spiritual world before His birth in this world.'[68]

Bahá'u'lláh also seems to allude to this pre-existent reality of the Prophets in the Kitáb-i-Aqdas when, in the course of enunciating His station and authority, He explains that the Prophets were created and were taught the realities of the spiritual world before the creation of the earth itself (or, perhaps, before the active process of bringing forth an 'ever-advancing civilization' began):

> Take heed that ye dispute not idly concerning the Almighty and His Cause, for lo! He hath appeared amongst you invested with a Revelation so great as to encompass all things, whether of the past or of the future. Were We to address Our theme by speaking in the language of the inmates of the Kingdom, We would say: 'In truth, God created that School ere He created heaven and earth, and We entered it before the letters B and E were joined and knit together.' Such is the language of Our servants in Our Kingdom; consider what the tongue of the dwellers of Our exalted Dominion would utter, for We have taught them Our

knowledge and have revealed to them whatever had lain hidden in God's wisdom. Imagine then what the Tongue of Might and Grandeur would utter in His All-Glorious Abode![69]

In light of these important differences between the reality of the Manifestations and that of ordinary human beings, we might find it helpful to think of these specialized individuals as visitors from the unseen world come in disguise to live among us and guide us without directly taking from us the reins of control in our lives. And yet we do well to appreciate that while they have no desire to possess temporal authority, their guidance, their wisdom, and their actions are infallible and unfailing standards for us to follow. Bahá'u'lláh thus observes that only the Manifestation has essential or inherent infallibility, what Bahá'u'lláh calls 'the Most Great Infallibility': 'He Who is the Dawning-place of God's Cause hath no partner in the Most Great Infallibility.'[70] 'Abdu'l-Bahá further explains this concept with the following:

> . . . the supreme Manifestations certainly possess essential infallibility, therefore whatever emanates from Them is identical with the truth, and conformable to reality. They are not under the shadow of the former laws. Whatever They say is the word of God, and whatever They perform is an upright action.[71]

Here 'Abdu'l-Bahá verifies that infallibility is an essential attribute of the Prophet (and therefore an inherent property from the beginning), but He also affirms that essential sinlessness is an inherent part of their condition and is *distinct* from infallibility. Thus everything the Prophets say is 'identical with the truth and 'whatever They perform is an upright action'. The concept of the Most Great Infallibility is, thus, not concerned solely with unquestioned authority or with moments of inspiration.

Does this perfection that is an inherent part of their essential reality also imply omniscience? After all, they perfectly manifest all the attributes of God and omniscience is an attribute of God. Such an inference seems logically unavoidable and, in fact, Shoghi Effendi states as much when he observes that the Prophet is 'omniscient at will'.[72]

But what about omnipotence? Is not omnipotence also an attribute of God? Do we dare ascribe this attribute to the Manifestations? Do the Prophets have the power to do anything they wish? Of course, since the Manifestations one and all profess that they subordinate their personal will to do the Will of God, we must presume that anything they choose to do is naught but the Will of God. But, in that capacity, could they literally do anything they wished so long as it was sanctioned by God?

Throughout the Bahá'í writings we find the passage that God does whatever He wishes, and since the Prophet is operating as God's 'viceregent', we might assume He too would possess such power, should it become necessary. For example, we find Bahá'u'lláh stating the following in the Kitáb-i-Aqdas regarding a law He has revealed: 'God hath removed the restrictions on travel that had been imposed in the Bayán. He, verily, is the Unconstrained; He doeth as He pleaseth and ordaineth whatsoever He willeth.'[73] Likewise, there is the familiar episode in the life of Bahá'u'lláh when in Baghdad He was taunted by the 'ulamá to produce a miracle if He were truly a Prophet of God.[74] While the assembled ecclesiastes 'failed to arrive at a decision, and had chosen to drop the matter',[75] Bahá'u'lláh had agreed to do whatever they requested. In effect, we must presume He would have been capable of fulfilling whatever miracle they could request.[76]

In fact, the Báb in the *Qayyúmu'l-Asmá'* alludes to Bahá'u'lláh as 'great and *omnipotent* Master' (emphasis added).[77] But perhaps the clearest indication that omnipotence is indeed an attribute of the Prophets is this astounding statement by Bahá'u'lláh Himself:

> Within the throat of this Youth there lie prisoned accents which, if revealed to mankind to an extent smaller than a needle's eye, would suffice to cause every mountain to crumble, the leaves of the trees to be discolored and their fruits to fall; would compel every head to bow down in worship and every face to turn in adoration towards this *omnipotent* Ruler Who, at sundry times and in diverse manners, appeareth as a devouring flame, as a billowing ocean, as a radiant light, as the tree which, rooted in

the soil of holiness, lifteth its branches and spreadeth out its limbs as far as and beyond the throne of deathless glory. (emphasis added)[78]

No doubt the reality of this power accounts for the meaning of the symbolic story of the temptation of Christ.[79] While we can presume that a Prophet would never accede to such temptation for worldly ascendancy, the fact is, theoretically, the Manifestation could use His powers for selfish purposes if He chose to do so. The importance in our understanding this attribute is to appreciate the degree of sacrifice and pain and humiliation the Prophets willingly endure for our sake when at any moment they could overcome any obstacle, should they choose to do so.

Of course, the Manifestations rarely employ miracles and other sensational displays of their power or capacity because their purpose is to conceal overt or obvious demonstrations of their divine capacity and power that the sincerity of the followers might be tested and trained. The point is, however, that we can only vaguely appreciate the true nature of their station, powers and capacities.

What the 'Station of Distinction' Really Means

If we have satisfactorily concluded that the Prophet is not an ordinary human being, we have not finished exploring precisely what is meant by the 'station of distinction'. For while we may have demonstrated that such a station does not designate an ordinary human condition, we have not exactly clarified what it does designate or how it works.

When we examine Bahá'u'lláh's definition of 'the station of distinction', we realize that He is alluding to the fact that each Manifestation, though an integral part of one 'school' of Prophets (a divinely coordinated team of educators working in perfect unity at the behest of the divine Will for the progress of humankind on this planet), must fashion everything He does and says to befit the particular conditions that exist at the time of His appearance. He must gauge the propriety of everything He does or says to the 'distinct' condition of humanity in general at that historical time, and, most immediately, He must respond to the followers of the previous Prophet in whose midst He appears.

As Bahá'u'lláh explains in the *Kitáb-i-Íqán*, each Prophet carefully relates His teaching to the historical context in which He appears. If He did not, He would not be an effective teacher, any more than an ordinary school teacher would be effective were he or she to enter a classroom and begin teaching nuclear physics without being aware of the age, the beliefs, the social and educational background, and the fundamental capacity of the class. One obvious indication of their awareness of this context are the Prophets' allusions to how they withhold much that they could tell (and perhaps would dearly love to share), because they must shape what they say to the capacity and limitations of humankind. Christ said, 'I have yet many things to say to you, but you cannot bear them now.'[80] Bahá'u'lláh repeatedly speaks of how He shapes what He says to the capacity of the hearer, not because of His own limitations:

> All that I have revealed unto thee with the tongue of power, and have written for thee with the pen of might, hath been in accordance with thy capacity and understanding, not with My state and the melody of My voice.[81]

In the Kitáb-i-Aqdas Bahá'u'lláh says much the same thing when He observes, 'These words are to your measure, not to God's . . . I swear by God, were We to lift the veil, ye would be dumbfounded.'[82]

This is a subtle issue – how the Manifestation gears His ministry to a distinct set of circumstances, how He must stretch us as far as we can go without going beyond the bounds of our capacity, something Bahá'u'lláh explains with the exquisite passage about timeliness in relation to revelation:

> How great the multitude of truths which the garment of words can never contain! How vast the number of such verities as no expression can adequately describe, whose significance can never

be unfolded, and to which not even the remotest allusions can be made! How manifold are the truths which must remain unuttered until the appointed time is come! Even as it hath been said: 'Not everything that a man knoweth can be disclosed, nor can everything that he can disclose be regarded as timely, nor can every timely utterance be considered as suited to the capacity of those who hear it.'

Of these truths some can be disclosed only to the extent of the capacity of the repositories of the light of Our knowledge, and the recipients of Our hidden grace.[83]

Among the numerous other events and statements that exemplify the self-imposed restraint the Prophet must exercise is Shoghi Effendi's description in *God Passes By* of Bahá'u'lláh's command that His amanuensis destroy hundreds of thousands of revealed verses because they were too advanced for this dispensation:

> No less an authority than Mírzá Áqá Ján, Bahá'u'lláh's amanuensis, affirms, as reported by Nabíl, that by the express order of Bahá'u'lláh, hundreds of thousands of verses, mostly written by His own hand, were obliterated and cast into the river. 'Finding me reluctant to execute His orders,' Mírzá Áqá Ján has related to Nabíl, 'Bahá'u'lláh would reassure me saying: 'None is to be found at this time worthy to hear these melodies.' . . . Not once, or twice, but innumerable times, was I commanded to repeat this act.'[84]

This anecdote raises an interesting question. If Bahá'u'lláh had omniscience, then He knew beforehand we would not be ready; why did He, then, bother to reveal these verses in the first place? The answer might be that some response to the revelation altered the course of history (i.e. the failure of religious leaders to accept the revelation). The more likely answer is that He was dramatically demonstrating that revelation is continuous, that there is always more for humanity to learn, and that the more we put to use what we have been taught, the more we can be shown.

Does the Point of Transformation Really have any Significance?

These explanations of the essential reality of the Prophets and the proper implications of the 'station of distinction' are most helpful by way of enabling us to appreciate the incredible nature of these emissaries from the invisible reality, but we are still left with the question of what is really intended by their allusions to the dramatic event associated with the beginning of their ministries. Neither do these discussions explain why they are still alluded to in some passages as human beings.

In the broadest sense, the Manifestations are human beings to the extent that They share things in common with human beings, much as human beings share things in common with the animal kingdom, though remaining distinctly superior. The Prophets have individual souls and personalities which, during their earthly lives, associate with physical bodies. They have families. They have jobs. They get sick. They feel sorrow. They feel pain. They love, grow old and die.

In short, they willingly undergo all the tribulations of human existence, even though they have the power any time they wish to exercise it to escape such limitations. This suffering they endure for our benefit. Their souls may be pre-existent, their knowledge transcendent, but their souls, like human souls, are also emanations from God. In this sense, the souls of the Prophets, though pre-existing in the spiritual realm, do have a beginning: the 'rational soul' of the Manifestation, like the soul of ordinary human beings, 'though it has a beginning, has no end'.[85] Unlike ordinary human souls, the soul of the Prophet is perfect from the beginning and therefore has the powers and capacities associated with a perfected soul (perfect knowledge, perfect will, perfect love, etc.).

So what does happen at the point when the Prophets experience what they portray as a type of transformation – when they manifest what 'Abdu'l-Bahá describes as 'the condition of the divine appearance and heavenly splendor'?[86]

While it might seem that this experience marks the beginning of such a 'condition', 'Abdu'l-Bahá states that this condition has neither beginning nor end, except in relative terms. For example, we speak of the moment when the divine Will reveals the Word of God through the Prophets as the beginning of their ministry. This is the point at which the Holy Spirit actively utilizes this specialized and sanctified soul to reveal the content of the new revelation.

In this sense, there is a point of beginning for the Prophet's ministry and for the new revelation, but it is not the point where an ordinary human being is transformed into a Prophet; it is the point at which the Prophet can now reveal His true identity and actively articulate the Word of God for the new dispensation:

> When beginning is spoken of, it signifies the state of manifesting; and, symbolically, the condition of silence is compared to sleep. For example, a man is sleeping – when he begins to speak, he is awake – but it is always the same individual, whether he be asleep or awake; no difference has occurred in his station, his elevation, his glory, his reality or his nature.[87]

We can infer from this statement that 'Abdu'l-Bahá is alluding to the point at which the Manifestation begins to be actively utilized to convey the new revelation. Prior to this point the Prophet is, relatively speaking, in a 'state of silence' or 'sleep' or concealment. After this point as the Prophet receives the revelation He is in a condition of 'wakefulness', even though the 'man sleeping or waking is the same man'.[88]

'Abdu'l-Bahá's analogy and its similarity to Bahá'u'lláh's description of His experience in the Síyáh-Chál in the Tablet to Náṣiri'd-Dín Sháh is no accident. In fact, 'Abdu'l-Bahá makes this allusion explicit by authoritatively interpreting those very passages in terms of this explanation:

> We come to the explanation of the words of Bahá'u'lláh when He says: 'O king! I was but a man like others, asleep upon My couch, when lo, the breezes of the All-Glorious were wafted over Me, and taught Me the knowledge of all that hath been. This thing is not from Me, but from One Who is Almighty and All-

Knowing.' This is the state of manifestation: it is not sensible; it is an intellectual reality, exempt and freed from time, from past, present and future; it is an explanation, a simile, a metaphor and is not to be accepted literally; it is not a state that can be comprehended by man.[89]

From this explanation we can appreciate that when Bahá'u'lláh speaks of Himself as 'asleep' and 'a man like others', He is not being literal; rather He is alluding to the point at which He can now reveal His true station.

'Abdu'l-Bahá confirms this interpretation by further elucidating the metaphorical nature of Bahá'u'lláh's statement: 'Sleeping is the state of silence; wakefulness is the state of speech. Sleeping is the state of mystery; wakefulness is the state of manifestation.'[90] He goes on to state that

> . . . the Holy Manifestations have ever been, and ever will be, Luminous Realities; no change or variation takes place in Their essence. Before declaring Their manifestation, They are silent and quiet like a sleeper, and after Their manifestation, They speak and are illuminated, like one who is awake.[91]

'Abdu'l-Bahá further explicates the meaning of Bahá'u'lláh's statement in His Tablet to the Sháh by explaining that it alludes to the physical condition of the Manifestation:

> We have mentioned that the Holy Manifestations have three planes. The physical condition, the individual reality, and the center of the appearance of perfection: it is like the sun, its heat and its light. Other individuals have the physical plane, the plane of the rational soul – the spirit and mind. So the saying, 'I was asleep, and the divine breezes passed over Me, and I awoke', is like Christ's saying, 'The body is sad, and the spirit is happy', or again, 'I am afflicted', or 'I am at ease', or 'I am troubled' – these refer to the physical condition and have no reference to the individual reality nor to the manifestation of the Divine Reality.[92]

This, then, is the primary significance of what has occurred: the Prophet has been in a state of silence, concealment, and when the time is ripe for Him to begin, He receives the divine summons and begins to receive the command to speak and act with authority. We might further presume that, though the Prophet has been aware that this point would come, the actual process of receiving the revelation is no less profound and astounding for Him.

A secondary wisdom in or explanation for these epiphanies (these dramatic accounts of the active receipt of the revealed Word) stems from the need to explain to the ordinary human beings around them why the Manifestations are suddenly speaking with divine knowledge and authority. Physically they are unchanged. They have never made such claims before. They have, for the most part, lived relatively ordinary, if exemplary lives. Some explanation is called for, some dramatic event which can serve, even if temporarily, to justify why they now assume a station that they did not claim before.

This explanation does not imply that they dissimulated nor that the accounts they give of this experience are false. They state that they have received a divine summons to reveal the Word of God. To accomplish this, they subordinate their will to the Will of God and speak as they are told. The proof of their station then becomes the effectiveness of the revelation, not some phenomenal demonstration of their special status or station. They may not have 'become' Manifestations (they always were), but they are now actively engaged in fulfilling the task that has awaited them.

The wisdom in this concealment is manifold. It protects them from harm. It causes those to whom they appear to examine the basis for such a claim. It tests and educates humankind in general, as Bahá'u'lláh explains at length in the *Kitáb-i-Íqán*.

The Importance of Studying the Station of Distinction

Even if we accept that the station of the Prophet is from the beginning, that the Prophets enter this life aware of their mission, recalling the celestial abode from which they come, infallibly knowledgeable about the secrets of existence, and awaiting the signal to break their silence, we still may question why it is so crucial that we be aware of the station of distinction. So long as we accept the authority of the words they utter after they break their silence and the station they occupy after they remove their concealment, why do we need to appreciate the historical circumstances of their lives or the context in which they reveal each work?

The answers to this are numerous, subtle and weighty. The most obvious meaning we have already discussed – the Prophet as the perfect educator shapes His message to befit our condition, as any wise educator must. Were the Word of God to be given in its fullness, none could be found to comprehend it, much less benefit from it or apply it. A second and somewhat less obvious significance to the station of distinction is that by coming to understand the specific conditions in which the Prophet appears, we necessarily must recognize the dynamic process of progressive revelation as a whole. For example, it is apparent that the primary audience for the new Manifestation are the followers of the previous Manifestation. Consequently, virtually everything the Prophet says and does is calculated to awaken those souls by alluding to their own beliefs and the admonitions given them by their own Prophet to forewarn them about the advent of the next Manifestation.

Before He publicly declares His station, therefore, Bahá'u'lláh's writing is thick with allusions to Muḥammad and to Qur'ánic verses and Islamic traditions. After His public declaration, He often directs His statements that are not to the believers themselves to the People of the Bayán (i.e. the as yet unconverted followers of the Báb). Towards the end of His ministry He more often directs His statements to the generality of humankind.

In other words, while the teachings of each Manifestation are intended for the whole world (or for as much of the world as could reasonably be affected during His dispensation), the Prophet invariably directs His revelation first of all to the followers of the previous Manifestation who, presumably, are awaiting the advent of the next teacher. Consequently, for one to accept and understand a Manifestation, one must necessarily become aware of the teachings and conditions of the previous revelation. In this vein, we can hardly appreciate fully Christ's teachings without first understanding the Jewish audience and society in which Christ spoke. To understand His 'station of distinction' is to appreciate how His appearance in the guise of a simple carpenter's son confounded the expectations of the Jewish scholars. Likewise, to understand Christ's 'station of distinction' is to appreciate why His teaching technique (parables) so challenged the legalistic Pharisees.

Similarly, to understand the revealed works of the Báb, one must first begin to understand the period of expectation in which the Báb appeared, the condition of Islam as an institution, and the particular conditions in Persia. One must then approach the plethora of allusions in the writings of the Báb to specific Qur'ánic verses and Islamic hadíth.

All in all, the 'station of distinction' relates to the inescapable fact that revelation, however divinely empowered and guided, is a thoroughly historical event and to the fact that history is, from a Bahá'í perspective, a thoroughly spiritual enterprise impelled forward by an unseen but demonstrable spiritual dynamic. To appreciate and understand the full impact and meaning of a revelation, the student of religion must also become a student of history since progressive revelation is an historical process.

Conversely, causal relationships among events in history cannot be fully understood apart from the dynamic motive force underlying historical processes (i.e. the advent of successive Manifestations which, in turn, fosters civilizations). The historian can still make important and valuable observations about events, just as the physicist might catalogue information about falling objects. But when the physicist understands the motive force of gravity or the historian appreciates the influence of the appearance of Prophets, each is able to appreciate the causal relationships that unify experience, something that is veiled from those who do not grasp how these unseen forces work in phenomenal reality.

In this context the Guardian stated that it will be the eventual task of American Bahá'ís to redeem Islam in the West so that its fundamental teachings and tremendous importance in the progress of Western history can be appropriately understood and appreciated:

The mission of the American Bahá'ís is, no doubt, to eventually establish the truth of Islám in the West.

The spirit of Islám, no doubt, was the living germ of modern Civilization; which derived its impetus from the Islamic culture in the Middle ages, a culture that was the fruit of the Faith of Muḥammad.[93]

The Guardian also affirms that the study of Islam is relevant now for any Bahá'í wishing to have a proper perspective on history:

> The truth is that Western historians have for many centuries distorted the facts to suit their religious and ancestral prejudices. The Bahá'ís should try to study history anew, and to base all their investigations first and foremost on the written Scriptures of Islám and Christianity.[94]

In *The Advent of Divine Justice* Shoghi Effendi further observes that the Bahá'ís must study Islam if they are to grasp fully the 'source and background of their Faith', if they are to be capable of becoming stalwart teachers of their beliefs:

> They must strive to obtain, from sources that are authoritative and unbiased, a sound knowledge of the history and tenets of Islám – the source and background of their Faith – and approach reverently and with a mind purged from preconceived ideas the study of the Qur'án which, apart from the sacred scriptures of the Bábí and Bahá'í Revelations, constitutes the only Book which can be regarded as an absolutely authenticated Repository of the Word of God. They must devote special attention to the investigation of those institutions and circumstances that are directly connected with the origin and birth of their Faith, with the station claimed by its Forerunner, and with the laws revealed by its Author.[95]

At least one important implication in these exhortations of the Guardian is that the Bahá'í scholar is privy to the divine logic and the unseen forces shaping history and is further privileged to know how those forces work. Consequently, with this bounty comes responsibility, the obligation to share with others the keys that unlock the mysteries so long veiled from the hungry human mind and heart. No doubt in the course of time these unseen forces will be discovered anyway, because these forces and the laws that describe relationships among them describe reality accurately. Stated another way, spiritual forces and spiritual laws are real and thus have a consistent effect in the phenomenal world; therefore, in time they become apparent and uncovered (discovered) by the unbiased scholar, much as any physical force is in time discovered and the laws associated with that force observed and formulated.

From this perspective, the informed Bahá'í scholar has the potential to offer a profound service to humankind. By virtue of the knowledge imparted by the revelation of Bahá'u'lláh regarding reality, the Bahá'í student (each in his or her own way a demi-Newton, a semi-Copernicus, a mini-Einstein) is capable of applying this insight to every conceivable field of study.

But the reverse of this is equally true, the danger of the inevitable *post hoc* fallacy[96] that necessarily occurs when these forces are ignored, when one attempts to describe reality without an understanding of these principles. For example, the student of religion who fails to recognize the divine station of Christ might logically conclude from studying solely the events accompanying the emergence of the Christian movement that Christianity was not a spiritual force, not a revelation from God, but merely an offshoot of Judaism which attempted some sort of reformation, much like Luther, who had no intention of starting a new religion – he wanted to purge the Roman Church of what he saw as flagrant abuses by church officials and as erroneous or spurious theological doctrines. The scholar who fails to recognize Christ as the Messiah might well be justified in viewing Christianity not as a divine intervention in history or as a source of human salvation, but as a flagrant rebellion by a charismatic law-breaker who refused to accept the sanctity and legitimacy of Judaic law and the established rule of the Sanhedrin.

Similarly, the scholar who does not recognize or acknowledge the station of distinction manifest in the Báb is equally susceptible to perceiving the Bábí movement not as the dawning of a new revelation, but as an attempt at religious reform. Ultimately, however, the secular scholar is forced to confront the specific claims of the founders of religions, the Prophets themselves – either the Manifestation speaks the truth or He does not:

> The point at issue is clear, direct and of utmost brevity. Either Bahá'u'lláh was wise, omniscient and aware of what would ensue, or was ignorant and in error.[97]

Either the Báb was the Qá'im (as He claimed to be in no uncertain terms[98]), or He was a stirrer of sedition, a blasphemer, and worthy of imprisonment.

A *post hoc* fallacy occurs when the scholar begins to examine these religious events to discover causes for their origin (and success) without considering the possibility that unseen but nonetheless actual spiritual forces play a part in the process. It is understandable that a scholar, writing critically in a secular milieu, might find it difficult to defend speculation about an unseen force at work, even when that force seems demonstrated by miraculous or otherwise unexplainable events, such as the ability of the Manifestation to write spontaneously lengthy discourses of stellar style and power or the capacity of the martyrs at Fort Ṭabarsí to perform deeds of unexplainable prowess and fortitude.

But when the Manifestations themselves make very explicit claims that this process of revelation is beyond anything they initiate or create, the scholar is obliged at least to acknowledge those claims. And if the scholar is to be objective, he or she must at least consider the possibility that such claims might be true. This obligation is particularly important because the only alternatives to the Prophet's veracity are either 1) delusion or 2) deception.

The historian who does not wish to become enmeshed in matters of theology is certainly free to abstain from speculation about the veracity of the claim or the causes that account for the progress of a religion – the scholar may simply describe events and claims. However, when one possible cause is chosen over another, then the scholar is not being accurate or even 'scholarly' if due consideration has not been given to the viability of both alternatives. Simply assuming that a secular/humanistic choice is the only valid theory (i.e. that any spiritual explanation is *a priori* unfounded or not worth consideration) is hardly logical or justified (even though it might be more acceptable among the majority of other scholars). This erroneous course of action becomes particularly noisome and grievous when the scholar compounds this assumed conclusion (i.e. that the claim for spiritual empowerment or anointment is *a priori* fallacious) with the *post hoc* fallacy of attributing the powers or capacities of the Prophet to some other cause without demonstrating the logical necessity of that cause being sufficient or even preferable to the alternative possibility – that the Prophet is being honest and accurate.

A brief example may serve to demonstrate the point as it relates to the station of distinction. Like every other Prophet, Muḥammad claims to have been divinely inspired and explicitly affirms that the Qur'án is not His own invention, but is the Word of God revealed to Him:

> But when our clear signs are recited to them, they who look not forward to meet Us, say, 'Bring a different Koran from this, or make some change in it.' Say: It is not for me to change it as mine own soul prompteth. I follow only what is revealed to me.[99]

Like the Báb, Muḥammad was unlearned, and, consequently, His sudden ability to speak with unsurpassed eloquence in an inimitable style was, for His own followers, a profound proof of Muḥammad's claims to be an Apostle of God.

The scholar, of course, may reject the claim or ignore it, but the scholar cannot ignore the fact that Muḥammad was suddenly able to do something that He had never been able to do before and which no one else could do. A related problem for the scholar is the fact that Muḥammad seems to demonstrate an exact knowledge of information to which He had no apparent access. For example, Muḥammad recounts the story of Joseph in exacting detail.[100] We may presume that Muḥammad, like Bahá'u'lláh, had instant access to the learning or writings of others, something Bahá'u'lláh describes in the *Lawḥ-i-Ḥikmat*:

> Thou knowest full well that We perused not the books which men possess and We acquired not the learning current amongst them, and yet whenever We desire to quote the sayings of the learned and of the wise, presently there will appear before the face of thy Lord in the form of a tablet all that which hath appeared in the world and is revealed in the Holy Books and Scriptures.[101]

But confronted with this problem of accounting for how Muḥammad could have such knowledge, given his background, the scholar and translator J.M. Rodwell decided that this ability 'clearly proves that Muḥammad must have been in confidential intercourse with learned Jews'.[102] In effect, Rodwell out of hand rejected Muḥammad's clear assertion that the verse was inspired and that, as an Apostle of God, He had divine access to all knowledge. Rodwell then assumed there must have been some external cause of this effect and he arbitrarily chose the one that best suited his personal bias.

Again, the scholar, especially the historian, is not obliged to make judgments about causal relationships when researching religious history, or any history for that matter. But having chosen to make statements about causality, the scholar is obliged not to make arbitrary inferences, either by commission (actively choosing one cause over another without sufficient justification) or by omission (failing to give appropriate consideration to obvious alternatives to an inference).

Conclusions

Infallibility is an essential attribute of the Prophet's soul. Consequently, the station of distinction alluded to by Bahá'u'lláh does not designate a point where such knowledge begins, but the historical context in which it appears. Likewise, the dramatic events surrounding the point of beginning in the ministry of a Prophet is not a point of transformation from one state to another (from a human being to a Manifestation), but a point where the Manifestation breaks His silence, reveals His true station and sets aside His concealment, even though He may retain the veil of a human persona.

Consequently, we may assume that it is the Manifestation (or God working through the Manifestation) who determines what devices He will employ, what allusions He will make, what style He will utilize in the station of distinction in which He must operate. He is not the sum total of those influences at loose in the society in which He dwells, nor is His motive the result of some subtle path towards self-aggrandizement. Were that the case, the Prophets would surely have chosen a course of action that would have rendered better results than condemnation, persecution, crucifixion, exile and imprisonment.

In this sense, the 'Most Great Infallibility', an infallibility that is an inherent attribute, is confined to the Prophets. This does not mean that the infallibility subsequently conferred upon the various institutions of the Cause (i.e. 'Abdu'l-Bahá, the Guardian and the Universal House of Justice) is any less infallible. Infallibility does not admit degrees – either one's knowledge and guidance complies unerringly with reality or it does not. If there is less than perfect compliance, then the term *infallible* is erroneous. Neither is the term *infallible* used solely to designate unquestioned authority or immaculate character. These attributes may also exist but they are clearly distinct in nature from the notion of what is intended by the concept of infallibility (i.e. without error).

These subtle matters of doctrine and theology, while logically explained and causally related, require an acceptance of a spiritual reality. They might thus seem to rely on proofs that must needs transcend assertions available to a strictly secular-humanistic analysis of religion or religious history. Such is not the case, as the articles in this collection proving the existence and nature of God help demonstrate. The scholar as historian may wish to avoid the difficulties of discussing these ineffable subjects that might seem the province of the theologian and the philosopher, and so long as the scholar is satisfied with merely recounting events, or with recitation of fact, there is no harm in this – immense benefit can be derived from such information. However, when the historian decides to make judgments – and it is most certainly appropriate for the historian to do this – then these judgments must be arrived at with scientific method if they are to be truly scholarly. The more the scholar forgoes considering *all* the alternative inferences, the more such analysis is in danger of becoming a polemic, even if that polemic is veiled with indirection, qualification and the trappings of academic form.

Unsealing the Choice Wine at the Family Reunion

John S. Hatcher

In the opening passage of the Kitáb-i-Aqdas we find a familiar but infinitely subtle statement of human purpose enunciated in terms of two duties: 1) the 'recognition of Him Who is the Dayspring of His Revelation' and 2) the observance of 'every ordinance of Him Who is the Desire of the world'.[1] On the surface, this mandate seems clear enough – it describes human responsibility in the eternal covenant. God provides continuous divine guidance through His Prophets and we, in turn, must attempt to recognize these teachers when They appear and follow their guidance. However, a more thorough examination of this obligation reveals a two-part paradigm that frames the entire process of divine enlightenment, defines the fundamental properties that distinguish all human activity, and establishes with clarity the unique position and status of the Kitáb-i-Aqdas in the evolution of humankind on our planet.[2]

Part of the subtlety in these twin duties derives from the fact that recognition and obedience are not two separate and independent actions but two parts of one integral process, something Bahá'u'lláh implies in this same preamble to the Kitáb-i-Aqdas when He states that neither action is sufficient or 'acceptable without the other'. If we apply this principle to the revelation of Bahá'u'lláh, for example, we might observe that it is not sufficient to recognize the station and authority of Bahá'u'lláh as personal lord and savior unless we express or signalize that recognition through the daily regimen of actions that Bahá'u'lláh has instituted to train us.

Consequently, obedience to the Prophet's guidance is not so much a distinct process as it is a completion of the process of recognition. Or stated conversely, without those actions that confirm one's willingness to accede to the beneficent wisdom of the Prophet, one cannot properly be said to have understood the authority, station and the essential purpose of the Manifestation.

Another even more subtle property of these twin duties is the implicit reciprocity between these inextricably related actions. For while there may be a primacy of order (one must know before one can act on that knowledge), the more one implements understanding in metaphorical acts (which is what the laws of the Prophet are designed to have us do), the more one comes to understand the spiritual principle underlying that action. For example, as one attempts to be fair and equitable with others, one comes to acquire a greater understanding of the abstract notion of justice itself. Spiritual awakening begets action; action induces a greater perception of the verity being acted out; and that enhanced understanding yields a more ample and complete expression of that abstraction in deeds.

While the interplay between these twin duties of recognition and obedience is evident throughout the Bahá'í sacred texts in a number of profound and revealing ways, perhaps the most succinct statement of this process is found in the short obligatory prayer and functions virtually as a credo for the Bahá'í: 'I bear witness, O my God, that Thou hast created me to know Thee and to worship Thee.'[3] For most Bahá'ís, this testimony of faith is hardly difficult to comprehend, but there is a subtlety here that may elude a casual reading.

Bahá'u'lláh observes in the *Kitáb-i-Íqán* that knowledge of God is achieved solely through the appearance of the Manifestations. Therefore, 'to know Thee' would necessarily imply recognition of Manifestation. But recognition in this context implies not merely the designation of a personality or historical figure as having a certain spiritual status. Recognition here clearly implies individual perception of the spiritual attributes of God as given earthly expression. Furthermore, the Bahá'í scriptures define worship as any act that expresses in concrete form our recognition of the Manifestation – work, for example.

Could we not infer, then, that the short obligatory prayer and the opening passage of the Kitáb-i-Aqdas are both describing precisely the same paradigm? Human purpose is a process of 1) coming to understand spiritual concepts as they are made apparent to us through the dramatic appearance of the Prophet (who is but a metaphorical statement of Godliness in human form) and then 2) expressing that perception in metaphorical acts which, when performed with pure motive, discipline and consistency, result in the transformation of the human soul.

But there is a corollary to this axiomatic statement of human purpose. Not only is this inescapable duty at the heart of any human endeavor; the capacity to accomplish these twin tasks is tantamount to a definition of the distinctive character of human reality. That is, the ability to discern abstractions metaphorized in concrete forms and then to reinvest the perceived concept with a personally initiated course of metaphorical action is a capacity unique to human beings among all physical creation:

> Having created the world and all that liveth and moveth therein, He, through the direct operation of His unconstrained and sovereign Will, chose to confer upon man the unique distinction and capacity to know Him and to love Him – a capacity that must needs be regarded as the generating impulse and the primary purpose underlying the whole of creation.[4]

Thus, when 'Abdu'l-Bahá observes that creation is eternal and that the human being as the fruit of that creation has always existed,[5] He is implying that there have always existed in the created universe beings capable of performing these two acts – recognition and obedience. Whether or not such beings have always had a physical appearance that we commonly associate with human existence or whether the expression of that recognition was always in terms that we might easily comprehend is largely irrelevant.

Because these twin capacities constitute an essential definition of human nature, we can discover how they underlie the entire Bahá'í paradigm of physical reality. For example, the Bahá'í writings are commonly perceived as portraying physical reality as transient, unreliable, a shadowy and illusive imitation of the eternal changeless spiritual reality:

> Know thou that the Kingdom is the real world, and this nether place is only its shadow stretching out. A shadow hath no life of its own; its existence is only a fantasy, and nothing more; it is but images reflected in water, and seeming as pictures to the eye.[6]

Yet a number of related axioms in the Bahá'í scriptures demonstrate the possibility of a radically different attitude. First, 'Abdu'l-Bahá asserts that physical reality is an eternal, essential and calculated expression of spiritual reality. In *Some Answered Questions* 'Abdu'l-Bahá observes that 'as the Essence of Unity (that is, the existence of God) is everlasting and eternal – that is to say, it has neither beginning nor end – it is certain that this world of existence, this endless universe has neither beginning nor end', even though parts of the universe 'may come into existence, or may disintegrate'.[7] Second, the Bahá'í writings assert that all creation has as its principle and animating purpose the rendering of spiritual attributes in sensually perceptible forms: 'Know thou that every created thing is a sign of the revelation of God. Each, according to its capacity, is, and will ever remain, a token of the Almighty.'[8] Third, Bahá'u'lláh observes that without this capacity 'the entire universe would become desolate and void'.[9] Fourth, the Bahá'í writings affirm that the physical world is a classroom designed specifically for human enlightenment: 'Out of the wastes of nothingness, with the clay of My command I made thee to appear, and have ordained for thy training every atom in existence and the essence of all created things.'[10]

But this essential purpose inherent in the relationship between the physical and the spiritual goes quite beyond the Platonic doctrine whereby the physical world functions solely to give us clues about the world of ideas and abstract forms. The commonly accepted Platonic perspective of the human goal in the physical life is to abstain from the things of this world and thereby escape from this illusory 'cave'[11] thereby ascending to the eternal realm.

The Bahá'í writings, on the other hand, portray the physical world as a thoroughly spiritualized expression of the unseen spiritual world, a 'Great Workshop',[12] a classroom not to be disdained, but to be respected, esteemed and utilized:

> The spiritual world is like unto the phenomenal world. They are the exact counterpart of each other. Whatever objects appear in this world of existence are the outer pictures of the world of heaven.[13]

This observation leads to yet another axiom – whatever inherent capacity the physical world may have to manifest the attributes of the divine reality, the most significant expression of divine principles in human existence is an evolutionary process, described by Bahá'u'lláh as a paradigm of social progress, 'an ever-advancing civilization'.[14] This continual advancement, He explains, is brought about through the critical linkage between divine ordination and human volition. Thus if we liken the relationship between the spiritual world and the physical world to the relationship between the human soul and the human body, we can observe that this linkage is from the beginning. It is an inherent property of creation itself.

This linkage or interplay between the two realities is clearly demonstrated in the Bahá'í concept of how human society advances through the process of progressive revelations. For example, it is a commonplace in discussions of Bahá'í theology to observe that the Manifestations bring two sorts of information – a reiteration of the eternal and changeless spiritual verities and an updating of laws, ordinances and institutions that translate these spiritual concepts into a daily regimen for the individual and into a social program for society as a whole. Bahá'u'lláh discusses this distinction as relating to the two stations of the Prophet. In the station of essential unity, the Manifestation is the eternal voice of God and indistinguishable from God or the other Prophets.[15] In the station of distinction, the Manifestation possesses a particular personality, appears in a particular social and historical context, and ministers to the exigencies of that age.[16] Each successive

Manifestation thus unveils ever more completely a vision of the spiritual world and ordains a course of action whereby that enhanced vision can be translated into an ever more complete concrete social expression of spiritual reality.

These two stations of the Prophet thereby parallel the twin aspects of the revelation, as well as the twin duties ordained in the Kitáb-i-Aqdas. In each case the purpose is constant, to clothe understanding with the garment of action, the unseen with visible representation. Similarly, in every expression of this duality neither part of this complementarity is acceptable or sufficient or complete without the other.

Christ alludes to this relationship in a series of potent analogies describing the need for a new edifice to contain the new revelation:

> No man putteth a piece of new cloth unto an old garment, for that which is put in to fill it up taketh from the garment, and the rent is made worse. Neither do men put new wine into old bottles: else the bottles break, and the wine runneth out, and the bottles perish: but they put new wine into new bottles, and both are preserved.[17]

So it is that when in the course of religious history the spiritual teachings of a dispensation become separated from or antithetical to the social laws and ordinances, or when one aspect of this duality excels or exceeds the other in its progress, the religious edifice as a whole is rent to pieces, its purposes perverted, the new wine poured out useless onto the dust.

It is in this context that Shoghi Effendi cautions against any perception of the spiritual or doctrinal teachings of the Bahá'í Faith as being distinct or separable from the laws or administrative principles:

> To dissociate the administrative principles of the Cause from the purely spiritual and humanitarian teachings would be tantamount to a mutilation of the body of the Cause, a separation that can only result in the disintegration of its component parts, and the extinction of the Faith itself.[18]

Certainly the schism between the essentially spiritual doctrines of Christ and of Muḥammad and the institutions and laws that now bear their names gives eloquent testimony to the mutilation that is wrought when these twin parts of the process of spiritualization are severed. Indeed, we in the modern age endure the inheritance of this schism in virtually every aspect of our lives, especially in the often adversarial relationship between religion and science, in the Western political dichotomy between church and state, in the fragmentation of our personal lives between spiritual and secular aspirations.

The revealed writings of Bahá'u'lláh, containing as they do explicit guidance for integrating the sacred and the secular aspects of human advancement, thus represent a strategic reunion for the human body politic. In fact, because this revelation signals the first instance in which a Prophet has securely established both the spiritual insight and an explicit edifice to disseminate that guidance through divinely ordained social structures, the new 'wine' of this revelation might well be thought of as the wine of reunion for our planet. Likewise, because the Kitáb-i-Aqdas provides the means by which that wine can be conveyed to the entire body politic through the creation of evolving social and administrative institutions, as well as a progressive daily regimen, the revelation of the Kitáb-i-Aqdas represents the completion or consummation of planetary social evolution:

> The emergence of a world community, the consciousness of world citizenship, the founding of a world civilization and culture – all of which must synchronize with the initial stages in the unfoldment of the Golden Age of the Bahá'í Era – should, by their very nature, be regarded, as far as this planetary life is concerned, as the furthermost limits in the organization of human society, though man, as an individual, will, nay must indeed as a result of such a consummation, continue indefinitely to progress and develop.[19]

The reunion thus symbolized by the revelation of the Kitáb-i-Aqdas is, from the perspective of religious history, the consummate fusion of the sacred with the secular, the spiritual kingdom of heaven translated into earthly form.

Here again the two-part paradigm is at the center of this process, particularly as regards the revelation of the Kitáb-i-Aqdas since this work is the repository of those laws, ordinances and institutions that will provide outward or visible aspect to the spiritual concepts enunciated in Bahá'u'lláh's doctrinal works, particularly the *Kitáb-i-Íqán*. Indeed, we can see in the relationship between these two works a symbolic representation of this twofold paradigm. As an enunciation of the eternal plan of God and as an explication of the divine rationale by which God manifests His attributes and the pre-existent word through divinely empowered Manifestations, the *Kitáb-i-Íqán* represents the new wine. In fact, Shoghi Effendi affirms that the *Kitáb-i-Íqán* has 'preeminence among the doctrinal'[20] works of Bahá'u'lláh. He also observes that the *Kitáb-i-Íqán* 'proffered to mankind the "Choice Sealed Wine", whose seal is of "musk"'.[21]

The 'Choice Sealed Wine' referred to here by Shoghi Effendi alludes to a passage of the Qur'án in which Muḥammad discusses the redemption of mankind at the time of the resurrection. In that day, Muḥammad observes, the faithless shall be made to understand the truth about what they have rejected: 'This is the (reality) which ye rejected as false!'[22] Whereas the righteous shall be greatly rewarded: 'Their thirst will be slaked with Pure Wine Sealed: The Seal thereof will be Musk.'[23] Since one purpose of the *Kitáb-i-Íqán* as the preeminent doctrinal work is to induce certitude by explaining the divine rationale and essential benignity underlying the divine process by which God educates humanity, we might well consider the *Kitáb-i-Íqán* as that choice wine. Of course, the 'wine' of Bahá'u'lláh's revelation is not contained solely in the *Kitáb-i-Íqán*; all of the essentially spiritual or doctrinal works of Bahá'u'lláh are part of that vintage. But as an essay explicating the station and methodology of the Prophets, the *Kitáb-i-Íqán* proffers to humanity the first clear statement of the abiding theological verities that govern human existence.

If the *Kitáb-i-Íqán* is that choice wine, however, the proffering of this wine of knowledge, while inducing a kind of certitude that might derive from an intellectual appreciation of the justice that pervades the divine plan, cannot by itself complete the process of resurrection and reunion alluded to by Muḥammad. We are proffered the vintage. We can behold it and become attracted by the musk of its seal, but we cannot yet imbibe this precious source of transmutation because the 'choice wine' is yet sealed. We still lack some means of unsealing the wine and a proper receptacle to contain its contents that we might convey it to our lips and become nourished by the wisdom it can induce.[24] Stated more plainly, it is not sufficient that the Manifestation unveil for us the divine logic underlying God's pedagogy. Resurrection and reunion can occur only when the Prophet provides us a means of applying that knowledge towards a useful course of social action.

This is precisely what Bahá'u'lláh does with the revelation of the Kitáb-i-Aqdas – enunciate in a series of laws, ordinances and exhortations the methodology for expressing the new knowledge in creative action. It is in this context that Bahá'u'lláh in the Kitáb-i-Aqdas refers to this work as the 'mother book' of His dispensation, as His 'Most Holy Book'. It is also in this context that He alludes to the Kitáb-i-Aqdas as the unsealing of the choice wine: 'Think not that We have revealed unto you a mere code of laws. Nay, rather, We have unsealed the choice Wine with the fingers of might and power.'[25]

The revelation of the Kitáb-i-Aqdas thereby completes the twofold process of recognition and obedience, of knowing and worshiping, by delineating a pattern of behavior that will give outer form to spiritual insight, a new wineskin for this choice wine of reunion. Here, too, we find several sorts of significance to the concept of 'reunion'. Through this twofold process individual believers are reunited with their Lord. Through the creation of a world commonwealth, Bahá'u'lláh has reunited the body politic of humankind. Through the establishment of a divinely ordained social order, the Manifestation has put in place the final stage whereby human society can be organized and administered according to spiritual principles (i.e. the divine kingdom becomes expressed in material form). Shoghi Effendi confirms this when he observes that the form of social organization revealed by

Bahá'u'lláh establishes the 'furthermost limit' of human social organization on this planet, as indicated above.

Of course, we can envision a future in which a paradigm of social order might transcend the limits of our planetary society – an interplanetary order or an intergalactic one. The point is that for this planet the future will consist of an ever more refined version of what Bahá'u'lláh has revealed, and it is perhaps in this sense that the revelation is aptly alluded to as the 'wine of reunion' because Bahá'u'lláh has introduced a 'divine economy' for our single household.

Consequently, in works penned after the revelation of the Kitáb-i-Aqdas in 1873, Bahá'u'lláh frequently employs this same metaphor to indicate that the choice wine has now been unsealed:

> Whoso faileth to quaff the choice wine which We have unsealed through the potency of Our Name, the All-Compelling, shall be unable to discern the splendors of the light of divine unity or to grasp the essential purpose underlying the Scriptures of God, the Lord of heaven and earth, the sovereign Ruler of this world and of the world to come. Such a man shall be accounted among the faithless in the Book of God, the All-Knowing, the All-Informed.[26]

In fact, in His final Tablet, *Epistle to the Son of the Wolf* penned in 1891, Bahá'u'lláh alludes to the 'Sealed Wine' as a symbol of God's Revelation in five different passages. In one of these He states:

> Ponder upon the things which have been mentioned, perchance thou mayest quaff the Sealed Wine through the power of the name of Him Who is the Self-Subsisting, and obtain that which no one is capable of comprehending.[27]

In still another passage, Bahá'u'lláh alludes to this choice wine as the 'Wine of Reunion': 'Take heed lest anything deter thee from extolling the greatness of this Day – the Day whereon the Finger of majesty and power hath opened the seal of the Wine of Reunion, and called all who are in the heavens and all who are on the earth.'[28]

But intriguing as the symbolism of this prophecy is regarding the unsealing of the choice wine of reunion, this is not the only major prophecy indicating how the Kitáb-i-Aqdas completes this twofold process of knowing and doing. 'Abdu'l-Bahá has discussed that the various biblical allusions to the advent of the 'the Holy City, the Jerusalem of God' symbolizes the 'Law of God' become manifest in human society.[29] Similarly, the 'new heaven' and the 'new earth' allude to the fundamental verities of the spiritual world clothed in the garment of human society and governance.[30]

Possibly the most potent and useful of these allusions to this twofold process as it pertains to the revelation of the Kitáb-i-Aqdas is the concept of the reunion of the bride with the bridegroom. Shoghi Effendi states in *God Passes By* that the Kitáb-i-Aqdas is 'the principal repository of that Law which the Prophet Isaiah had anticipated, and which the writer of the Apocalypse had described as . . . the "Bride"'.[31] We may recall from 'Abdu'l-Bahá's explication of the Adamic myth in *Some Answered Questions* that the beloved or the bride in some poetic traditions often symbolizes the spiritual or intellectual aspect of the self, while the male represents the physical dimension. The adorned bride in this prophecy might thus represent that same spiritual insight symbolized by the choice wine. In fact, this bride may well be the same veiled maiden whose image is for Bahá'u'lláh the source of the Word of God:

> There, in a vision, the 'Most Great Spirit', as He Himself has again testified, appeared to Him, in the guise of a 'Maiden' 'calling' with 'a most wondrous, a most sweet voice' above His Head, whilst 'suspended in the air' before Him and, 'pointing with her finger' unto His head, imparted 'tidings which rejoiced' His 'soul'.[32]

This marriage or wedding of the bride (the unseen world) with the bridegroom (the visible or physical world) likewise serves as a powerful metaphor alluding to the marriage or reunion of the twofold aspect of the human reality. In fact, in the concluding passages of the *Hidden Words*, a work composed mostly of spiritual axioms, Bahá'u'lláh alludes to the mystic bride as having revealed the truth, but concludes that it is now the duty of the believer to flesh out that understanding with deeds:

> The mystic and wondrous Bride, hidden ere this beneath the veiling of utterance, hath now, by the grace of God and His divine favor, been made manifest even as the resplendent light shed by the beauty of the Beloved. I bear witness, O friends! that the favor is complete, the argument fulfilled, the proof manifest and the evidence established. Let it now be seen what your endeavors in the path of detachment will reveal.[33]

It is obvious, then, that applications of this two part paradigm are pervasive throughout the Bahá'í revelation and are endlessly fascinating. In the Bahá'í administrative order we find evidence of this complementarity, for example, in the conjoining of the 'learned' (the appointed institutions such as Hands of the Cause, Counsellors, Auxiliary Board members and their assistants) and the 'rulers' (the elected institutions such as the Universal House of Justice, the Secondary and Local Houses of Justice).[34]

I suspect that it is this very same process that is being alluded to when Bahá'u'lláh in the long obligatory prayer refers to the Manifestation as the one 'through Whom the letters B and E (Be) have been joined and knit together'.[35] That is, the Prophet of God links the eternal, changeless world of the spirit with the contingent reality by creating a social edifice capable of translating that unseen reality into a visible but divine artifice, an organic form wherein we ourselves collaborate as artisans, or to use one of 'Abdu'l-Bahá's favorite metaphors, as fellow laborers in the Vineyard of God.[36]

The Kitáb-i-Aqdas: The Causality Principle in the World of Being*

William S. Hatcher

Introduction

The usual articulation of the well-known Bahá'í principle that prejudices are truly immoral and not just socially troublesome affective attitudes tends to obscure another, cognitive defect of prejudice: prejudiced thinking is lazy thinking, signifying the subject's refusal to come to grips with the object as it truly is, in all its dimensions. Prejudiced thinking is stereotypical thinking in which we try to assimilate or reduce something new to a previously known category. Such a reductionist approach to life deprives new experiences of their capacity to transform or change us. In our rigidity and self-satisfaction, we require that each newly encountered phenomenon somehow accommodate itself to our preconceived categories of thought and experience.

Nowhere else will the reductionistic approach to life be more disastrous than if applied in our attempt to understand the Kitáb-i-Aqdas, Bahá'u'lláh's Most Holy Book, for this work can in no way be assimilated to any previous category of religious writing or any pre-existing conception of religious thought. It sees spiritual laws neither as social conventions nor as divinely imposed rules of behavior but rather as exact expressions of fundamental, objective relationships inherent in the very structure of reality.

* Reprinted by kind permission of the Universal House of Justice from *The Bahá'í World 1993-4*.

Thus, the worldview of the Kitáb-i-Aqdas is fundamentally scientific. It considers that reality is structured by objective relationships of cause and effect (i.e. laws) which can be rationally understood and articulated. The very purpose of the Kitáb-i-Aqdas is the articulation of some of the most basic laws of spiritual reality. However, an adequate understanding of these laws also involves some knowledge of the overall philosophical framework of the Bahá'í Faith. The next four sections seek to provide the essentials of this framework, after which we will undertake a more direct and detailed study of the Kitáb-i Aqdas itself.

Levels of Existence: The Material World

The Bahá'í writings affirm that reality is an integrated whole but that this wholeness is a unity in diversity, not a uniformity. In particular, within the context of overall wholeness, there are distinct levels of being. The lowest of these levels is the natural or material world, where the principle of existence is one of composition of elements. As 'Abdu'l-Bahá has expressed it:

> Nature is that condition, that reality, which in appearance consists in life and death, or, in other words, in the composition and decomposition of all things.
>
> This Nature is subjected to an absolute organization, to determined laws, to a complete order and a finished design, from which it will never depart – to such a degree, indeed, that if you look carefully and with keen sight, from the smallest invisible atom up to such large bodies of the world of existence as the globe of the sun or the other great stars and luminous spheres, whether you regard their arrangement, their composition, their form or their movement, you will find that all are in the highest degree of organization and are under one law from which they will never depart.[1]

'Abdu'l-Bahá further explains that this natural order, though objective, is an expression of the will of God: 'Nature, which has neither perception nor intelligence, is in the grasp of Almighty God, Who is the Ruler of the world of Nature; whatever He wishes, He causes Nature to manifest.'[2] Bereft of the capacity for thought (intelligence) or experience (perception), the material world also lacks the power of will: '... when you look at Nature itself, you see that it has no intelligence, no will.'[3] In other words, the material world totally lacks the capacity of consciousness or self-awareness.

One of the consequences of the composite principle of existence in the material world is that all material systems are temporary; they have a finite life span. A material entity is born when the particular combination of elements that determines its existence is established. As long as the relationships necessary to sustain this configuration are maintained, the material entity exists, and when these relationships are destroyed it dies or decomposes, i.e. ceases to exist:

> The whole physical creation is perishable. These material bodies are composed of atoms; when these atoms begin to separate decomposition sets in, then comes what we call death. This composition of atoms, which constitutes the body or mortal element of any created being, is temporary. When the power of attraction, which holds these atoms together, is withdrawn, the body, as such, ceases to exist.[4]

Another feature of the material world is that it is dynamic; it is in continual movement:

> Absolute repose does not exist in nature. All things either make progress or lose ground. Everything moves forward or backward, nothing is without motion. From his birth, a man progresses physically until he reaches maturity, then, having arrived at the prime of his life, he begins to decline, the strength and powers of his body decrease, and he gradually arrives at the hour of death ... All material things progress to a certain point, then begin to decline.[5]

As explained here, the nature of movement in the material world is a reciprocal, back-and-forth motion both of progress and of regress. This, 'Abdu'l-Bahá explains, is because the material world is a tension of opposites, an arena of opposing forces: 'The world of mortality is a world of contradictions, of opposites; motion being compulsory everything must either go forward or retreat.'[6]

Thus, the dynamic of the material world is one of *continual motion within fixed limits.* This kind of motion is called *periodic* or *cyclic,* and it is the fundamental characteristic of all material phenomena. From the beating of the human heart, to the movement of the planets around the sun, the material world exhibits this cyclic feature. Periodic motion is the way God has chosen to endow the material world with both dynamism and stability. Dynamism without stability produces an unbridled, purely quantitative (and ultimately catastrophic) growth, while stability without dynamism is death.

Even though the material world, and all material composites, are on the same ontological level, there is nonetheless an ordering or hierarchy among physical systems resulting from the relative complexity of their structure, the lower systems being less structured (or ordered) and the higher more structured. At the top of this hierarchy is the human body, which constitutes the most complex and highly structured physical system: 'The body of man, which is composed from the elements, is combined and mingled in the most perfect form; it is the most solid construction, the noblest combination, the most perfect existence.'[7]

That the human body is indeed the most complex of all systems in the known physical universe has also been confirmed and validated by modern neuroscience.[8]

The Knowledge of Material Reality

According to the Bahá'í teachings, God has not only established the laws that govern material reality, but He has also given to humanity the power for the rational and systematic understanding of these laws. This power is what we call 'science':

> The outcome of this [human] intellectual endowment is science, which is especially characteristic of man. This scientific power

investigates and apprehends created objects and the laws surrounding them. It is the discoverer of the hidden and mysterious secrets of the material universe and is peculiar to man alone. The most noble and praiseworthy accomplishment of man, therefore, is scientific knowledge and attainment.[9]

'Abdu'l-Bahá makes it clear that science is not just a serendipitous accident of history but a divine, supernatural endowment:

> All blessings are divine in origin, but none can be compared with this power of intellectual investigation and research, which is an eternal gift producing fruits of unending delight. Man is ever partaking of these fruits. All other blessings are temporary; this is an everlasting possession ... it is an eternal blessing and divine bestowal, the supreme gift of God to man.
> ... science or the attribute of scientific penetration is supernatural ...[10]

As we have already noted, material reality is composed of physical systems in continual movement. Through science, we gain knowledge of the laws governing the evolution of these systems and also of their current, particular conditions (states). This scientific knowledge enables us to determine and predict – not perfectly but with a practically significant degree of accuracy – the future states of these systems, given some particular set of initial conditions. This, in turn, enables us to act in the present so as to bring about a desired future configuration of a system: by deliberately establishing, in the short run, certain particular conditions of a system, we can bring about, in the long run, certain desired future states of the system, i.e. configurations that are favorable to our goals and our (perceived) interests. This is the power that scientific knowledge gives us, the power to control our future – to participate in the processes of the natural world and not just endure them. In other words, scientific knowledge has the effect of *increasing our autonomy with regard to the natural world.*

Of course, what we perceive to be in our own interest will, in itself, depend on our knowledge of reality, including the reality that is within us, the reality of our own selves. But whatever we perceive our interest to be, we generally seek to bring about those configurations that will, according to our present knowledge of reality, maximize the joy and pleasure of life and minimize its pain and suffering. Thus, scientific knowledge is a knowledge of the relationship of cause and effect in material reality, and this knowledge, when properly used, *gives us the power to produce or increase our material happiness and well being.*

This power of scientific knowledge to produce happiness and to increase our autonomy depends fundamentally on two things: 1) that the material world is regulated by objective laws, and 2) that we are able to apprehend these laws, if not absolutely, at least to a degree sufficient to allow for reasonably accurate predictions and manipulations of future events. These two features of the material world are all we need if our goal in life is to maximize our well-being and our autonomy. The other particular features of the material world (e.g. periodic motion, the temporary existence of objects) are incidental to this fundamental, binary goal.

Spiritual Reality

Above and beyond material reality lies a second level of existence that is not directly accessible to physical observation. In the Bahá'í writings this is called *spiritual reality* or the *spiritual world.* Like material reality, spiritual reality has objective existence and is governed by lawful, cause-and-effect relationships. However, the laws governing spiritual reality, and the structure resulting from the operation of these laws, are significantly different from the laws and structures of material reality, mainly because the principle of existence in the spiritual world is different from that of the material world: spiritual entities exist as undivided wholes rather than as composites; and chief among these spiritual entities is the soul or spirit of each human being: 'The soul is not a combination of elements, it is not composed of many atoms, it is of one indivisible substance and therefore eternal. It is entirely out of the order of the physical creation; it is immortal!'[11]

Because spiritual entities are noncomposite, there is no tension of opposites in spiritual reality, and thus no retrogression:

In the world of spirit there is no retrogression. The world of mortality is a world of contradictions, of opposites; motion being compulsory everything must either go forward or retreat. In the realm of spirit there is no retreat possible, all movement is bound to be towards a perfect state. 'Progress' is the expression of spirit in the world of matter. The intelligence of man, his reasoning powers, his knowledge, his scientific achievements, all these being manifestations of the spirit, partake of the inevitable law of spiritual progress and are, therefore, of necessity, immortal.[12]

Thus, in contrast to the movement of physical systems which, as we have seen above, is cyclical and always within fixed limits, the motion of the soul is unidirected, irreversible and potentially infinite:

Now let us consider the soul. We have seen that movement is essential to existence; nothing that has life is without motion. All creation, whether of the mineral, vegetable or animal kingdom, is compelled to obey the law of motion; it must either ascend or descend. But with the human soul, there is no decline. Its only movement is towards perfection; growth and progress alone constitute the motion of the soul.

Divine perfection is infinite, therefore the progress of the soul is also infinite.[13]

The Bahá'í writings teach that the fundamental capacities of the soul are those of knowledge, of love and of will. That is, the soul has the intellectual capacity of *understanding* or *mind,* the affective capacity of *feeling* or *emotion,* and the voluntary capacity of *willing* or *acting.* Because the soul is a noncomposite entity, it has no parts. Thus, the soul's capacities are inherent in its very nature, rather than being alienable parts of it.

This characteristic of the soul constitutes an extremely important difference from a physical system such as the body. The higher-order properties of the physical body are entirely due to its relative complexity in terms both of the number of its components (i.e. the cells of the body) and the complex nature of the relationship between these components. Any such composite entity has parts which may be alienated from the organism without necessarily destroying the organism. For example, a person may well survive the amputation of both his legs. But he will have lost the function of autonomous ambulation.

According to the Bahá'í writings, the intrinsic capacities of the individual's soul (called his 'spiritual' capacities) are eternally fixed. They can never be diminished or alienated from the soul, nor can they be increased; they can only be *developed*:

> Know thou that all men have been created in the nature made by God, the Guardian, the Self-Subsisting. Unto each one hath been prescribed a pre-ordained measure, as decreed in God's mighty and guarded Tablets. All that which ye potentially possess can, however, be manifested only as a result of your own volition.[14]

Thus, the soul can never lose any of its capacities, unless it be totally destroyed, which, we are assured, God will never do.

This fundamental difference between the nature of the soul and the nature of the physical body is important for an understanding of the difference between the laws governing spiritual reality and those governing material reality. Because it is such a delicate and complex system, the physical body is fragile and vulnerable. It is more or less continually threatened by the possibility of either a partial or total loss of functioning (i.e. death). But the soul is threatened by neither of these possibilities.

However, the soul does face a different kind of threat: it is threatened by the possibility of a relative underdevelopment of its intrinsic capacities. To say that the soul cannot retrogress is not to say that its progress is automatic:

> My hope for you is that you will progress in the world of spirit, as well as in the world of matter; that your intelligence will develop, your knowledge will augment, and your understanding be widened.
>
> You must ever press forward, never standing still; avoid stagnation . . .[15]

The process of developing the intrinsic capacities of the soul is called 'spiritual growth' or 'spiritual progress'. Such a process implies both an increase in spiritual autonomy and an increase in spiritual happiness and well-being.

The Bahá'í writings affirm that learning how to grow spiritually is the fundamental purpose of our existence. We accomplish this purpose by first understanding the laws that govern spiritual reality and then by applying them to the particular circumstances of our life. Just as scientific knowledge of the laws of physical reality enables us to act in the present in such a way as to produce a desired future state of increased material happiness, so a knowledge of the laws governing spiritual reality enables us to act in the present in such a way as to produce a desired future state of increased spiritual happiness. Thus, we progress towards spiritual happiness by increasing our knowledge of spiritual reality, and this, in turn, represents an increase in our spiritual autonomy. This accretion of spiritual happiness and spiritual autonomy is just another name for spiritual growth, or the development of the intrinsic capacities of our souls.

The Knowledge of Spiritual Reality

In the foregoing, we have seen that science is the means God has given us for the understanding of material reality. Scientific method is based on direct observation of the physical world followed by logically sound deductions based on such observations. But spiritual reality is not directly observable. We do not have direct access to spiritual reality, only an indirect access through observation of the effects of the action of spiritual forces on observable phenomena, such as the action of the soul on the physical body. God has therefore ordained a second source of valid knowledge about reality: religion.

The Bahá'í writings make it clear that religion and science are just two different segments of a continuum of knowledge about reality. Since the laws governing spiritual reality are objective, they are potentially discoverable by scientific method. However, because of the relative inaccessibility of spiritual phenomena to spontaneous human observation, it would take us an impractically long time to discover even the simplest of spiritual laws by an unassisted application of scientific method. Thus, religion operates by *revelation* in which God freely explains or 'reveals' to us certain of the laws and principles governing spiritual reality. We are thus spared the pain and effort that would be involved in discovering these truths for ourselves. However, these spiritual truths are objective and can therefore be tested experientially and applied practically when once understood.

Thus, in the Bahá'í conception, religion, like science, is most correctly viewed as a knowledge-generating enterprise, rather than a belief-affirming or rule-making enterprise: 'religion is the essential connection which proceeds from the realities of things . . . [it] is the necessary connection which emanates from the reality of things . . .'[16]

This conception of religion clearly differs from the received idea that science is an expression of reason and rationality while religion operates on 'blind' faith and unreasoned belief. Indeed, the Bahá'í writings define faith as the deliberate implementation of consciously-acquired knowledge: 'Although a blind man produceth a most wonderful and exquisite art, yet he is deprived of seeing it . . . By faith is meant, first, conscious knowledge, and second, the practice of good deeds.'[17]

The Bahá'í Faith teaches that the revelation of religious truth (that is, of valid knowledge of the laws and structure of spiritual reality) is a progressive phenomenon in which God periodically communicates with humanity through the agency of a specially chosen human being or *Manifestation*. These Manifestations are none other than the great religious Founders of history, some of whose names we know (such as Moses, Jesus, Buddha, Zoroaster, Muḥammad, the Báb and Bahá'u'lláh, Founder of the Bahá'í Faith). These unique beings are endowed by God with a direct knowledge of spiritual reality, and this endowment allows them to become the teachers of the laws of spiritual reality to humanity:

> Briefly, the supreme Manifestations of God are aware of the reality of the mysteries of beings. Therefore, They establish laws

which are suitable and adapted to the state of the world of man
... the supreme Manifestations of God are aware of the mysteries
of beings, therefore, They understand this essential connection
[emanating from the reality of things], and by this knowledge
establish the Law of God.[18]

In further elaboration of this point, 'Abdu'l-Bahá explains:

> Knowledge is of two kinds. One is subjective and the other objective knowledge – that is to say, an intuitive knowledge and a knowledge derived from perception.
>
> The knowledge of things which men universally have is gained by reflection or by evidence ... The circle of this knowledge is very limited because it depends upon effort and attainment.
>
> But the second sort of knowledge, which is the knowledge of being, is intuitive; it is like the cognizance and consciousness that man has of himself [i.e. of his own being or existence] ... This knowledge is not the outcome of effort and study. It is an existing thing; it is an absolute gift.
>
> Since the Sanctified Realities, the supreme Manifestations of God, surround the essence and qualities of the creatures, transcend and contain existing realities and understand all things, therefore, Their knowledge is divine knowledge, and not acquired – that is to say, it is a holy bounty; it is a divine revelation.[19]

In other words, in the same way that ordinary human beings have the spontaneous knowledge of their own being and existence, the Manifestations of God are endowed with the spontaneous knowledge of the laws of all being. In fact, the Manifestations constitute a distinct ontological level intermediate between God and ordinarily-endowed humans: 'Know that the conditions of [conscious] existence are limited to the conditions of servitude, of prophethood, and of Deity, but the divine and the contingent perfections are unlimited [on each level of existence].'[20]

Elsewhere, it is explained that the Manifestations can be thought of as absolutely perfected human beings – as human beings all of whose spiritual capacities have been developed to the maximum degree possible. They thus represent an ideal or model of the ultimate limits of human spiritual development. However, the Manifestations are created in this state of absolute perfection, whereas ordinary humans can only progressively approximate this condition through the process of spiritual growth. As 'Abdu'l-Bahá has stated, there is 'progress in perfection but not in state'.[21] In other words, 'progress' never implies a change from one level of being to another, only a progressive unfolding of the potential inherent in a given level of being.

We can thus sum up the Bahá'í teachings concerning the levels of existence as follows: Within the framework of the overall wholeness of reality, there are four distinct levels of being. The first and highest level is that of the essence or being of God. The second level is that of the Manifestation of God, who perfectly manifests or incarnates all of the attributes of God but not His essence. The third level is that of the human soul, which has consciousness and the capacity to reflect progressively all of the attributes of God. Finally, the lowest level is that of the material world, which is totally devoid of consciousness and will.

The third level, that of the human soul, is the only level of being that exhibits true irreversible progress. God and the Manifestations are already in perfect states of existence on Their respective levels of being and therefore have no need of progression. The material world exhibits continual movement within fixed limits, which involves temporary progression, but a progression that is always followed sooner or later by retrogression and degeneration. However, the human soul, while created in an unperfected state, has the potential for perfection. After being freed from the constraints of the material world, the only movement of the soul is an irreversible progression towards God. The rate of progression, however, is specific for each person and depends on the quality and appropriateness of that person's response to the circumstances of his life.

The Bahá'í writings further explain that, from the point of view of human spiritual development, the material world functions as the womb of preparation for birth into the purely spiritual world. The special conditions in the physical womb of our mother enable us to progress from a one-celled organism to a mature human form – effectively compressing five hundred million years of biological evolution into nine short months. In the same way, it is explained, the tests and trials of this material world provide us with the possibility of compressing an immense quantum of spiritual growth into the short period of a human physical lifetime.

However, whereas the physical growth and development in the maternal womb is an automatic process, our spiritual growth during our earthly lives depends on the efforts we make in response to the conditions of our lives. Moreover, during our earthly life, but not afterwards, our souls are subject to the effect of material forces that serve as a resistance against which we struggle in our efforts to grow spiritually. It is this aspect of the material world, the tension of opposition between spiritual and material forces, that provides the opportunity for rapid spiritual growth. But a necessary concomitant of this configuration is that both spiritual progression and spiritual retrogression can occur in this life, whereas (relative) progression alone is the movement of the soul in the next life.

Thus, the fundamental task of our earthly lives is to understand and apprehend the laws governing the process of spiritual growth so that we may generate the appropriate, growth-inducing responses to the circumstances of our lives and thereby profit from the unique opportunities for spiritual growth with which God has endowed this life. This knowledge and understanding can only come from religion and, more particularly, from the holy books of the Manifestations, which explain and expound the principles of spiritual reality.

The experience of five hundred million years of biological evolution is genetically encoded in the DNA of the human genome, and it is this 'knowledge' that enables the human fetus to profit from the special environment of the maternal womb and accomplish its astonishing development from a single fertilized egg to a multi-billion-celled mature and complex organism. The teachings of the Manifestations may be thought of as the spiritual counterpart of the genetic code. These teachings are recorded (encoded) in the holy writings of the great religions, and when the knowledge they contain is implemented, genuine spiritual growth is the result.

The revelation of God to humanity is progressive because spiritual growth is both collective and individual, and the knowledge appropriate to one stage of spiritual growth may not be appropriate to a later stage. Thus, as the most recent Manifestation of God, Bahá'u'lláh represents the most appropriate and mature expression of our understanding of spiritual laws and principles, and the Kitáb-i-Aqdas is the Most Holy Book of Bahá'u'lláh – the book that epitomizes His divinely-inspired articulation of the laws governing spiritual reality.

Because spiritual growth is collective as well as individual, the laws and principles of the Kitáb-i-Aqdas are partly social and partly individual. Indeed, Bahá'u'lláh explains that religion has always had these two fundamental aspects:

> God's purpose in sending His Prophets unto men is twofold. The first is to liberate the children of men from the darkness of ignorance, and guide them to the light of true understanding. The second is to ensure the peace and tranquillity of mankind, and provide all the means by which they can be established.[22]

According to Bahá'u'lláh, the history of the last few thousand years has been the history of the childhood and youth of humanity, during which most social forms and structures have had a temporary, experimental quality. We are now in late adolescence, in the transition towards full maturity, when all the potential latent within the human being will be actualized. Thus, the social laws of the Kitáb-i-Aqdas seek to provide the basis for this transition, as well as to establish the framework for the emerging, mature and stable world order, founded on spiritual principles.

The Kitáb-i-Aqdas therefore represents the culmination not only of the revelation of Bahá'u'lláh, but also of the process of progressive revelation itself. Humanity now stands on the brink of its maturity, and we are now in the throes of the greatest single transition in the history of the human race: the transition from our collective adolescence to our collective maturity. The Kitáb-i-

Aqdas reveals to us the knowledge necessary for the successful completion of this transition.

The Laws of Spiritual Reality

In *God Passes By,* Shoghi Effendi describes the Kitáb-i-Aqdas as, among other things:

> ... the principal repository of that Law which the Prophet Isaiah had anticipated, and which the writer of the Apocalypse had described as the 'new heaven' and the 'new earth', as 'the Tabernacle of God', as the 'Holy City', as the 'Bride', the 'New Jerusalem coming down from God', this 'Most Holy Book', whose provisions must remain inviolate for no less than a thousand years, and whose system will embrace the entire planet ... as the brightest emanation of the mind of Bahá'u'lláh, as the Mother Book of His Dispensation, and the Charter of His New World Order.[23]

In the light of this, and other similarly exalted descriptions of the Kitáb-i-Aqdas, one might expect to be confronted with a formal legal text in an inflated style. Instead, one finds nothing less than an extended love letter from God to humanity, an outpouring of tenderness and concern for every detail of human existence such as to dispel any possible doubt of God's overwhelming love for His creatures. Moreover, the Kitáb-i-Aqdas exhibits a remarkable harmony of content and style that heightens this impression of God's love and concern for us.

The development of ideas in the Kitáb-i-Aqdas is not strictly linear but rather cyclical or spiral. The Author discusses certain questions, then turns to other issues, and later returns to the initial questions, amplifying and elaborating with each subsequent discussion. There is also an ongoing alternation between the abstract and the concrete, the general and the specific, the universal and the particular. Nevertheless there is an overall progression throughout this dialectical development.

Fundamentally, the Kitáb-i-Aqdas views life as a continual

dialogue between God and humanity. Thus, not only does the content of the Kitáb-i-Aqdas treat a wide spectrum of life's questions, the work's very form reproduces our experience of life, in which profound philosophical and moral issues are continually juxtaposed with practical and concrete questions of everyday life. By reproducing this existential juxtaposition within the text itself, Bahá'u'lláh allows us to see how the most significant and abstract philosophical and spiritual questions are indeed related to the most homely issues of our material existence. Also, these textual juxtapositions help the reader make logical connections that might otherwise remain obscure. This, in turn, increases the reader's autonomy in confronting and understanding the Kitáb-i-Aqdas, enabling him to 'see with his own eyes and hear with his own ears'.[24]

According to Bahá'u'lláh, our dialogue with God is pursued on both the individual and the collective level; it is initiated by God, who also establishes its parameters, but its success is dependent upon our ability to generate an appropriate response to God's overtures. Thus, the laws and principles of the Kitáb-i-Aqdas are presented in the form of a *covenant* or agreement in which God requires certain things from us but solemnly promises that spiritual growth, progress and happiness will inevitably follow if these actions and attitudes on our part are forthcoming.

The opening paragraph of the Kitáb-i-Aqdas states that the fundamental duty of man towards God is 'the recognition of Him Who is the Dayspring of His Revelation and the Fountain of His laws' and that the second duty is 'to observe every ordinance of Him Who is the Desire of the world'. It is then stated that 'These twin duties are inseparable. Neither is acceptable without the other.'[25]

Thus, the individual dialogue takes place within the framework of the collective dialogue. The collective dialogue is initiated by God's sending of the Manifestations, and the first response required of us is to recognize and accept the spiritual authority of these figures. Indeed, if God has taken the trouble to send the Manifestations to give us valid knowledge of the laws governing spiritual reality, then the minimal acceptable response on our part is to turn to them and follow their instruction. In particular, we must signify our true acceptance by implementing the laws and principles they teach.

Following this opening statement, paragraphs 2 to 5 of the Kitáb-i-Aqdas constitute a powerful articulation of the importance generally of obeying and implementing the laws of God and of the benefits to be derived from such obedience. For example:

> O ye peoples of the world! Know assuredly that My commandments are the lamps of My loving providence among My servants, and the keys of My mercy for My creatures . . . 'Observe My commandments, for the love of My beauty.' Happy is the lover that hath inhaled the divine fragrance of his Best-Beloved from these words, laden with the perfume of a grace which no tongue can describe.[26]

This portion of the text culminates (paragraph 5) in the following metaphor for the whole of the Kitáb-i-Aqdas itself: 'Think not that We have revealed unto you a mere code of laws. Nay, rather, We have unsealed the choice Wine with the fingers of might and power . . . Meditate upon this, O men of insight!'[27] The symbolic use of 'Wine' in this passage powerfully conveys the notion that implementation of the laws of spiritual reality produces an effect of spiritual euphoria – thus of extreme spiritual happiness. Bahá'u'lláh's choice of image here is particularly significant given the fact that, subsequently in the Kitáb-i-Aqdas, He strictly forbids the drinking of wine and other intoxicants (paragraph 119), stating, 'It is inadmissible that man, who hath been endowed with reason, should consume that which stealeth it away.'[28]

Thus, true happiness – spiritual euphoria – comes not from the abandonment of rationality but by its disciplined application to an understanding of the laws governing spiritual reality. Divine proscriptions are not intended to deny us genuine joy but rather to teach us the conditions under which the greatest and most enduring joy can be obtained. What is being given us is no less than the keys to a true and lasting paradise.

In this way, the opening five paragraphs of the Kitáb-i-Aqdas lay out the general parameters of the dialogue, or covenant, between God and humanity: God initiates the dialogue by sending the Manifestations to teach us the fundamental laws of spiritual reality. We respond by recognizing the spiritual authority (validity) of the Manifestation and obeying His laws. The result is increased spiritual development leading to increased happiness and, ultimately, to a state of extreme and enduring joy.

The Kitáb-i-Aqdas also affirms that the implementation of the laws of spiritual reality increases the individual's spiritual autonomy, which Bahá'u'lláh calls 'true liberty':

> Say: True liberty consisteth in man's submission unto My commandments, little as ye know it. Were men to observe that which We have sent down unto them from the Heaven of Revelation, they would, of a certainty, attain unto perfect liberty. Happy is the man that hath apprehended the Purpose of God in whatever He hath revealed . . . Say: The liberty that profiteth you is to be found nowhere except in complete servitude unto God, the Eternal Truth.[29]

In this and other passages, Bahá'u'lláh makes unequivocally clear that God does not seek an obedience of childlike weakness but a mature, intelligent obedience based on deliberate individual choice. We must submit our wills to God's, but this submission results from a disciplined accretion of spiritual power to the individual, not from a helpless capitulation.

The Covenant and the Universal House of Justice

Before examining some specific laws and principles contained in the Kitáb-i-Aqdas, it is important to understand several fundamental features of Bahá'u'lláh's Covenant, which, as mentioned above, constitutes the basic framework for the dialogue between God and humanity. The first concerns the question of the interpretation of Bahá'u'lláh's writings and, in particular, the interpretation of the Kitáb-i-Aqdas. Bahá'u'lláh Himself wrote elucidations of several passages of the Kitáb-i Aqdas during His lifetime, many of which are included in the current English edition. Given the fact that certain laws of the Kitáb-i-Aqdas 'have been formulated in anticipation of a [future] state of society destined to emerge from the chaotic conditions that prevail today', Bahá'u'lláh foresaw the necessity of providing for further authoritative interpretation of His writings after His death.[30] He therefore appointed His eldest son, 'Abdu'l-Bahá, as the 'Center of the Covenant', the authorized interpreter of Bahá'u'lláh's writings, and as the perfect exemplar of Bahá'í teachings. 'Abdu'l-Bahá survived Bahá'u'lláh by 29 years during which time He wrote a number of texts, including explanations of certain passages of the Kitáb-i-Aqdas. 'Abdu'l-Bahá in turn appointed His eldest grandson, Shoghi Effendi, to succeed Him as the authorized interpreter of the Bahá'í writings.

Beginning in 1921, Shoghi Effendi's ministry continued for 36 years until his death in 1957. During this period, Shoghi Effendi generated an extensive corpus of detailed commentary and interpretation of the writings of Bahá'u'lláh, including the Kitáb-i-Aqdas. Certain portions of Shoghi Effendi's commentary are likewise included in the present English edition of the Kitáb-i-Aqdas.

Thus, in a certain sense, 'the Kitáb-i-Aqdas' is not just the relatively brief (but extraordinarily concentrated) text of the Kitáb-i-Aqdas itself, but also includes the extensive body of authoritative commentaries by Bahá'u'lláh, 'Abdu'l-Bahá and Shoghi Effendi.

Another fundamental aspect of Bahá'u'lláh's Covenant derives from Bahá'u'lláh's declared intention of establishing a system of divine governance adequate for the needs of humanity for at least a thousand years. Such a system must take into account permanence, stability and order, on one hand, and change, progression and dynamism, on the other. The specific laws of the Kitáb-i-Aqdas constitute the permanent or stable underpinnings of Bahá'u'lláh's system; they are to remain inviolate for at least a thousand years. To provide for change and flexibility in His system, Bahá'u'lláh has established a supreme legislative organ, called the Universal House of Justice.

According to the specific texts of Bahá'u'lláh and 'Abdu'l-Bahá, the Universal House of Justice is invested with the authority to legislate on all matters not specifically dealt with in the Kitáb-i-Aqdas or elsewhere in the Bahá'í sacred writings. Moreover, the Universal House of Justice can repeal or alter any of its previous decisions. This feature provides Bahá'u'lláh's system with a great flexibility and adaptability. As the conditions of humanity change and as scientific progress alters various social realities, the Universal House of Justice can legislate in order to take into account this evolution.

For example, the Kitáb-i-Aqdas specifically proscribes murder, defined as the willful taking of another human life. This, then, is an absolute prohibition. However, while specifying certain penalties for murder (either execution or life imprisonment), Bahá'u'lláh leaves the Universal House of Justice free to determine their application. Moreover, He also leaves to the Universal House of Justice the task of establishing various degrees of murder and the appropriate penalty for each degree. Or, to take another example, the laws of the Kitáb-i-Aqdas do not deal directly with the question of birth control, leaving the House of Justice free to legislate (or not) in this area. It is therefore logically possible for the Universal House of Justice to legislate in a certain manner regarding this question and later, perhaps in the light of changed demographic circumstances, repeal or alter this legislation.

Though the Universal House of Justice cannot repeal or alter any of the laws of the Kitáb-i-Aqdas, it is nevertheless empowered by Bahá'u'lláh to oversee the gradual and progressive application of those laws. The Universal House of Justice is also invested with the quasijudicial function of rendering an authoritative and final verdict in all disputes or controversies that arise within the Bahá'í community. These functions are summed up in the following passage from the Will and Testament of 'Abdu'l-Bahá:

> It is incumbent upon these members (of the Universal House of Justice) to gather in a certain place and deliberate upon all problems which have caused difference, questions that are obscure and matters that are not expressly recorded in the Book. Whatsoever they decide has the same effect as the Text itself. And inasmuch as this House of Justice hath power to enact laws that

are not expressly recorded in the Book and bear upon daily transactions, so also it hath power to repeal the same ... The House of Justice is both the initiator and the abrogator of its own laws.[31]

The House of Justice was first elected in 1963 in the manner outlined by 'Abdu'l-Bahá and has functioned continually since that date. Election of the membership of the House of Justice is held every five years.

In the Kitáb-i-Aqdas Bahá'u'lláh also establishes local Houses of Justice, which have administrative jurisdiction on a local – usually municipal or county – level. Acting on the authority given Him by Bahá'u'lláh, 'Abdu'l-Bahá established secondary Houses of Justice on an intermediate – national or regional – level. Membership in these governing councils is also by election.[32]

Thus the administrative structure of the Bahá'í community exists at three levels: local, national and international. Decisions of local Houses of Justice can be altered by the secondary House of Justice on which they depend, and the Universal House of Justice can change a decision of any local or secondary House of Justice.

Underlying all the laws and community structures in the Bahá'í Faith is a group decision-making process called *consultation.* This process was instituted by Bahá'u'lláh himself in the Kitáb-i-Aqdas and further elaborated and explained by 'Abdu'l-Bahá and Shoghi Effendi. Essentially, Bahá'í consultation involves a frank but loving exchange of opinions by members of a group with a view towards the determination of the objective truth of some matter and the consequent establishment of a genuine group consensus. In particular, consultation is the basic mode of functioning of the Houses of Justice. Thus, in Bahá'u'lláh's system of governance, all decision-making authority derives from consultative bodies. No individual has decision-making authority unless such authority has been specifically granted by an appropriate consultative decision of a collective organ functioning under one of the Houses of Justice.

The central role that consultation plays throughout Bahá-

'u'lláh's system, and Bahá'í community life in general, gives a non-authoritarian, collaborative spirit to the functioning of the Bahá'í community at all levels. The ideal of Bahá'í consultation is to arrive at a unanimous decision of the consultative group. In the instances where such unanimity is not forthcoming, a vote is taken and the majority view prevails.

Unity, the Fundamental Goal of the Bahá'í Faith

It is important here to stress that all of the laws, institutions and principles that Bahá'u'lláh has established are expressions of the two fundamental principles of justice and love. Justice has to do with the recognition of and respect for the role, status and worth of a given individual, of a given social function or of a given institution or principle. Justice provides the component of stability and order to the social fabric and to human relationships generally. Love is the underlying dynamic and motivating force of the whole of creation. Without love, justice degenerates into dry formalities, and without justice love may be improperly channeled and therefore unproductive of effective results.

The principles of justice and love are thus complementary and each is essential to the fundamental Bahá'í goal of establishing the unity of humanity at all levels of human interaction. Indeed, the unity of the material world itself results from the natural laws (justice) which regulate the dynamic interactions (love) among the different physical forces and entities. According to Bahá'u'lláh, the ultimate expression of the unity of humanity will be the organization of the life of the entire planet into one coherent social system based on justice and cooperation: 'The well-being of mankind, its peace and security, are unattainable unless and until its unity is firmly established.'[33]

Given the breathtaking scope of Bahá'u'lláh's vision of the future of mankind, we might anticipate that His system would exalt justice over love, order over dynamism. However, we will see that, if anything, the opposite is true: love is the most fundamental principle of all and the laws of the Kitáb-i-Aqdas reflect the fact that, in all of God's creation, justice is the servant of love.

As 'Abdu'l-Bahá has expressed it:

> Know thou of a certainty that Love is the secret of God's holy Dispensation, the manifestation of the All-Merciful, the fountain of spiritual outpourings. Love is heaven's kindly light, the Holy Spirit's eternal breath that vivifieth the human soul. Love is the cause of God's revelation unto man, the vital bond inherent, in accordance with the divine creation, in the realities of things. Love is the one means that ensureth true felicity both in this world and the next ... Love is the most great law that ruleth this mighty and heavenly cycle, the unique power that bindeth together the divers elements of this material world, the supreme magnetic force that directeth the movements of the spheres in the celestial realms ... Love is the spirit of life unto the adorned body of mankind, the establisher of true civilization in this mortal world, and the shedder of imperishable glory upon every high-aiming race and nation.[34]

The Individual Dialogue with God

Having established, in the opening passages, the fundamental premise of the Kitáb-i-Aqdas – the collective and individual dialogue or covenant between God and humanity – Bahá'u'lláh now turns, in paragraphs 6 to 15, to the first specific and most basic law of the Kitáb-i-Aqdas, the law of prayer. Prayer is the foundation of the individual dialogue between God and man. Through it, the individual establishes a direct, unmediated, inner connection between his soul and God. Moreover, this relationship is *the most fundamental of all relationships accessible to the individual.* Unless this relationship be correctly and firmly established, all other relationships, whether with other individuals, with society or with nature, will be essentially flawed.

The following statement, written on behalf of Shoghi Effendi, illustrates the importance that Bahá'u'lláh gives to prayer:

> How to attain spirituality is indeed a question to which every young man and woman must sooner or later try to find a satisfactory answer ...

Indeed the chief reason for the evils now rampant in society is the lack of spirituality. The materialistic civilization of our age has so much absorbed the energy and interest of mankind that people in general do no longer feel the necessity of raising themselves above the forces and conditions of their daily material existence. There is not sufficient demand for things that we call spiritual to differentiate them from the needs and requirements of our physical existence . . .

The universal crisis affecting mankind is, therefore, essentially spiritual in its causes . . . the core of religious faith is that mystic feeling which unites Man with God. This state of spiritual communion can be brought about and maintained by means of meditation and prayer. And this is the reason why Bahá'u'lláh has so much stressed the importance of worship . . . The Bahá'í Faith, like all other Divine Religions, is thus fundamentally mystic in character. Its chief goal is the development of the individual and society, through the acquisition of spiritual virtues and powers. It is the soul of man which has first to be fed. And this spiritual nourishment prayer can best provide.[35]

Among the various prescriptions Bahá'u'lláh gives concerning prayer is a specific, daily obligatory prayer. This prayer has three forms: short, medium and long. Bahá'u'lláh makes it clear that the individual is entirely free to choose, each day, whichever of the three forms he prefers, but is spiritually and morally obligated to offer an obligatory prayer at least once every 24 hours. The text of the short prayer is as follows:

I bear witness, O My God, that Thou has created me to know Thee and to worship Thee. I testify, at this moment, to my powerlessness and to Thy might, to my poverty and to Thy wealth.

There is none other God but Thee, the Help in Peril, the Self-Subsisting.[36]

A detailed study of the obligatory prayers is beyond the scope of the present article, but one main feature is already clear from the content of the short obligatory prayer: the key to spiritual happiness and autonomy is *recognition* of our total dependence on God. In other words, spiritual growth is not a process of becoming more dependent on God but of becoming more aware of our dependence on God.

The obligatory prayers, as well as other prayers, are offered individually in private. The Bahá'í Faith has no priesthood or clergy, and each individual believer is responsible before God for his own spiritual development.

The habit of regular prayer is collateral with other spiritual disciplines such as the daily reading of and meditation upon the texts revealed by Bahá'u'lláh. For example, in paragraph 149 of the Kitáb-i-Aqdas, Bahá'u'lláh says: 'Recite ye the verses of God every morn and eventide. Whoso faileth to recite them hath not been faithful to the Covenant of God and His Testament.'[37] Thus prayer, meditation and the thoughtful study of the holy writings constitute the fundamentals of the individual covenant or dialogue between God and ourselves.

However, it is important to realize that the daily obligatory prayers constitute only a spiritual minimum, not a maximum or an optimum. Bahá'u'lláh stresses throughout His writings that we should pursue communion with God at every moment of our existence, in such wise that the attitude of prayerfulness pervades our entire life and all of our human interactions. As Shoghi Effendi has expressed in a letter written on his behalf: 'We must become entirely selfless and devoted to God so that every day and every moment we seek to do only what God would have us do and in the way He would have us do it.'[38]

A second key element of individual spiritual discipline is fasting, and Bahá'u'lláh mentions the law of fasting in paragraph 16, immediately following His initial discussion of the obligatory prayers. He later elaborates the details of the law of fasting: Bahá'ís are to fast from sunrise to sunset for 19 successive days during the same period (2 March to 21 March) each solar year. This periodic, temporary suspension of eating and drinking allows the individual to experience his soul as an entity separate from the body. In this way, the individual's soul or spirit becomes a palpable reality and not just an intellectual abstraction.

Most of the other prescriptions pertaining to individuals are related, in one way or another, to prayer and fasting. For example,

Bahá'u'lláh stresses physical cleanliness, stating that it has an effect on spiritual purity and thereby on the heart's receptivity to communion with God. As mentioned above, He also forbids recourse to alcohol, opium and other substances which distort perception and thus inhibit the individual's capacity to maintain an ongoing state of communion with God.

The importance Bahá'u'lláh gives to our individual relationship with God and the centrality of this relationship within Bahá'u'lláh's system are expressions of the fundamental role that the love of God plays in all human relationships.

Lateral Relationships; Marriage

The vertical relationship between each individual and God is the necessary basis for harmonious and productive lateral relationships between and among human beings. Of all these lateral relationships, the most fundamental is that between husband and wife. Indeed, society comes forth from the family and the family from the couple. Ultimately, society cannot be more healthy than its families nor families more healthy than the relationship between wife and husband. Thus, Bahá'u'lláh devotes a portion of the Kitáb-i-Aqdas to laying out the fundamental parameters of the marriage relationship.

As viewed by Bahá'u'lláh, the relationship between husband and wife is governed by two basic principles: equality (or reciprocity) and fidelity. The principle of equality is the expression of justice within the marriage and the principle of fidelity is an expression of love. We will discuss each in turn.

The equality of women and men is a fundamental principle of the Bahá'í Faith. This principle implies not only social equality but total reciprocity within the marriage relationship. In making decisions that are not purely individual – that relate to the married couple as a social entity – the marriage partners are enjoined to use consultation. As mentioned in our brief discussion of Bahá'í consultation above, the goal is to seek a consensual view of the matter at hand and to abide by a majority view when such a consensus cannot be attained. When, as in the case of husband and wife, no non-unanimous majority is possible, then the couple must find a creative way of making a given decision when differences of opinion persist. This may involve either one deferring to the other in certain given instances, but in the Bahá'í conception of the marriage relationship, there is no presumption that either party should ever dominate the other or impose his or her will by force or manipulation.

Consultation, and the pursuit of justice within the marriage relationship, is best thought of as a lateral extension of the intimate dialogue between each individual and God. Viewed in this way, consultation between the couple becomes a sort of collective prayer: in the same way that the individual seeks the truth through his internal dialogue with God, so the couple must seek the truth in their intimate dialogue with each other.

Clearly, this conception of the relationship between marriage partners represents a certain challenge to the maturity of their relationship. But this can be seen as a healthy challenge, conducive to spiritual growth and thus to the purpose of human existence.

The second basic principle governing the relationship between husband and wife is absolute fidelity. Among other things, the Kitáb-i-Aqdas specifically states that a sexual relationship is spiritually legitimate only between a man and a woman who are married to each other. Thus, sexual relationships outside of the marriage bond are proscribed in the Kitáb-i-Aqdas, and those who violate this prohibition are subject to a penalty which, in the case of consenting adults, is the payment of an identical fine by both parties, the amount being doubled with each subsequent offense. The penalty for other particular violations of this law, such as rape, incest or adultery, are to be determined by the Universal House of Justice.

Bahá'u'lláh's conception of loyalty between the marriage partners implies not only the act of sexual faithfulness but also an attitude of mind in which each partner continually gives priority to the well-being of the other in all circumstances. The importance Bahá'u'lláh gives to loyalty within marriage is apparent from His first mention of the principle in paragraph 19: 'Ye have been forbidden to commit murder or adultery, or to engage in backbiting or calumny; shun ye, then, what hath been prohibited in the holy Books and Tablets.[39]

Just as murder is the most grievous possible violation of the sanctity of individual life, so adultery is the most grievous possible violation of the sanctity of the marriage relationship. Backbiting and calumny destroy the individual by assassinating his character and reputation rather than his physical person. Similarly, other more subtle forms of unfaithfulness may assassinate the marriage relationship. But sexual faithfulness is the minimum challenge to be met by the marriage partners.

Probably most people would agree that the combination of sexual chastity before marriage and faithfulness within marriage will serve to strengthen the marriage bond. However, many may also feel that this discipline will impose an intolerable hardship on the individual. The accepted idea in many quarters is that men especially cannot be seriously expected to restrain themselves sexually before marriage or to confine themselves to only one partner after marriage.

Clearly, Bahá'u'lláh does not agree with such notions. To begin with, there is no trace whatsoever of any sexual double standard in the Kitáb-i-Aqdas. Marriage is monogamous, the principles of chastity and fidelity are equally binding on men and women, and all penalties for violations of these principles between consenting adults apply equally to both partners. Moreover, a number of special conditions regarding prayer and fasting apply to women only, such as special prayers to be said in lieu of fasting for menstruating women. The overall result – confirmed in other writings of Bahá'u'lláh as well – is to exalt the position of the woman as the bearer and nurturer of life, while maintaining total social equality between women and men in all other respects.

As to the question of sexual discipline, Bahá'u'lláh considers this to be a particular means God has provided for our spiritual development. If God has so freely endowed us with the precious and potent gift of sexuality, He has also endowed us with the capacity for its disciplined and responsible use. Throughout His writings, Bahá'u'lláh insists that one of the basic principles God has established in His dealings with humanity is that He never requires from us anything of which we are not truly capable: 'He will never deal unjustly with any one, neither will He task a soul beyond its power.'[40] Indeed, explains Bahá'u'lláh, everything God imposes upon us is for our benefit alone, for there is no self-interest on the part of God. God is totally self sufficient and His love for us is absolutely pure.

Thus, according to Bahá'u'lláh, the sexual discipline of chastity and fidelity contained in the Kitáb-i-Aqdas is for our benefit and fully within our God-given power to accomplish. Had God withheld the gift of so powerful a sexuality from us, we would have been spared the tensions sometimes involved in the exercise of sexual discipline, but we would have been denied the opportunities for substantial and rapid spiritual growth this discipline affords. Thus Bahá'u'lláh's prescriptions regarding sexuality constitute a prime example of teachings that can be understood only in the light of Bahá'u'lláh's conception of human purpose.

Although the prescription of chastity and fidelity are not original with the Bahá'í teachings, historical attempts to practice these disciplines have been marred by several factors. First is the often unspoken assumption that human sexuality is animalistic, dirty or debased. The Bahá'í teachings specifically contradict this notion, teaching that all of the naturally-given human capacities – both physical and spiritual – come from God and are good in themselves. Any evil connected therewith is strictly a result of our misuse of them. Human sexuality is divine and sacred, not animal and exploitative, unless we debase it through willful misuse. Moreover, Bahá'u'lláh specifically states that there is no moral value whatsoever in celibacy itself. Not only does the Kitáb-i-Aqdas condemn asceticism and other forms of extreme self-denial, it criticizes harshly anyone who, for example, 'hath secluded himself in the climes of India, denied himself the things that God hath decreed as lawful, imposed upon himself austerities and mortifications', stating that such a person 'hath not been remembered by God, the Revealer of Verses'.[41]

A second feature that has prevented mankind from benefitting appropriately from the disciplines of chastity and fidelity has been the historic inequality between men and women. Polygamous marriage (specifically forbidden in the Kitáb-i-Aqdas), the sexual double standard (in which, curiously, women are blamed for male promiscuity) and the dominance of women by men generally have prevented the marriage relationship from reaping anything like the full benefits of sexual discipline, even when it was sincerely practiced. However, the channeling of sexual expression into long-term, stable marriage relationships, in conjunction with the Bahá'í practice of equality, reciprocity and consultation between the marriage partners, will undoubtedly allow marriage relationships to achieve unprecedented levels of harmony, loyalty, intimacy and satisfaction. Indeed, 'Abdu'l-Bahá is reported to have said that no human can conceive of the union and harmony that God has destined for husband and wife.[42] In Bahá'u'lláh's view, such a consummation is more than adequate compensation for whatever temporary frustrations must be endured in the practice of sexual discipline before marriage.

Importantly, the Kitáb-i-Aqdas allows divorce:

> Should resentment or antipathy arise between husband and wife, [they must] bide in patience throughout the course of one whole year, that perchance the fragrance of affection may be renewed between them. If, upon the completion of this period, their love hath not returned, it is permissible for divorce to take place. God's wisdom, verily, hath encompassed all things.[43]

It is often true that whatever has great potential for good when properly implemented also has great potential for evil if misused. Thus Bahá'u'lláh exalts the station of marriage and its positive spiritual potential but recognizes that there is no spiritual value – and, in fact, much potential spiritual harm – in forcing a couple to maintain the formalities of a relationship that no longer exists in fact. Notice that the grounds for divorce are 'resentment or antipathy', not necessarily a specific act of (sexual or other) unfaithfulness. As with other aspects of marriage, both husband and wife have an equal right to divorce, when once the year of waiting has been accomplished. Neither party can block or refuse divorce to the other.

The Family

We have seen that the two basic parameters of marriage – equality and fidelity are particular instances of the two fundamental pillars of all human relationships, justice and love. We now want to see how these same principles operate in the context of the next most intimate category of human relationships, namely the relationships within the family.

Equality and reciprocity are the expression of justice within the marriage relationship because Bahá'í marriage is conceived as a completely symmetrical relationship between two equally mature and competent adults. But other relationships within the family, and in particular the relationship between parents and children, are not symmetrical. Therefore, the expression of justice within the family involves certain subtleties and nuances, which Bahá'u'lláh addresses in the Kitáb-i-Aqdas.

To begin with, Bahá'u'lláh makes it clear that the primary purpose of spiritually healthy marriages is to bring forth spiritually healthy children. Indeed, a high quality of relationship between the marriage partners provides an appropriate milieu for the healthy growth and development of each member of the family and, in particular, for the children: 'Enter into wedlock, O people, that ye may bring forth one who will make mention of Me amid My servants. This is My bidding unto you; hold fast to it as an assistance to yourselves.'[44] Thus the purpose of the family is not just the physical propagation of children but also their spiritual education. The emphasis which Bahá'u'lláh places on the parents' responsibilities is indicated by the following commentary of Bahá'u'lláh:

> Unto every father hath been enjoined the instruction of his son and daughter in the art of reading and writing and in all that hath been laid down in the Holy Tablet. He that putteth away that which is commanded unto him, the Trustees are then to take from him that which is required for their instruction if he be wealthy

and, if not, the matter devolveth upon the House of Justice. Verily we have made it a shelter for the poor and needy. He that bringeth up his son or the son of another, it is as though he hath brought up a son of Mine; upon him rest My glory, My loving-kindness, My mercy, that have compassed the world.[45]

Elsewhere it is explained that the spiritual and moral obligation to educate children devolves equally upon both parents, but in different ways. The mother is declared to be the 'first educator' of the child, and she has the right to material support from the father in this task. Indeed, each succeeding generation of the human race is founded on the willingness of its mothers to dedicate themselves to the best interests of their children. This pivotal role of motherhood is stressed throughout the Bahá'í writings. It means that society in general, and men in particular, must arrange their affairs so that mothers receive all of the necessary recognition, support and reward for their accomplishment of this sacred task.

For example, Bahá'u'lláh states that sons and daughters must be educated equally (and, according to 'Abdu'l-Bahá, with the same curriculum), but that whenever choices must be made in the education of children, preference is given to daughters because it is they who, upon becoming mothers, will be the first educators of the next generation. This principle shows clearly a shift of values away from the traditional view that the primary goal of education is to prepare males for economic or material success and towards the view that education must serve the primary goal of fostering the spiritual development of the entire future generation.

Thus, according to Bahá'u'lláh's view of the family, children have certain rights, such as the right to education, which the parents are obliged to respect. In a commentary on the Kitáb-i-Aqdas, Bahá'u'lláh states that a parent who neglects these sacred obligations may be declared by the House of Justice to have lost his rights of parenthood: 'Should a father neglect this most weighty commandment [to educate one's children] laid down in the Kitáb-i-Aqdas by the Pen of the Eternal King, he shall forfeit rights of fatherhood, and be accounted guilty before God.'[46]

Thus, children are not viewed as chattels or possessions of their parents, and parents do not have absolute authority over their children. Appropriate community agencies and authorities, under the guidance of the House of Justice, can intervene when necessary for the protection of children. According to Bahá'u'lláh's prescriptions, children reach the age of discretion at 15, after which they are held individually responsible for their actions and for the fulfillment of all adult spiritual responsibilities. Fifteen is also the age at which individuals are free to contract marriage.

A counterpart to these spiritual obligations devolving upon parents are similar obligations on children to respect the rights and station of their parents. Bahá'u'lláh has said:

> Well is it with him who in the Day of God hath laid fast hold upon His precepts and hath not deviated from His true and fundamental Law. The fruits that best befit the tree of human life are trustworthiness and godliness, truthfulness and sincerity; but greater than all, after recognition of the unity of God, praised and glorified be He, is regard for the rights that are due to one's parents ... Observe how loving kindness to one's parents hath been linked to recognition of the one true God![47]

The mutual respect for the rights and obligations of each member of the family provides a framework of justice which allows for true and enduring love to exist within the family. In the past, family relationships have too often been based on power rather than love. If the power of the parents is dominant, then the family falls into an authoritarian mode in which children can become virtual slaves to their parents' purely egotistical wishes. If the power of the children is dominant, the family tends to become indulgent and degenerates into anarchy and chaos.

In Bahá'u'lláh's conception of the family, none have dominance over others. Rather, the entire family and its members are subject, one and all, to the spiritual authority of Bahá'í principles and laws. In particular, parents recognize and acknowledge that they also are guided by a moral law greater than their own individual will. This acknowledgement confers upon them the necessary moral authority to direct, guide and teach their children. Thus the parents function as instruments or vehicles for the spiritual education of their children, not as tyrants or dictators who rule over them.

Of course, this quality of education requires continual and significant sacrifice on the part of the parents. Thus, children are obliged to show forth respect and kindness for their parents as a recognition of the sacrifice their parents make for the sake of the children's education. The experience of many Bahá'í families has been that children respond positively to principles to which their parents also submit, whereas the common experience of humanity is that children tend to resent the imposition of principles and rules they perceive as arbitrary dictates of their parents as individuals. Indeed, is it not the gap between deeds and words that so often leads the younger generation to view the older generation as hypocritical?

Because of the great sacrifice parents make for the spiritual education of their children, and because of the seriousness of marriage and its centrality to the human enterprise, Bahá'u'lláh requires that a couple, *once they have freely chosen each other as future marriage partners,* must seek the blessing and permission of their parents for the marriage. This requirement serves the fundamental Bahá'í goal of promoting unity. It can also be seen both as a formal recognition of the contribution the parents have made to the person's spiritual development, as well as a protection against a hasty choice of marriage partner, perhaps made under a spell of infatuation. Here is Bahá'u'lláh's statement of this principle in paragraph 65 of the Kitáb-i-Aqdas:

> . . . marriage is dependent upon the consent of both parties. Desiring to establish love, unity and harmony amidst Our servants, We have conditioned it, once the couple's wish is known, upon the permission of their parents, lest enmity and rancor should arise amongst them. And in this We have yet other purposes. Thus hath Our commandment been ordained.[48]

Those who have some knowledge of the immense cultural diversity abroad in the world today can appreciate the fineness and wisdom with which Bahá'u'lláh has established these various parameters of marriage and family relationships. One cultural extreme places the emphasis on absolute parental authority, where marriages are forced and arranged for economic or cultural reasons having little or nothing to do with the quality of spiritual relationship between the marriage partners. This has led to such terrible abuses as bride selling, bride burning and involuntary surrogate motherhood. Thus Bahá'u'lláh makes it absolutely clear that, unless and until the marriage partners have made a personal decision that they desire to marry, the parents have no right to interfere in the process. Furthermore, the Kitáb i-Aqdas strictly limits any dowry to a symbolic amount, thereby permanently removing any basis for the infernal manipulations so widespread in many parts of the world today.

At the other end of the cultural spectrum, as for example in North America, marriage is usually viewed as an absolute free choice between two individuals, without regard for the perceptions or wishes of the parents. As a consequence of this pattern, marriages are often entered into for immature and frivolous reasons, and frequently without the vital and necessary support of the families involved. Consequently, marriages may begin under conditions of intolerable stress, leading to early and acrimonious divorce, with attendant destabilization of the family milieu and catastrophic effects on the children involved. By making marriage conditional upon parental consent, 'once the couple's wish is known', Bahá'u'lláh maximizes the possibility that marriages will begin under conditions of loving family support and that young people will be protected from immature choices.

Interestingly and significantly, Bahá'u'lláh has not made divorce conditional on the approval of others, once the year of waiting and attempted reconciliation has been faithfully observed. Thus, on one hand, Bahá'u'lláh optimizes the possibility that marriages will be spiritually healthy and successful, and, on the other, He allows for the possibility that sincere mistakes can and will occur. Such a balanced, responsible and reasonable approach to the whole question of marriage and family shows the faith that

Bahá'u'lláh has in the human potential for mature and responsible spirituality.

The Bahá'í principles regarding marriage and family life are not the only examples where the Kitáb-i-Aqdas deals with the question of cultural relativity and conflicting cultural traditions. Indeed, many of the ordinances in the Kitáb-i-Aqdas represent liberalizations and abolitions of past practices. For example, in paragraphs 74 to 76 of the Kitáb-i-Aqdas, Bahá'u'lláh states:

> God hath decreed, in token of His mercy unto His creatures, that semen is not unclean . . .
> God hath, likewise, as a bounty from His presence, abolished the concept of 'uncleanness', whereby divers things and peoples have been held to be impure . . .
> God hath enjoined upon you to observe the utmost cleanliness, to the extent of washing what is soiled with dust, let alone with hardened dirt and similar defilement.[49]

Thus, with one stroke of His pen, Bahá'u'lláh completely abolishes the whole, hoary fetish of ritual uncleanness, which has lain at the root of centuries – indeed millennia – of superstitious and obsessive social practices in many parts of the world. He likewise stresses the importance of genuine physical cleanliness.

There are a number of other instances in the Kitáb-i-Aqdas where Bahá'u'lláh specifically declares previous religious practices to have been based on superstition or gross misinterpretation of previous holy texts such as the Qur'án or the Bible.

The Extended Family: The Larger Society

In a certain sense, all of the challenges of human relationships are reproduced within the milieu of each extended family. The dynamics of family relationships are subtle and constantly changing. As time passes, the parents, who were once young, vigorous and powerful become weak, fragile and vulnerable; whereas the children, who were dependent, vulnerable and untutored become strong, virile and accomplished. The children no longer see their parents as god-like – as representing the ultimate in human accomplishment. They began to achieve things their parents have not or could not have achieved. When the parents approach old age, there is almost a complete reversal of roles in which they become, in some ways, like dependent children to the same younger generation they have propagated. Nevertheless, as grandparents, uncles and aunts, they have various other important roles to play, providing a needed sense of historical perspective and continuity to the family. Under stable social conditions, the experiential oral history of a family can encompass almost a hundred years, involving three or even four generations.

These same dynamics exist within the larger society, in which roles and interdependencies are constantly shifting. This raises, in a very sharp way, the question of how to maintain the cohesion, the stability and progressiveness of social systems, while giving ample scope for individual freedom and initiative. Bahá'u'lláh articulates two fundamental principles that are necessary to the spiritual health of society: cooperation and service. These are the general social expression of justice and love. To the degree that society, at any level, is founded on cooperation and service, it will succeed and prosper, spiritually and materially. And, in the same way, the extent to which competition displaces cooperation and self-seeking displaces service in human motivation, society will degenerate. Here is one strong statement Bahá'u'lláh makes concerning the destructive effects of competition and self-seeking in human society:

> And amongst the realms of unity is the unity of rank and station. It redoundeth to the exaltation of the Cause, glorifying it among all peoples. Ever since the seeking of preference and distinction came into play, the world hath been laid waste. It hath become desolate. Those who have quaffed from the ocean of divine utterance and fixed their gaze upon the Realm of Glory should regard themselves as being on the same level as the others and in the same station. Were this matter to be definitely established and conclusively demonstrated through the power and might of God, the world would become as the Abhá Paradise.

Indeed, man is noble, inasmuch as each one is a repository of the sign of God. Nevertheless, to regard oneself as superior in knowledge, learning or virtue, or to exalt oneself or seek preference, is a grievous transgression. Great is the blessedness of those who are adorned with the ornament of this unity and have been graciously confirmed by God.[50]

Although most people would admit that competition does indeed have negative aspects, the extreme individualism and competitiveness of modern Western society are often justified as an evil that is necessary for the achievement of excellence. However, Bahá'u'lláh and 'Abdu'l-Bahá strongly reject this view. The pursuit of excellence proceeds by vertical comparisons between the performances of the same individual at different times; whereas competition proceeds by the horizontal comparison of the performances of different individuals at the same time. As a basic motivation, pure competition may sometimes stimulate the pursuit of excellence but it may also generate efforts to sabotage or undermine the performance of others (by the passive refusal to collaborate, if not through more active means). The Bahá'í writings stress that the underlying motivation for the pursuit of excellence should be to put our God-given talents at the service of others. When this intrinsic motivation is dominant, individuals strive to enhance their performance for greater development both of society and self, regardless of whether this leads them to outperform other individuals.

The other pillar of the spiritualization of society is service. Service involves not only a general attitude towards others but also the discipline of daily work at a chosen profession:

> O people of Bahá! It is incumbent upon each one of you to engage in some occupation – such as a craft, a trade or the like. We have exalted your engagement in such work to the rank of worship of the one true God. Reflect, O people, on the grace and blessings of your Lord, and yield Him thanks at eventide and dawn. Waste not your hours in idleness and sloth, but occupy yourselves with what will profit you and others.[51]

Other statements in the Bahá'í writings make it clear that the obligation to work is a spiritual law equally binding on everyone, regardless of the degree of material necessity. Homemaking is considered a noble profession and, accordingly, an act of worship. However, this in no way precludes mothers' and homemakers' engaging in other professions outside the home.

The Bahá'í view of work as worship brings us back again to the theme that the fundamental purpose of the laws and principles of the Kitáb-i-Aqdas is to foster the spiritual and material development of humanity. Bahá'í morality is thus not a morality of avoidance and withdrawal but a proactive dynamic of accomplishment and progression, motivated by the principles of justice and love, service and cooperation, reciprocity and loyalty.

Inheritance Laws; Ḥuqúqu'lláh

The application of the general social principles of service and cooperation can take many forms in particular contexts. In most instances, Bahá'u'lláh has left to individual judgment, and to the Universal House of Justice, the task of establishing or defining the implementation of these important principles. With regard to the age-old question of the distribution of wealth, 'Abdu'l-Bahá has enunciated the general principle that gross accumulation of wealth, whether by individuals or groups within society, should be avoided. He states that such overconcentration of wealth is harmful not only for society but also for the individuals involved. In the light of this principle, Bahá'u'lláh has instituted certain practical measures that, while allowing the necessary latitude for entrepreneurial initiative and individual freedom of economic action, nevertheless help to avoid extremes both of poverty and of excessive wealth.

One of these measures is called Ḥuqúqu'lláh or 'the right of God'. In summary form, this measure stipulates that every believer must pay, once only, 19 percent of the value of his possessions, less various exempt items, such as one's home and its furnishings. Bahá'u'lláh extols the spiritual benefits of Ḥuqúqu'lláh and states, 'By this means He [God] hath desired to purify what ye possess and to enable you to draw nigh unto such stations as none can comprehend save those whom God hath willed.'[52]

Ḥuqúqu'lláh is paid to the Universal House of Justice and thus sums derived from it can be redistributed and redeployed to maximum social benefit. One can imagine, for example, that favorable local conditions could create an economic boom in one area of the planet while difficult financial conditions elsewhere generate poverty. The Universal House of Justice could use the sums derived from the Ḥuqúqu'lláh paid in the prosperous region to help alleviate economic hardship in the depressed zone. Since such patterns of economic boom and bust are often temporary and shifting, it might be that, subsequently, the operation of redistribution of wealth will take place in the opposite direction. In any case, the Universal House of Justice, as the supreme governing organ of the entire Bahá'í world, will have the necessary information to assess accurately the situation and the necessary authority to implement the appropriate measures.

Through the payment of Ḥuqúqu'lláh, the believer 'purifies' his savings. Bahá'u'lláh institutes another tax, called Zakát, through which the believer purifies his means of sustenance: 'It hath been enjoined upon you to purify your means of sustenance and other such things through payment of Zakát.[53] The term 'Zakát' derives from the Qur'án and refers to an obligatory tax levied for the relief of the poor and other charitable purposes. Bahá'u'lláh has left to the Universal House of Justice the freedom to determine the various parameters of Zakát (e.g. exemptions, categories of income, scales of rates, frequency of payment).

Ḥuqúqu'lláh and Zakát, together with the general mandate given the Universal House of Justice, provide the necessary measures for the 'horizontal' adjustment of gross economic disparities within each generation. However, there is also the question of 'vertical' inequities resulting from the gradual overconcentration of wealth over succeeding generations. Bahá'u'lláh addresses this issue by specifying certain principles for the distribution of inheritance in the absence of a will on the part of the deceased: 'We have divided inheritance into seven categories.'[54] With respect to the decease of a given individual, these categories are children, wife or husband, father, mother, brothers, sisters and teachers. Bahá'u'lláh specifies the proportion of a given inheritance that is to be allotted to each category. *However; this distribution is obligatory only in the case that the individual dies without writing a will.* Moreover, Bahá'u'lláh has specifically enjoined each individual to make a testament establishing the manner of distribution of that person's accumulated wealth after his or her passing:

> A person hath full jurisdiction over his property. If he is able to discharge the Ḥuqúqu'lláh, and is free of debt, then all that is recorded in his will, and any declaration or avowal it containeth, shall be acceptable. God, verily, hath permitted him to deal with that which He hath bestowed upon him in whatever manner he may desire.[55]

Of course, it is presumed that, in writing his will, the individual will take into account the general Bahá'í principle of avoiding the overconcentration of wealth in the hands of a few individuals.[56]

Gender Equality and the Membership of the Universal House of Justice

As is well known, and as already mentioned above in the discussion of marriage and the family, one of the fundamental principles of the Bahá'í Faith is the equality of men and women. The Bahá'í writings affirm unequivocally that women have historically been dominated and subjugated by men, creating a disastrous imbalance in society. For example, both Bahá'u'lláh and 'Abdu'l-Bahá attribute the prevalence of war and bloodshed in human history primarily to the predominance of aggressiveness, which has tended to characterize men, over compassion and common sense, which have been more characteristic of women. If women had been allowed to achieve the same level of education as men and contribute on an equal basis to civilization, then many historic injustices, such as slavery and child labor, would have been greatly diminished if not avoided altogether. Here is one of the many strong statements in the Bahá'í writings concerning these questions:

> The world in the past has been ruled by force and man has dominated over woman by reason of his more forceful and aggressive qualities both of body and mind. But the scales are already shifting, force is losing its weight, and mental alertness, intuition, and the spiritual qualities of love and service, in which woman is strong, are gaining ascendancy. Hence the new age will be an age less masculine and more permeated with the feminine ideals, or, to speak more exactly, will be an age in which the masculine and feminine elements of civilization will be more properly balanced.[57]

Not only does this passage acknowledge the imbalances of the past, it asserts that women tend to possess certain qualities to a degree superior to men. Elsewhere, 'Abdu'l-Bahá stresses that women possess all intellectual and creative abilities exhibited by men and that any lack of achievement on the part of women is due only to lack of adequate access to education: 'If given the same educational opportunities or course of study, [women] would develop the same capacity and abilities [as men]' and this 'whether in scientific research, political ability or any other sphere of human activity.'[58] Moreover, 'Abdu'l-Bahá underlines the necessity for women to enter all arenas of social and public life:

> So it will come to pass that when women participate fully and equally in the affairs of the world, when they enter confidently and capably the great arena of laws and politics, war will cease; for woman will be the obstacle and hindrance to it. This is true and without doubt.[59]

In the light of these and other strong statements in the Bahá'í writings concerning the capacity and role of women, it is surprising, and somewhat puzzling at first, that the Kitáb-i-Aqdas restricts the membership of the Universal House of Justice, but not the local and secondary Houses of Justice, to men alone. Indeed, in all other public functions and roles instituted by Bahá'u'lláh, women and men have equal access. The only exception at any level is membership in the Universal House of Justice. Moreover, there is no indication whatsoever, in any statement of Bahá'u'lláh or 'Abdu'l-Bahá, that exclusion of women from membership on the Universal House of Justice is based on any presumed incapacity of women to serve in this way.

The perception of paradox is reinforced when we recall that, as the supreme institution of Bahá'u'lláh's world order, the Universal House of Justice is the chief promulgator of all Bahá'í principles, including the principle of the equality of men and women. Why, one may reasonably ask, has Bahá'u'lláh excluded women from membership in the one institution that bears the primary responsibility for promoting the cause of the equality and rights of women?

This feature of Bahá'u'lláh's system has long given rise to discussion and speculation. When questioned on this subject, 'Abdu'l-Bahá only reiterated His affirmation that this restriction had nothing to do with the capacities of women and that the reason for their exclusion from membership in the Universal House of Justice would, in time, become absolutely clear to everyone.

Conclusions

The task of exploring the implications of so profound a work as the Kitáb-i-Aqdas is ongoing and progressive. Certainly the present article cannot claim to be more than a modest, initial contribution to this enterprise. Nevertheless, the fundamental outlines of Bahá'u'lláh's vision of a global planetary order can already be clearly seen. The goal is a unified, universal society, founded on spiritual principles and allowing for both stability and dynamism, global order and individual initiative. This world order has two fundamental components, one personal and spiritual, the other social and structural.

The personal component is based on the direct relationship between each human soul and the God who has created us all. The Kitáb-i-Aqdas instructs us in the fundamental parameters of this relationship. Bahá'u'lláh thereby tells us that the ultimate category of existence, Being Itself, is not an abstract principle but a loving Person who seeks intimate communion with each human being.

This vertical relationship between each individual and God is the necessary source of the love and compassion that must infuse all human relationships. But this great force of love must be properly harnessed if it is to produce a truly progressive and stable society. The Kitáb-i-Aqdas therefore institutes appropriate, just social structures, at every level of society, to allow for the free and unhampered flow and diffusion of love. These structures constitute a system of rights and obligations within marriage, the nuclear family, the extended family, and ultimately the whole of society. They involve potent institutions which allow for the implementation, at all levels of society, of decisions taken through consultation. These structures also provide the basis of a stable but dynamic economic system which, while not imposing the unrealistic and unhealthy norm of total economic egalitarianism, nevertheless eliminates the extremes of poverty and the gross accumulation of wealth.

Human history has witnessed a wide variety of social systems. Some have crushed individual freedom and initiative either through dictatorship or else an extreme collectivism that attributes little intrinsic value to the individual person. At the other extreme are highly individualistic systems in which interpersonal competition tends to permeate every aspect of society. Such systems are certainly dynamic but tend to be volatile and unstable.

Social philosophers have often held that there is an intrinsic, logical opposition between the good of the individual and the good of society as a whole. As a consequence of this view, most social systems are seen as a compromise in which some degree of individual self-realization must be sacrificed for the sake of social order.

Bahá'u'lláh's vision of society challenges this received idea. In His view, there can be no contradiction between what is truly good for the individual and what is truly good for the collectivity. Indeed, Bahá'u'lláh conceives that the very purpose of society is to create a milieu that optimizes the opportunities for the spiritual growth and development of each of its members. In the Kitáb-i-

Aqdas we have the balanced conception of a society that is founded on the sacred, intrinsic value of each individual human soul, independently of the role that person may play within society. At the same time, the Kitáb-i-Aqdas lays the structural foundations of a stable and progressive social life that favors the maximum degree of self-realization for everyone.

Now that the publication of the full, annotated edition of the Kitáb-i-Aqdas is accomplished, the eyes of the Bahá'í world are turned towards the institution of the Universal House of Justice whose sacred task it is to oversee the wise, gradual but steady implementation of the laws and principles of the Kitáb-i-Aqdas, which are nothing less than the laws governing the spiritual world, the world of being. But the ultimate responsibility for the implementation of these laws and principles lies not with any institution. Rather it lies with each of us, in whose hearts and minds the intimate communion with our Creator must be diligently pursued. This is an immense responsibility but also a unique privilege given us by God that we can participate, to whatever degree we choose, in the building of the mighty spiritual edifice of a world united on the basis of the very law of causality God has inscribed in the innermost recesses of reality.

Some Thoughts on Gender Distinction in the Kitáb-i-Aqdas: The Bahá'í Principle of Complementarity

John S. Hatcher

Among the most distinguishing features of the Bahá'í Revelation is the concept of revelation itself, the belief delineated in the *Kitáb-i-Íqán* that the historical purpose of religion is gradually to raise human consciousness to the realities of the spiritual world. From such a view, religion consists of two distinct but inextricably linked processes: the unveiling of eternal verities and the subsequent application of that enlightenment to human social structures.

As a corollary of this twofold process, the Bahá'í scriptures teach that knowledge of truth is inseparable from deeds but not simply because action gives dramatic form to understanding. The concretizing of a verity in the construct of human society heightens our perception of that truth and thereby gives rise to more ample expression. Indeed, this reciprocity of causality is at the heart of the Bahá'í belief in the evolution of human society.

The interdependence of knowledge and deed is, thus, no mere moral dictum, but a thoroughly practical relationship ordained for the training of humanity and its connection with the principle of the equality of women with men is crucial. For while we are only now beginning to come to terms with how to translate this revealed truth into human relationships and institutions, the principle itself is eternal. Bahá'u'lláh states unequivocally that 'Women and men have been and will always be equal in the sight of God'.[1] Therefore, inasmuch as this verity is eternal, we cannot in one sense say that either Bahá'u'lláh or the Bahá'í Faith has caused women to be equal to men – they always have been. But by unveiling this eternal truth to humanity and by further inaugurating laws and institutions that embody this spiritual reality, the Manifestation empowers us to make this relationship, which already exists in the 'sight of God', extant in every aspect of human society.

Of course, it is important to understand that while Manifestations of the past may not have given explicit utterance to the principle of equality of gender, the emergence in various religious cultures of beliefs contrary to this principle is not attributable to the Prophets. These are distortions, perversions and misunderstandings of their teachings. Thus Christ never advocated the sort of subordination of women that we find implicit in some Pauline letters and explicit in the antifeminist treatises of St Jerome and other patristic leaders of early Christianity, and yet such beliefs still afflict much of contemporary Christian thought.

Therefore, to appreciate the divine methodology whereby certain principles must await the fullness of time to be made explicit, we need to understand more generally the concept of timeliness in regard to revealed truth. For example, no doubt some of the Iranian Bahá'í women may have been troubled upon receiving 'Abdu'l-Bahá's letter early in this century stating that they should 'now engage in matters of pure spirituality and not contend with men'.[2] At the time, this advice may have seemed to contradict His other statements about women having an equal role in all aspects of human society and governance but the pragmatic benefits derived from this temporary delay later became apparent. Indeed, 'Abdu'l-Bahá's wisdom calls to mind Bahá'u'lláh's general statement about the timeliness of revealed truth:

> How manifold are the truths which must remain unuttered until the appointed time is come! Even as it hath been said: 'Not everything that a man knoweth can be disclosed, nor can everything that he can disclose be regarded as timely, nor can every timely utterance be considered as suited to the capacity of those who hear it.[3]

Accordingly, we may safely presume that Bahá'u'lláh's revelation and explicit directives regarding the equality of women implies that humanity presently has both the experience and capacity to comprehend this relationship as well as the appropriate social circumstances to implement it.

Such logic seems to underlie 'Abdu'l-Bahá's observation that 'The world in the past has been ruled by force, and man has dominated over woman by reason of his more forceful and aggressive qualities both of body and mind'.[4] And yet humanity some time ago emerged from a primitive state wherein survival depended on physical prowess. Furthermore, even among the animal kingdom, and in many tribal societies, there exists distinction of function between male and female without any attendant sense of oppression, disdain or subordination. Consequently, we can infer a third requisite for the timeliness of revealed truth, the emergence of a universal need that arises from a state of imbalance, ill-health and functional disorder, a condition that occurs whenever operant spiritual laws are ignored or violated. In short, humankind is now thoroughly motivated to acknowledge the equality of women because we are experiencing the dire crisis that has resulted from a society's domination by males and so-called male attributes (i.e. the emphasis on territoriality, materialism, acquisitiveness, aggression, etc.).

From the Bahá'í view, then, the timeliness of the principle of equality of women with men is not simply that this is one among a myriad of newly revealed verities. The very pathology and ecology of the contemporary human crisis is significantly attributable to the violation of this fundamental principle because the need for a complementary balance between male and female aspects of ourselves and of our collective enterprise is essential to creating a just and functional society, as several statements of 'Abdu'l-Bahá confirm:

> In past ages humanity has been defective and inefficient because it has been incomplete. War and its ravages have blighted the world . . .[5]

... it is well established that mankind and womankind as parts of composite humanity are coequal and that no difference in estimate is allowable...[6]

The world of humanity consists of two parts: male and female. Each is the complement of the other. Therefore, if one is defective, the other will necessarily be incomplete and perfection cannot be attained.[7]

... the new age will be an age less masculine and more permeated with the feminine ideals...[8]

At first, it might seem that the entire remedy for this disease would be relatively obvious and simple – to offset the imbalance by increasing the status of women, and indeed numerous statements in the Bahá'í writings affirm that this is a crucial part of the solution:

... the education of woman will be a mighty step toward [war's] abolition and ending, for she will use her whole influence against war.[9]

Only as women are welcomed into full partnership in all fields of human endeavor will the moral and psychological climate be created in which international peace can emerge.[10]

Similarly, the writings state that the only reason this imbalance has occurred is the deprivation women have experienced in educational opportunity:

In all human powers and functions they are partners and coequals. At present in spheres of human activity woman does not manifest her natal prerogatives, owing to lack of education and opportunity. Without doubt education will establish her equality with men.[11]

But noble and salutary as have been the efforts on the part of Bahá'ís and others to remedy this imbalance in opportunity, such responses are, by themselves, inadequate, incomplete and even possibly unfortunate when they are pursued without a clear understanding of the overall truth underlying the relationship between the sexes in a healthy society. For example, one understandable reaction to the injustices that erroneous ideas of gender distinction have produced has been the perception that all notions of gender are unnecessary, illogical, artificial and condemnable. One might even infer from some passages in the Bahá'í writings that this is a correct assumption:

> Equality of the sexes will be established in proportion to the increased opportunities afforded woman in this age, for man and woman are equally the recipients of powers and endowments from God, the Creator. God has not ordained distinction between them in His consummate purpose.[12]

However, the term 'distinction' in this passage clearly refers not to difference in function but degree of status or equality of human powers, such as reason, intellect, enlightenment, spirituality. It is similar to 'Abdu'l-Bahá's use of the term when He states, 'the sex distinction which exists in the human world is due to the lack of education for woman . . .'[13] 'Abdu'l-Bahá is not here implying that there is no difference between the sexes but that the unjust distinctions which currently obtain are baseless and unfounded.

Another similarly understandable but likewise counter-productive response to the injustice and subordination created by traditional gender roles has been the tacit re-creation of women in the image of men, even while we acknowledge that the male role is unbalanced, unhealthy and the cause of much of humanity's contemporary dilemma. Instead of inducing balance, such a response can exacerbate the very imbalance that has so afflicted human society by producing even more human beings in the mold of the stereotypical male.

What, then, is distinctive about the Bahá'í notion of a cure for this imbalance and what is further unique about the Bahá'í paradigm for a natural, proper, healthy and balanced relationship between women and men? As with other social problems, the

Bahá'í position is not an Aristotelian mean between extremes, not a point of moderation between those on the one hand who deem gender itself as a meaningless distinction and those on the other who view the woman's role as confined to some narrow province of domestic duties. It is, instead, a simple yet subtle principle of co-equal complementarity. The principle is simple because it retains a sense of gender distinction as natural while affirming the absolute equality of status. It is subtle because we have often confused notions of functional identity with women's rights, yet the House of Justice states forthrightly that 'equality of status does not imply identity of function'[14]

It is of utmost importance, therefore, that we have a clear understanding of how equality of status can coexist with distinction of function and perhaps the best place to begin is with 'Abdu'l-Bahá's often cited comparison of humanity to a bird:

> The world of humanity has two wings – one is women and the other men. Not until both wings are equally developed can the bird fly.[15]

We should note that in this analogy humanity is neither male nor female. It is an independent organism that utilizes two distinct faculties – men and women. We should further note that neither wing has any meaning or purpose without the other; they have a completely complementary relationship. Most important of all, we should observe that the primary objective of the bird is neither the amalgamation of one wing with the other nor solely the possession of two wings, particularly two of the same type (two left wings or two right wings). The goal of the organism is flight, and flight is achieved only when each wing retains its distinct identity and function but is precisely equal with the other in power and status: 'The solution provided in the teachings of Bahá'u'lláh is not . . . for men to become women, and for women to become men. 'Abdu'l-Bahá gave us the key to the problem when He taught that the qualities and functions of men and women "complement" each other.'[16]

This Bahá'í concept of gender distinction coexisting with

absolute equality of status is thus at the heart of any perception of this revealed truth, and it must be understood and appreciated before we can hope to approach the second of our twin duties, the implementation of this principle in Bahá'í laws and relationships. But we quickly discover that even if we have a relatively clear sense of the principle in theory, the application of this concept of complementarity to social relationships requires careful consideration. For example, we must begin by disabusing ourselves of the inherited responses we all share with regard to traditional gender distinction because gender roles have so often been promulgated for the purpose of suppression and subordination of women: the male had his province (the world of business, politics, the running of society); and the woman hers (the home, the children). Let us attempt, therefore, an objective look at some of the most obvious gender distinctions with regard to function in the Bahá'í society to understand how a division of duties can exist without unjust and inappropriate distinctions of status or authority.

We find in the Bahá'í writings statements that attribute 'primary responsibility for the financial support of the family' to the man, and statements which describe the woman as 'chief and primary educator of the children'.[17] Certainly we can observe this distinction in the laws of inheritance in the Kitáb-i-Aqdas as regards someone who has died intestate.[18] We may understandably blanch at the assignment of these duties solely on the basis of sexual distinctions because connotatively these duties call to mind contexts in which similar role distinctions have been used to circumscribe and suppress women. We may have an equally skeptical response to the statement by the Universal House of Justice that 'Homemaking is a highly honorable and responsible work of fundamental importance for mankind'.[19] If we take these gender distinctions out of the Bahá'í context, lump them together with some other gender distinctions in Bahá'í law regarding such things as dowry, inheritance, exemption from military engagements[20] and membership of the House of Justice, we may infer a general contradiction between the enunciation of the egalitarian relationship and the implementation of that truth in Bahá'í society.

To appreciate the distinguishing characteristics of the Bahá'í paradigm, we must first realize that there in no single issue or explanation that governs all distinctions of function as regards gender. The exigencies of family life dictate parental roles, whereas the restriction of membership on the House of Justice to men has its own special wisdom. For example, let us approach the rationale for gender distinction with regard to functions in the Bahá'í family. In Bahá'í society, parental responsibility is in many ways the most essential and pivotal function of community life since the training of children is viewed as the primary means by which the bird of humankind takes flight and an 'ever-advancing civilization' is fostered. As a result of this priority, the duties of both parents are carefully focused on this crucial task. Thus, because of physiological fact, the woman as mother has obligations regarding children that men do not have to the same degree, 'for it is the mother who rears, nurtures and guides the growth of the child'.[21] Likewise, and we may presume to facilitate the mother's duty, the father has obligations that the mother does not have – 'primary responsibility for the financial support of the family'.[22]

But we must immediately note that these are 'primary' areas of responsibility and are in the context of a marriage in which there are children. Such distinctions most emphatically do *not* imply that the man has no parental responsibilities or that the woman is less capable than the man of earning a living or that the woman does not have full and equal part in making all financial decisions. Indeed, the House of Justice notes that these relationships and responsibilities must be worked out within the exigencies of each individual family, that 'Family consultation will help to provide the answers',[23] and, of course, in such consultation, neither sex has primacy of authority or status. In addition, the House of Justice notes that the role of the woman as mother 'does not by any means imply that the place of woman is confined to the home'.[24]

The reason for gender distinction as it regards parental or familial functions thus seems centered around the essential goal of society to advance itself by training its children and the pivotal role of the family as a divinely ordained organism in accomplishing that task, a duty that 'Abdu'l-Bahá states is so important that the neglecting of this duty is a 'sin unpardonable'.[25] It is perhaps understandable, then, that the crucial nature of this function dictates that the woman be released from financial responsibilities to accomplish the initial stages of this process. We might also assume that the man's right of inheritance with regard to intestacy is likewise bound up in his special financial responsibilities in Bahá'í family life, obligations which might render the appellation of 'head' of the family appropriate to the father as it relates to his special financial duties: 'it can be inferred from a number of the responsibilities placed upon him, that the father can be regarded as the 'head' of the family'.[26]

However, this designation carries with it no special authority but rather demonstrates that because the family as an organic enterprise is 'a very special kind of "community"',[27] it reflects a division of duties according to the exigencies of this function:

> The members of a family all have duties and responsibilities towards one another and to the family as a whole, and these duties and responsibilities vary from member to member because of their natural relationships. The parents have the inescapable duty to educate their children – but not vice versa; the children have the duty to obey their parents – the parents do not obey the children; the mother – not the father – bears the children, nurses them in babyhood, and is thus their first educator, hence daughters have a prior right to education over sons and, as the Guardian's secretary has written on his behalf: 'The task of bringing up a Bahá'í child, as emphasized time and again in Bahá'í Writings, is the chief responsibility of the mother, whose unique privilege is indeed to create in her home such conditions as would be most conductive to both his material and spiritual welfare and advancement. The training which a child first receives through his mother constitutes the strongest foundation for his future development.' A corollary of this responsibility of the mother is her right to be supported by her husband – a husband has no explicit right to be supported by his wife. This principle of the husband's responsibility to provide for and protect the family can be seen applied also in the law of intestacy which provides that

the family's dwelling place passes, on the father's death, not to his widow, but to his eldest son; the son at the same time has the responsibility to care for his mother.[28]

Thus, when the term 'head' of the family is used in a Bahá'í context to designate the father, it must be understood to have none of the conventional authoritarian implications that the term heretofore has so often connoted because in the Bahá'í family the husband does not have any authority, privilege or status that the wife does not share equally:

> The atmosphere within a Bahá'í family as within the community as a whole should express 'the keynote of the Cause of God' which, the beloved Guardian has stated, 'is not dictatorial authority but humble fellowship, not arbitrary power, but the spirit of frank and loving consultation'.[29]

To understand the term in relation to the concept of complementarity, the term 'head' in the Bahá'í context designates the nature of the husband's function, not a hierarchy of status:

> Indeed, to use the human temple as the example, if the husband is the head, the wife can well be regarded as the heart of the family. When the husband and the wife work cooperatively and complementarily, the well-being, health and proper functioning of the unity can be ensured.[30]

> The House of Justice has stated previously, in response to a question from a believer, that use of the term 'head' does not confer superiority upon the husband, nor does it give him special rights to undermine the rights of the other members of the family. It has also stated that if agreement cannot be reached following loving consultation, 'there are times . . . when a wife should defer to her husband, and times when a husband should defer to his wife, but neither should ever unjustly dominate the other'; this is in marked contrast to the conventional use of the term 'head' with which is associated, frequently, the unfettered right of making decisions when agreement cannot be reached between husband and wife.[31]

In short, regardless of what appellations we use for family members, authority is equally distributed between the husband and wife, and, in fact, the primacy of duties is attributed to the mother, both with regard to her having first rights to education and in relation to her essential worth to human society:

> The woman is indeed of the greater importance to the race. She has the greater burden and the greater work. Look at the vegetable and the animal worlds. The palm which carries the fruit is the tree most prized by the date grower.[32]

Therefore, although the duties in the Bahá'í family relate in certain circumstances to gender, there is no intent whatsoever that the woman's role be inferior or subordinated to the man's role. Quite the opposite is the case, though clearly these distinctive Bahá'í gender roles can only be fully understood, appreciated and effected 'in the context of Bahá'í society, not in that of past or present social norms'.[33]

But even with our present limited insights about the future evolution of Bahá'í community life, we would do well to note at least one major characteristic of these gender distinctions with regard to Bahá'í relationships and institutions. These differences seem to result from such distinctions as circumstantial conditions and physiological fact. They are in no wise attributable to distinctions in human capacities or powers. To confirm this fact, 'Abdu'l-Bahá points out that in a sane, just and healthy society women will have full status and function in every human endeavor:

> In no movement will they be left behind. Their rights with men are equal in degree. They will enter all the administrative branches of politics. They will attain in all such a degree as will be considered the very highest station of the world of humanity and will take part in all affairs.[34]

With this clear statement of the equality of women and men, let us consider a distinction of duties that seems unrelated to matters of rearing children, the crucial role of membership of the Universal House of Justice.[35] How can we not infer from this distinction of function a sense of the woman as less capable in some as yet unknown capacity?

If we approach this issue by asking ourselves what it is that qualifies men that does not qualify women, or the converse, what capabilities do women not have that men have, then we have already strayed from the logic and integrity of the Bahá'í paradigm. Once we have established that there is absolutely no distinction in human capacity between men and women, such questions automatically become illogical and unfounded. We can infer as much from 'Abdu'l-Bahá's statement that 'ere long' the wisdom of this distinction will be 'manifest as clearly as the sun at high noon'.[36] We may presume that at such a time we will exclaim, as have the women of Iran regarding 'Abdu'l-Bahá's advice to them, 'This was indeed supreme wisdom!' In the meantime, we must necessarily confine our speculation to answers that deal with circumstantial explanations or do not imply difference in any essential human capability, an inference confirmed by the fact that women are ordained to serve on every other Bahá'í institutional and administrative body.

But even if we accept that there is a special logic and just explanation for every gender-based distinction of function in the Bahá'í community (the wisdom of each of which we will in time behold), what can we conclude about the nature of gender itself quite apart from the assignment of duties? Which attributes that we ascribe to women and men are real and which are artificially derived from antiquated notions of status and function?

Most probably we must conclude that for the present we cannot know with certitude anything much about true gender traits in the human species, since we approach such questions from the perspective of our own limited background and biases and since the emergence of valid and healthy distinctions, whatever they may turn out to be, must await a social context which is itself conducive to fostering such distinctions.

In some passages 'Abdu'l-Bahá seems to imply inherent and permanent gender traits. He states that 'woman has greater moral courage than the man; she has also special gifts which enable her to govern in moments of danger and crisis',[37] that the woman is 'more tender-hearted, more receptive, her intuition is more intense',[38] and that 'in sciences and arts, in virtues and perfections ye shall become equal to man, and as regards tenderness of heart and the abundance of mercy and sympathy ye are superior'.[39] Likewise, in describing the changes in society resulting from the ascent of the influence of women, 'Abdu'l-Bahá seems to distinguish certain attributes as belonging to women:

> But the balance is already shifting; force is losing its dominance, and mental alertness, intuition, and the spiritual qualities of love and service, in which woman is strong, are gaining ascendancy.[40]

Of course, these distinctions may be appropriate only to our present circumstance wherein men have largely lost a sense of their so-called feminine traits, but it is interesting that in each of these distinctions the feminine attributes cited are viewed not as signs of weakness or as alternative virtues, but as indications of superiority. Therefore, we might well conclude that the superior human being is one whose feminine self is highly developed.

We may find one helpful key to understanding more generally this principle of co-equal complementarity in the metaphorical appellation Bahá'u'lláh and the Master used in addressing women. They sometimes employed the epithet 'leaves' – Bahíyyih Khánum, of course, was titled 'the Greatest Holy Leaf'. Certain men, on the other hand, have been designated 'branches' and 'twigs'. If the tree represents the attributes of God given phenomenal form, or the 'Anísá' (the Tree of Life), or possibly the human race itself, what is the relationship between the branch and the leaf? Is one superior to the other, one more vital than the other in the thriving of the tree?

Their functions are distinct yet reciprocal and co-equal. Each is necessary for the survival of the other, even as 'Abdu'l-Bahá has observed that the husband and wife 'are two helpmates, two intimate friends, who should be concerned about the welfare of each other'.[41] Furthermore, it is only when both leaf and branch are functioning so as to complement the other that the tree can prosper. The branch channels raw fluids and nutrients to the leaf (perhaps as the father of a household provides the sheer financial wherewithal for the family), and the leaf takes that potentiality and through photosynthesis changes the raw substance into kinetic chemical energy. As we know, photosynthesis takes place because the leaf is capable of utilizing sunlight, and in the scriptures, sunlight symbolizes spiritual and intellectual guidance. Metaphorically, then, the appellation 'leaf' seems to designate the woman as the key instrument by which the enlightenment and evolution of human society takes place, possibly because it is she who in instructing the children translates the potentialities of the Revelation into virtues.

Finally, we are faced with the existential dilemma of responding to our present condition of trying to live in two worlds at the same time – one dying and suffering in the pangs of that death, and the other not yet fully born. We are challenged, therefore, to discover for ourselves the illusive and constantly changing point of balance between trying on the one hand to respond courageously to present injustice and, on the other hand, attempting to fashion, however embryonically, the society envisioned in the Bahá'í commonwealth which alone can ultimately elucidate and fully implement the equality of women and men. Of course, this is a dilemma Bahá'ís face with every social problem, since Bahá'ís perceive a social ecology wherein no single issue can be resolved piecemeal as an isolated or autonomous pathology. For example, we cannot curtail drug abuse until we create a society sufficiently healthy that it no longer needs to escape from the reality of its existence. In the same way, we can with only limited effectiveness pursue the equality of women and men until we fashion a just and healthy social context to nurture that organic relationship:

> The principle of the equality between women and men, like the other teachings of the Faith, can be effectively and universally established among the friends when it is pursued in conjunction with all the other aspects of Bahá'í life.[42]

Put another way, our goal is to establish a healthy human society, something that can only be accomplished when the full potentialities of women are released. But health is not simply the absence of disease; it is the presence of a vital energy and direction. In Noah's day the true workers for social justice were not those so immersed in pursuing what they deemed to be their own best interest that they were deaf to the Prophet's guidance and admonitions, strange as His advice may have seemed at the time, but those noble few who listened and believed and labored with Noah to fashion board by board the Ark of their own salvation.

The Model of Penology Implied in the Kitáb-i-Aqdas

John S. Hatcher

Though the Kitáb-i-Aqdas (The Most Holy Book) is often alluded to as Bahá'u'lláh's book of laws, Bahá'u'lláh is careful to forewarn us early in the work that this is 'no mere code of laws'[1] and even a cursory glance confirms this for the reader. Martha L. Schweitz has pointed out that, from the standpoint of legal documents, the work is more like a constitution than a code of law.[2] From my own perspective as a student of literature, the work seems more a moral dialogue or poem than a legal document.

Structurally it proceeds like a variegated tapestry into which Bahá'u'lláh has woven His vision of a global civilization. Within this vision are very specific images of the 'refined'[3] individual, the product of an harmonious and well-ordered family, itself an integral part of a spiritually based and highly organized local community.

Woven into the fabric of this vision of future society are laws, scattered like luminescent jewels. Some laws seem to appear almost randomly, as if to shock us into thought. Some establish a theme after which follows a discourse or meditative exemplum. Other laws conclude a moral commentary, as if to punctuate a theme.

What also becomes apparent as we consider this work is that Bahá'u'lláh's purpose seems not so much to establish basic rules of comportment (although it certainly does that as well) as it is to set forth models on which future law can be devised and administered. In this context, the House of Justice observes that the laws of the Kitáb-i-Aqdas 'constitute the kernel of a vast range of law that will arise in centuries to come. This elaboration of the law will be enacted by the Universal House of Justice under the authority conferred upon it by Bahá'u'lláh Himself.'[4]

Because these laws establish a basis for future law, we do well to appreciate that the manner in which the laws are presented is sometimes as important as the specific behavior they ordain. A brief examination of the model of penology implicit in the Kitáb-i-Aqdas will demonstrate that in the Kitáb-i-Aqdas Bahá'u'lláh is primarily concerned with establishing patterns of response, not merely specific punishments for a handful of offenses.

The Various Levels of Response to Law

One indication that the laws set forth paradigms rather than codes is the fact that so many laws involve various levels or patterns of response rather than a single specific dictum. For example, Bahá'u'lláh makes daily prayer obligatory, but reveals three different obligatory prayers for that purpose, each one distinctly different from the other two in tone and length. He then leaves it to the individual to decide which one to use – there is no rank or preference in this – and He further gives a number of exemptions from this obligation.

The law regarding the payment of dowry is also variable, though not arbitrarily so. Marriage is conditioned on the payment of dowry of nineteen mithqáls of gold from the husband to the bride. However, villagers can pay the same amount in silver,[5] and if the husband cannot afford to pay his bride this amount, 'a promissory note to his bride at the time of the wedding ceremony' is sufficient.[6] In other words, the concept of the dowry as a symbol of the wife's right to have her own money seems more important than the precise terms of the agreement so that the law would never prevent a couple from marrying because they are poor.

The law regarding renewing 'the furnishings of your homes after the passing of each nineteen years' also contains exemptions. After stating the principle behind this law – that God is 'desirous of refinement, both for you yourselves and for all that ye possesses' – Bahá'u'lláh states, 'Whoso findeth that his means are insufficient to this purpose hath been excused by God, the Ever-Forgiving, the Most Bounteous'.[7] And as with so many of the laws of personal conduct and refinement, the determination of compliance is left to individual judgment and conscience.

While a number of the laws offer various avenues of compliance, and for a variety of reasons, the abiding rationale for all variable responses would seem to lie in Bahá'u'lláh's demonstration of the fairness, the justice and the educative function of law in general. For example, some laws involve a minimal standard coupled with a more lofty alternative. Bahá'u'lláh establishes the minimum period of time a wife must wait after the absence of her husband when he fails to return after a promised time. Should her husband not return by the promised time, 'it behoveth her to wait for a period of nine months, after which there is no impediment to her taking another husband; but should she wait longer, God, verily, loveth those women and men who show forth patience'.[8]

Perhaps one of the clearest examples of the fairness and flexibility demonstrated in the laws is Bahá'u'lláh's commandment that His followers 'allow no trace of dirt to be seen upon your garments'.[9] He goes so far as to state that should the 'garb of anyone be visibly sullied, his prayers shall not ascend to God, and the celestial Concourse will turn away from him'.[10] And yet, in the midst of discussing this apparently severe consequence for being unmindful of proper decorum and comportment, Bahá'u'lláh states, 'Whoso falleth short of this standard with good reason shall incur no blame. God, verily, is the Forgiving, the Merciful.'[11] The overall implication of this command would thus seem to be that God's justice considers every deed according to individual motive and circumstances, standards which, we must presume, He would expect the House of Justice to use in devising and implementing its own laws.

The Violation of Law

In general, we can infer from the Kitáb-i-Aqdas that all religious law, whether personal and private or civil and public, has as its animating purpose the education of the human soul: 'Throughout, it is the relationship of the individual soul to God and the fulfillment of its spiritual destiny that is the ultimate aim of the laws of religion.'[12]

It might seem, then, that penology as a process of punishing an individual for violation of law would primarily concern those laws that overtly affect the public good, those laws that protect the rights of the citizenry. But the laws of Bahá'u'lláh do not make any rigid distinction between civil or secular law and religious or sacred law. The reason for this, of course, is that a spiritually based society, essentially theocratic in form, makes no such distinction – all law is related to both aspects of human existence, the social/physical and the private/spiritual.

The introduction to the Kitáb-i-Aqdas does cite three general areas that the laws govern:

- the individual's relationship to God
- physical and spiritual matters which benefit the individual directly and
- relations among individuals and between the individual and society.[13]

But since all religious law has as its raison d'etre the reinforcing of the 'individual's relationship to God', and since Bahá'u'lláh devises a spiritually based social order, all law might seem to fall within the rubric of this first category, the individual's relationship to God. Yet the obvious meaning here, as confirmed by Bahá'u'lláh, is that laws governing purely personal matters (e.g. prayer and fasting) are not the proper concern of the administrative bodies and are not subject to penology, though the neglecting of these laws may well have negative consequences.

My point is that the Bahá'í perception of what laws are 'purely personal' as opposed to those that are not is distinct from most contemporary views of jurisprudence and from most Western notions of individual rights and freedoms. The best example of this might be Bahá'u'lláh's ordination of punishment for fornication, something that would be unthinkable in most contemporary societies. At the same time, Bahá'u'lláh makes the law of Ḥuqúqu'lláh (what would seem to be one of the primary means of taxation in the future Bahá'í commonwealth), a strictly personal matter between the individual and God, even though He specifies in exacting detail the process by which one determines what one owes to God.

There are other laws, of course, which may or may not be of administrative concern. For example, Bahá'u'lláh's strict laws regarding drugs and alcohol are, under some circumstances, personal and private (between the individual and God). In other circumstances, the violation of these laws may become the proper concern of the houses of justice. In effect, the judicial system Bahá'u'lláh has devised in place of a code of law is capable of responding to an infinite variety of variables. He has devised a judicial system to replace a strict code or canon, or even a rigid system of case law.

Four Punishments as a Pattern of Penology

Bahá'u'lláh states throughout His writings that justice and order (as well as individual training) derive from the application of the twin stimuli of reward and punishment: 'That which traineth the world is Justice, for it is upheld by two pillars, reward and punishment. These two pillars are the sources of life to the world.'[14] Bahá'u'lláh goes on to remark in this same passage that the application of this remedy to the human body politic is, in this day, the responsibility of the Universal House of Justice:

> Inasmuch as for each day there is a new problem and for every problem an expedient solution, such affairs should be referred to the Ministers of the House of Justice that they may act according to the needs and requirements of the time.[15]

In guiding the House of Justice on how to devise future punishments, Bahá'u'lláh does not in the Kitáb-i-Aqdas make explicit His principles of penology. However, He does ordain the punishment for four specific offenses, and, like some of the laws previously cited, these punishments establish patterns or models for a future penal code because in the course of enunciating these punishments, He also alludes to the principles governing these responses.

Perhaps the first important observation we can derive from the paradigm established by these four laws is the rationale behind their selection. Of all the laws or violation of laws which Bahá'u'lláh could have discussed, why does He choose to specify punishment for stealing, fornication,[16] arson and murder?

The most obvious link among these violations is that each represents a different degree of the same fundamental action – the injustice of taking that which does not belong to the offender. In fact, Hand of the Cause Faizi in a talk in 1974 observed that it is this same principle of justice that Bahá'u'lláh alludes to in the medium obligatory prayer when the supplicant repeats while washing his hands, 'Strengthen my hand, O my God, that it may take hold of Thy Book with such steadfastness that the hosts of the world shall have no power over it. Guard it, then, from meddling with whatsoever doth not belong unto it.'[17]

A second possible relationship among these four violations is that they represent a fairly complete range of severity as regards the violation of this fundamental principle of justice (i.e. 'laying hands' on the property of others). Or stated in terms of the prayer, one lays his hands on the possessions of another (stealing); one lays his hands on a body that does not belong to him (fornication); one lays his hands on the home, the possessions and possibly the life of another (arson); one takes the life of another (murder).

A further indication that Bahá'u'lláh chose these violations as emblematic of penology in general is the way in which He incorporates variable responses with these punishments. The punishment for stealing ranges from 'exile and imprisonment' for the first offenses to placing a mark on the brow of the individual for the third offense 'so that, thus identified, he may not be accepted in the cities of God and His countries'.[18]

The punishment for adultery (fornication) is a fine of nine mithqáls of gold, a fine which doubles with each subsequent offense. Of course, it does not take profound mathematical skills to realize that if this fine increases exponentially, nine mithqáls would quickly mount into a substantial sum for those who become recidivists.

For the crime of murder Bahá'u'lláh ordains capital punishment or life imprisonment, and the punishment for arson may also be life imprisonment or death by fire: 'Should anyone intentionally destroy a house by fire, him also shall ye burn . . .'[19] As the notes to the Kitáb-i-Aqdas explain, the details in both of these punishments are left to the House of Justice to decide in the context of future society:

> The details of the Bahá'í law of punishment for murder and arson, a law designed for a future state of society, were not specified by Bahá'u'lláh. The various details of the law, such as degrees of offense, whether extenuating circumstances are to be taken into account, and which of the two prescribed punishments is to be the norm are left to the Universal House of Justice to decide in light of prevailing conditions when the law is to be in operation. The manner in which the punishment is to be carried out is also left to the Universal House of Justice to decide.
>
> In relation to arson, this depends on what 'house' is burned. There is obviously a tremendous difference in the degree of offense between the person who burns down an empty warehouse and one who sets fire to a school full of children.[20]

Punishment is determined, then, according to the severity of the crime, the number of offenses one has committed and other extenuating circumstances. But the essential purpose of penology in Bahá'í law is constant, and it is not retribution or retaliation but deterrence: 'Man has not the right to take vengeance, but the community has the right to punish the criminal; and this punishment is intended to warn and to prevent so that no other person will dare to commit a like crime.'[21]

The Social Aspect of Penology

Thus far we have alluded only to the physical or tangible aspects of the punishment. Perhaps more important are the social and spiritual ramifications of these punishments. For example, as the notes to the Kitáb-i-Aqdas indicate, the application of these laws awaits a future society, and the society envisioned in that future is not a vast and impersonal federal system but a commonwealth of autonomous and closely knit communities, much like tribal communities in the collaboration and close association among their members.

And similar to a tribal ethos, the process of socialization in the future Bahá'í community becomes a mighty force for education and enforcement of law. In such a tightly knit community, one perceives himself as an integral part of a collective endeavor. Consequently, to be regarded as 'anti-social' becomes a grievous punishment in itself, something 'Abdu'l-Bahá comments on at length in His discussion on 'The Right Method of Treating Criminals' in *Some Answered Questions*:

> . . . it is possible to educate the masses so effectively that they will avoid and shrink from perpetrating crimes, so that the crime itself will appear to them as the greatest chastisement, the utmost condemnation and torment. Therefore, no crimes which require punishment will be committed.[22]

Because of this social component in these penal laws, we do well to observe that for each of these laws there is a strong sense of community response implicit in the punishment itself. For the thief, there is imprisonment but there is also 'exile'; in a tribal ethos, expulsion from the group (whether through exile, excommunication or other forms of ostracism) is far more grievous than any purely physical torment. How much worse that exile would be to live within the society but to bear a mark designating one as untrustworthy, as tainted. Here again, in terms of contemporary standards, such punishment might be deemed ludicrous. Wearing a mark on the forehead might well be worn with pride by gang members in America, some of whom currently wear tattoos at the corner of the eye to indicate with derision they have killed a member of an opposing gang.[23]

An important social component is also present in the punishment for 'adultery' or fornication. Compared to societies in which adulterers are executed, Bahá'u'lláh's ordination of a fine seems lax, almost casual. But we must keep in mind that Bahá'u'lláh is here alluding not to a breech of the marriage laws but any sexual intercourse outside the bounds of marriage. Furthermore, the fine has as its central purpose the public humiliation of the offenders:

> ['Abdu'l-Bahá] indicates that the aim of this law is to make clear to all that such an action is shameful in the eyes of God and that, in the event that the offense can be established and the fine imposed, the principal purpose is the exposure of the offenders – that they are shamed and disgraced in the eyes of society. He affirms that such exposure is in itself the greatest punishment.[24]

In one sense, then, the community as the extended family of the criminal responds forcefully to recalcitrant behavior, thereby protecting itself and, it is to be hoped, fostering the spiritual education of the individual. This social aspect of penology is, properly understood, a microcosmic example of the process of 'collective security' that Bahá'u'lláh has instituted to protect the global commonwealth as a whole.

The Spiritual Aspect of Penology

Of course, it is difficult to see the punishment for arson or for murder as having a social dimension in the sense of the loss of reputation, though one would hardly want to leave behind such a wretched legacy for one's progeny to bear. But these punishments seem calculated primarily to accomplish two obvious things – to remove permanently the criminal from the community and to deter others from committing like offenses. Yet there is also a spiritual dimension to these punishments that might well elude a casual assessment.

For example, the thief, by being removed from the society of his community, is led to consider the reality that existential happiness as well as spiritual development are totally dependent on interaction with the body politic to which each of us is inextricably linked. This subtle aspect of the punishment may not be enunciated or consciously understood by the malefactor, but the lesson will, if properly administered, gradually be inferred by the citizenry.

The spiritual lesson for those who violate the laws of sexual propriety is more explicit – Bahá'u'lláh states the spiritual effects of this punishment with an awful clarity. The most severe ramifications of this deed will be experienced in continuation of one's life beyond the physical realm because 'in the world to come He hath ordained for them [adulterers or fornicators] a humiliating torment'.[25] Of course, the torment itself is never explained, thus making it all the more fearful to consider, but Shoghi Effendi reaffirms that 'Bahá'u'lláh says adultery retards the progress of the soul in the afterlife – so grievous is it'.[26]

It is clear, then, that as we assess the spiritual dimension of penology, we are enunciating a principle at work that also underlies the physical and social aspects of Bahá'í penology as well – the universal acknowledgement that we are essentially spiritual beings and that the consequences of our actions committed in our physical lives remain with us eternally (beyond physical reality). Or stated more succinctly, the belief in the spiritual nature of our existence logically instigates the very 'fear of God' so often cited in Bahá'í scripture as that essential ingredient for fostering all human advancement:

> The fear of God hath ever been the prime factor in the education of His creatures. Well is it with them that have attained thereunto![27]

> You ask him about the fear of God: perhaps the friends do not realize that the majority of human beings need the element of fear in order to discipline their conduct? Only a relatively very highly evolved soul would always be disciplined by love alone. Fear of punishment, fear of the anger of God if we do evil, are needed to keep people's feet on the right path. Of course we should love God – but we must fear Him in the sense of a child fearing the righteous anger and chastisement of a parent; not cringe before Him as before a tyrant, but know His mercy exceeds His justice![28]

Consequently, Bahá'u'lláh's allusion to this unnamed punishment in the afterlife might far exceed as a deterrent any physical or social consequence but only if one has confirmed belief in a spiritual reality, in which case the crime might not have occurred in the first place.

The most obvious importance of appreciating the spiritual dimension to penology concerns the possibility of capital punishment for the murderer and the arsonist. Most arguments against capital punishment hinge on this distinction: if the purpose of punishment is to instruct, how can one learn if one is dead? Other arguments consider the horror of punishing the wrong person, though such objections seem to disregard how often each minute the 'wrong person' (the innocent victim) is executed by uncaring villains.

Punishment based on the reality of the continuity of human life responds to both these concerns. If by chance an innocent person is executed, no doubt the station of that person in the next world would be tantamount to that of all those who have in perfect innocence sacrificed their lives for the progress of human society, whether as victims of crime or tyranny or as willing heroes and heroines. Hopefully such a mistake would occur rarely, if ever, but clearly the weight of such a rare injustice would be minuscule compared to the thousands of innocent lives that would be spared by effective deterrence.

Consequently, it is with the education and progress of the soul of the arsonist or murderer that we should primarily concern ourselves. As we just noted, the Bahá'í perspective recognizes that progress is not confined to this life. Furthermore, the fundamental guide for personal justice in Bahá'í scripture is Bahá'u'lláh's upgrading of the golden rule in the Kitáb-i-Aqdas: not only are we forbidden to strike another, to backbite another or contend with another, we are forbidden even to wish for another what we would not wish for ourselves, though in this command Bahá'u'lláh removes the punishment formerly prescribed in the Persian Bayán by the Báb:

> A fine of nineteen mithqáls of gold had formerly been prescribed by Him Who is the Lord of all mankind for anyone who was the cause of sadness to another; in this Dispensation, however, He hath absolved you thereof and exhorteth you to show forth righteousness and piety. Such is the commandment which He hath enjoined upon you in this resplendent Tablet. Wish not for others what ye wish not for yourselves; fear God, and be not of the prideful.[29]

In light of this standard, it is easy to appreciate that the most effective educative component in a penal law is a process that would bring about this realization by enabling the criminal to have empirical knowledge of the pain he has inflicted on others. Since the consciousness and memory of the arsonist or murderer will endure beyond the demise of his physical life, capital punishment will allow the criminal to attain this experience. Bahá'u'lláh thus observes, 'It is clear and evident that all men shall, after their physical death, estimate the worth of their deeds, and realize all that their hands have wrought.'[30]

Having achieved this insight, the criminal enters the next stage of life cleansed from this sin, partially absolved, and ready for growth. 'Abdu'l-Bahá seems to confirm this inference when He says that those murderers who are punished in this life will receive no further punishment in the continuation of their lives:

> As to the question regarding the soul of a murderer, and what his punishment would be, the answer given was that the murderer must expiate his crime: that is, if they put the murderer to death, his death is his atonement for his crime, and following the death, God in His justice will impose no second penalty upon him, for divine justice would not allow this.[31]

From these observations we must conclude, then, that a proper assessment of the Bahá'í model of penology implicit in the Kitáb-i-Aqdas would be impossible without first appreciating the relationship that punishment has in connection with Bahá'í beliefs about the essentially spiritual nature and purpose of the human existence.

Individual Responsibility versus Community Obligations

To conclude this brief assessment of what we can infer about penology from the Kitáb-i-Aqdas, we would do well to consider the clear distinctions that are made in the Bahá'í writings between how an individual responds to criminal behavior and how society as an institution responds, because it is in making this distinction that 'Abdu'l-Bahá clarifies the purpose of penology.

According to 'Abdu'l-Bahá, it is the first obligation of the administrators of the community to secure justice and order. I would presume that it is in this context that Bahá'u'lláh in the Kitáb-i-Aqdas admonishes, 'Beware lest, through compassion, ye neglect to carry out the statutes of the religion of God; do that which hath been bidden you by Him Who is compassionate and merciful.'[32] Coming immediately after His statement about punishing the thief, this caution would seem primarily aimed at Bahá'í houses of justice, as opposed to individuals, since compassion and forgiveness are precisely what the individual should demonstrate, whereas the institutions are directed to have a different response. In short, the purpose of the community as an administrative institution is to provide justice, not mercy and forgiveness.

This does not mean society is intent on seeking vengeance. As 'Abdu'l-Bahá notes, punishment is not a form of vengeance or retaliation; it is an expression of justice, and upon this principle, the 'tent of existence is upheld'.[33] Furthermore, Bahá'u'lláh states in the Kitáb-i-Aqdas that forgiveness must come from God; one cannot be absolved by confessing sins to others. Therefore, forgiveness is not something the community can give even if it thought it mete to do so.[34]

The penological response of the community is thus distinct from the response of the individual, which, 'Abdu'l-Bahá observes, should be to repay injustice by another with forgiveness and mercy. 'Abdu'l-Bahá goes on to explain that the individual Bahá'í should do as Christ bade, to 'return good for evil, and not only forgive, but also, if possible, be of service to his oppressor'.[35] For if the victim responds by inflicting harm on the perpetrator, his action is no different from that of the criminal: 'The two actions are equivalent; if one action is reprehensible, both are reprehensible. The only difference is that one was committed first, the other later.'[36]

Bahá'u'lláh in the Kitáb-i-Aqdas makes this same distinction. The individual is forbidden to strike another or carry weapons. Bahá'u'lláh further states, 'Ye have been forbidden in the Book of God to engage in contention and conflict, to strike another, or to commit similar acts whereby hearts and souls may be saddened.'[37]

However, the response and responsibility of the institutions is different – it is their responsibility to protect the community, to maintain order, tranquility and security for those in its care. Consequently, the 'constitution of the communities depends upon justice, not upon forgiveness':

> As forgiveness is one of the attributes of the Merciful One, so also justice is one of the attributes of the Lord. The tent of existence is upheld upon the pillar of justice and not upon forgiveness. The continuance of mankind depends upon justice and not upon forgiveness. So if, at present, the law of pardon were practiced in all countries, in a short time the world would be disordered, and the foundations of human life would crumble. For example, if the governments of Europe had not withstood the notorious Attila, he would not have left a single living man.[38]

It is too often the case in the present Bahá'í community that these roles become reversed – individuals seek to retaliate and punish others and the administrators of the community think to help the criminal by showing forgiveness:

> There is a tendency to mix up the functions of the Administration and try to apply it in individual relationships, which is abortive, because the Assembly is a nascent House of Justice and is supposed to administer, according to the Teachings, the affairs of the community. But individuals toward each other are governed by love, unity, forgiveness and a sin-covering eye. Once the friends grasp this they will get along much better, but they keep playing Spiritual Assembly to each other and expect the Assembly to behave like an individual . . .[39]

When the community ignores its responsibility to punishment the criminal, it is neglecting its obligation to 'protect the rights of man'.[40] Yet even for the community vengeance is abhorrent. 'Abdu'l-Bahá thus distinguishes between vengeance and chastisement, noting that vengeance is never appropriate but that chastisement is a means by which justice and order are secured:

> Man has not the right to take vengeance, but the community has the right to punish the criminal; and this punishment is intended to warn and to prevent so that no other person will dare to commit a like crime. This punishment is for the protection of man's rights, but it is not vengeance; vengeance appeases the anger of the heart by opposing one evil to another. This is not allowable, for man has not the right to take vengeance.[41]

'Abdu'l-Bahá goes on to observe that for the community to fail to punish the criminal (and thus demonstrate mercy) is to deprive others in the community of the right to security. He also notes that the community applies this punishment not out of vengeance or retaliation or hatred for the criminal:

> But the community has the right of defense and of self-protection; moreover, the community has no hatred nor animosity for the murderer: it imprisons or punishes him merely for the protection and security of others. It is not for the purpose of taking vengeance upon the murderer, but for the purpose of inflicting a punishment by which the community will be protected.[42]

Finally, as we noted earlier, penology is most effective when it is wielded as a process of socialization and education. 'Abdu'l-Bahá states that if individuals are properly educated and the society spiritually based, then one's desire not to be regarded as a criminal is the greatest deterrent to crime. 'Abdu'l-Bahá does not state that penal institutions have an obligation to educate the criminal, but He does make one poignant observation about the unfortunate nature of present attitudes about penology:

> . . . communities are day and night occupied in making penal laws, and in preparing and organizing instruments and means of

punishment. They build prisons, make chains and fetters, arrange places of exile and banishment, and different kinds of hardships and tortures, and think by these means to discipline criminals, whereas, in reality, they are causing destruction of morals and perversion of characters. The community, on the contrary, ought day and night to strive and endeavor with the utmost zeal and effort to accomplish the education of men, to cause them day by day to progress and to increase in science and knowledge, to acquire virtues, to gain good morals and to avoid vices, so that crimes may not occur.[43]

He goes on to state that 'the communities must think of preventing crimes, rather than of rigorously punishing them'.[44] The concept of penology implied in the Kitáb-i-Aqdas thus recognizes this same principle by envisioning a society in which one feels loved, appreciated, cared for and in which rebellion against the community would be tantamount to rebellion against one's own family, and, by extension, against one's own integrity and well-being.

The Concept of Spirituality

William S. Hatcher[1]

Introduction

Human history has witnessed the birth, proliferation and death of countless religions, belief systems and philosophies. Though the generating impulse for each of these systems is undoubtedly related to numerous particular cultural and psychological factors, there runs through virtually all of them the common idea that man is not, in his naturally given human state, whole or complete. The concomitant to this belief is the idea that man must undergo some process of completion, some discipline of self-definition. Such a process is usually regarded by its exponents as the basic purpose of man's existence, for through it man is seen to acquire or develop what is essential and universal, and not merely accidental and local, within the range of human potentiality. By this process, he defines what he truly is by becoming what he most truly can be. The process is often described as one of 'salvation', of being lifted above the condition of unregeneration (or spiritual death) to the plane of a superior reality.

The revealed religions have been major sources of such salvation concepts, spiritual philosophies and spiritual disciplines. Historically, the revealed religions would seem to be united in affirming, each in its own particular way, that there is an objectively real spiritual dimension to the universe, and that this spiritual dimension of existence is for man the most fundamental and the most important aspect of reality. However, the revealed religions also appear, at least at first glance, to exhibit a disturbing degree of difference in their respective views of the exact nature of this spiritual reality and of how man should relate properly to it. Moreover, most of the traditional systems of religious belief appear now to have crystalized into rigid social patterns and dogmatic attitudes of thought and belief with which the modern ethos of rapid social and intellectual change seems incompatible.

The changes in modern-day society are being wrought primarily by a highly efficient, powerful and established science which owes little or nothing to established religion. Whereas the religions, for the most part, continue to press harder and harder their mutually contradictory claims each to possess an absolute and unchanging truth which admits no compromise, science is based squarely on the idea that truth is relative and progressive, that what is useful and productive in the realm of ideas and techniques today may be obsolete and unproductive tomorrow. Thus traditional religion has come to abhor and fear change while science thrives upon it.

Yet science and technology have not given man the sense of wholeness he has so long been seeking, even though they have given him a vastly increased power to control and manipulate his physical environment. The sense of incompleteness and the conscious need for transcendence, for contact with some deep spiritual reality, are widespread in our society. Indeed, hardly at any other time of history or in any other culture has the sense of spiritual inadequacy been so acute as is currently the case in industrialized, high-technology, Western culture. But if contemporary man turns to religion for enlightenment, he too often finds dogmatism, which his mind cannot accept, or mindless emotionalism, which is not worthy of acceptance.

From the modern perspective, each of the great religions appears as a system which was largely successful in satisfying the spiritual and social needs of a certain people or culture during a previous era of history but which is no longer adequate to meet the needs of humanity in the present critical period of history. Thus modern man is caught in a serious dilemma with regard to fundamental spiritual questions. On the one hand, the highly efficient science he has so successfully developed serves in part to deepen his moral and spiritual needs – needs that science alone cannot satisfy.[2] On the other hand, most of the traditional religious forms, attitudes and concepts now appear obsolete and irrelevant.

This modern dilemma is addressed by several of the fundamental principles of the historically recent Bahá'í Faith. The Bahá'í principle of the unity of science and religion holds that religious truth, like scientific truth (or truth in general), is relative and progressive. It accepts unreservedly that 'if religious beliefs and opinions are found contrary to the standards of science they are mere superstitions and imaginations'.[3] In particular, with regard to spiritual questions the Bahá'í Faith rejects a dogmatic approach: It affirms that there are spiritual realities governed by lawful relationships and it invites each individual to assume a scientific attitude and to seek out and test for himself these spiritual truths.[4] Concerning the great world religions, the Bahá'í Faith teaches that they all derive from one common source, namely, that one, ultimate, creative force responsible for the phenomena of the universe, that force we call God. Bahá'ís hold that the founding figures of these great religious systems (e.g. Moses, Buddha, Jesus, Zoroaster, Muḥammad) were all chosen channels or true spokesmen for this unique God, and that differences in their teachings are due primarily to the varying requirements of the cultures and ages in which these systems were originally promulgated. Other significant doctrinal differences among these systems, as they are currently elaborated, are attributed to inaccuracies and distortions gradually introduced by their followers in the course of their evolution as social systems after the death of their founders.[5] However, the essential spiritual message of these systems is affirmed to be universal and common to all.

The Bahá'í Faith views itself as deriving from the most recent of these revelation events, as the latest chapter in the (unending) book of religion, so to speak. Bahá'u'lláh (1817-92), founder of the Bahá'í Faith, put forth these and other teachings in a series of over a hundred books and manuscripts written primarily between 1853 and His death in 1892.

Thus Bahá'ís feel that traditional religions are perceived by modern man as so unsatisfactory partly because some of their teachings are laden with culture-bound patterns and concepts (e.g. the dietary and penal laws of Judaism and Islám) and partly because of man-made distortions and corruptions which have crept in over the years. Religious dogmatism represents the arrogant attempt to transform a relative and partial conception of truth into an absolute and unchanging system, binding the whole of mankind for all human history. According to the Bahá'í understanding of the dynamics of God-created human nature, no such fixed system could ever be adequate for mankind. The Bahá'í system itself is viewed as responding to the needs of mankind in the present hour, but not for all future history.

Bahá'ís hold that the basic spiritual message common to the revealed religions is progressively elaborated and more fully articulated in each successive revelation. One would therefore expect that the Bahá'í Faith, if it is indeed the most recent divinely inspired articulation of spiritual truth to mankind, would contain a fuller elaboration and a deeper expression of this truth.

I believe that such is the case, and in the following pages I have quoted liberally, and sometimes at length, from the Bahá'í writings in an effort to convey to the reader some of the incredible spiritual riches they contain. Yet all of the ideas and opinions expressed herein should be strictly regarded as nothing beyond the attempt of one mind to grasp some of the deeper meanings latent in the profound writings of Bahá'u'lláh, 'Abdu'l-Bahá and Shoghi Effendi. In an effort to limit the scope of this article to reasonable proportions and to achieve an orderly exposition, I have consistently focused on the concept of spirituality, that is, on an intellectual and logical understanding of spirituality. This work does not attempt in any way to be a manual for attaining spirituality but seeks only to gain, insofar as is possible, a clearer conception of what is implied in attaining it.

Of course, attaining any goal is easier when we have a clear conception of what its attainment involves. I have offered the present text for publication only in the hope that it may contribute in some measure to the common task we all have of trying to express our spiritual understanding to each other, especially as I have already richly benefitted from the insights and reflections of so many in this regard.

The Nature of Man

The Basic Components of Man's Character

The Bahá'í writings articulate a model of human nature and functioning which sees man as the product of two basic conditions, the physical (material) and the spiritual (nonmaterial). The physical dimension of man's existence derives from his genetic endowment, determined at conception, plus the interaction of this configuration with the environment. This interaction produces an internal, physical milieu which is unique to each individual, though sharing common features with all members of the human species. The spiritual dimension of man's nature derives from the existence of a nonmaterial entity, the soul, which is individualized, it is explained, at the moment of conception. Just as the physical body of man has various physical capacities, so the soul has its capacities, called *spiritual* capacities of man. Among the most important spiritual capacities mentioned in the Bahá'í writings as characteristic of man are those of the intellect or understanding, the heart or feeling capacity, and the will (the capacity to initiate and sustain action).

The interactions of the individual with his environment affect not only his body but his soul as well. They develop both the genetically given physical capacities and the initially given spiritual capacities. These interactions may be called *learning* or *education,* and they give rise to a third aspect of man's total character, an aspect that is both physical and spiritual.

In sum, there are three essential aspects of the character of man: his genetic endowment, which is purely physical; his soul and its capacities, which are purely spiritual; and education, which is both physical and spiritual.[6]

In *Some Answered Questions,* 'Abdu'l-Bahá speaks of these three basic aspects of man's character:

> He [man] has the innate character, the inherited character, and the acquired character which is gained by education.
> With regard to the innate character, although the divine creation is purely good, yet the varieties of natural qualities in

man come from the difference of degree; all are excellent, but they are more or less so, according to the degree. So all mankind possess intelligence and capacities, but the intelligence, the capacity and the worthiness of men differ . . .

The variety of inherited qualities comes from strength and weakness of constitution – that is to say, when the two parents are weak, the children will be weak; if they are strong, the children will be robust . . .

But the difference of the qualities with regard to culture is very great, for education has great influence . . . Education must be considered as most important, for as diseases in the world of bodies are extremely contagious, so, in the same way, qualities of spirit and heart are extremely contagious. Education has a universal influence, and the differences caused by it are very great.[7]

From this, and other similar passages in the Bahá'í writings, it is clear that the innate character derives from the capacities of the soul while the inherited character derives from the individual's genetic endowment. Once fixed, these two elements of man's character remain unchanged, but the process of education enables man to develop these capacities either to a relatively high degree or to a relatively low degree, thus producing significant differences in character not attributable solely either to heredity or to innate spiritual capacity.

Spirituality Defined

We have used the word 'capacity' in referring both to the spiritual and to the physical endowments of the individual. The word connotes a potential, something to be fulfilled or accomplished (and something that is capable of fulfillment and accomplishment). Indeed, it is clear that the individual, at his birth into this world, is capable of manifesting very few of the qualities possessed by the mature adult human being. We know, moreover, that unless the infant is properly cared for and provided with a host of support systems and a growth-inducing milieu, he will never exhibit such qualities. Life, then, is a growth process. Man begins the process as a little bundle of potential and proceeds, for better or worse, to develop his potential through the process of education (considered broadly as the sum of all environmental influences on the individual plus the individual's reaction to these influences).

According to Bahá'í teachings, the very purpose of man's life is the proper, harmonious and full development of spiritual capacities. This is the most worthwhile possible goal since spiritual capacities, being part of the immortal soul, will eternally endure while the body and its capacities will not. However, the body is the instrument of the soul's development in this earthly life, and so physical health and development cannot be safely neglected but rather must be made to serve the primary goal of fostering the soul's progress.

Bahá'u'lláh expresses this truth succinctly and powerfully:

> Through the Teachings of this Day Star of Truth [the Manifestation or Prophet of God] every man will advance and develop until he attaineth the station at which he can manifest all the potential forces with which his inmost true self hath been endowed. It is for this very purpose that in every age and dispensation the Prophets of God and His chosen Ones have appeared amongst men, and have evinced such power as is born of God and such might as only the Eternal can reveal.[8]

The process of developing one's spiritual capacities is called *spiritual growth* or simply *spirituality*. We can thus formulate a working (operational) definition of the concept of spirituality as follows: Spirituality is the process of the full, adequate, proper and harmonious development of one's spiritual capacities. Unspirituality, by contrast, is either the lack of development of these capacities, their imbalanced or inharmonious development (e.g. the development of one to the exclusion of others), or else the false (improper) development and/or use of these capacities.

With this definition of spirituality in mind, we can also formulate a working definition of Bahá'í morality: That which fosters and advances the process of spiritual development is good, and that which tends to inhibit it is bad. Every law, counsel or behavioral norm contained in the writings of the Bahá'í Faith can be understood in large measure from this perspective.

The Duality of Human Nature

The only component of man's character capable of change is that which is acquired through education, where the latter term is understood broadly as the sum of all environmental influences on the individual together with the individual's reaction to these influences. However, the human situation is such that not every influence, and most certainly not every one of our reactions to these influences, is conducive to spiritual progress. Thus, the process of spiritual growth involves learning how to make appropriate responses to various circumstances and how to initiate certain kinds of actions: Spiritual growth is an educational process of a particular sort.

The experience of our life during the period when the body and the soul are linked is one of a tension between contradicting and opposing forces. 'Abdu'l-Bahá explains that this tension results from the duality of the physical and the spiritual in man's nature. On the one hand, man's body has legitimate physical needs which cry for satisfaction: food, shelter, companionship and protection from threatening forces. However, in seeking to satisfy these needs, man is easily led to be possessive, aggressive and insensitive to the needs of others. On the other hand, man's soul also has intrinsic needs which cry for satisfaction. These needs are metaphysical and intangible. They incite the individual to seek meaning and purpose in life and to establish the proper relationship with God, with himself and with his fellow humans. Though this proper relationship may, and indeed must, be expressed through physical means, it also is essentially intangible. It involves submission to the Will of God, the acceptance of our dependence on a power higher than ourselves. It implies self-knowledge, the discovery both of our limitations and of our particular talents and capacities. And it requires recognition of and respect for the rights of others. This means that we realize and understand that all other men have needs similar to our own and that we accept all the implications of this fact in our relations with and actions towards others.

Of course, the Bahá'í Faith is certainly not the first belief system to recognize this duality in man's nature. But the Bahá'í view of this duality is significantly different from certain views frequently attributed to other belief systems, for the Bahá'í Faith does not superimpose an absolute (good-evil) value judgment upon the duality, viewing all things spiritual as good and all things material as bad. The Bahá'í writings make clear that man can misuse his spiritual faculties just as easily as he can misuse his material ones. At the same time, the material faculties of man (indeed all of man's natural capacities) are viewed as God-given and therefore intrinsically (metaphysically) good. As moral categories, good and evil are relative terms: A given action on the part of an individual is relatively less good than another action if that other action would have been more favorable to the process of spiritual growth. Moreover, the Bahá'í writings lead us to understand that God judges human actions only with regard to those actions which are truly logically possible for the individual in the given circumstances. To judge otherwise would be tantamount to requiring of man that which is beyond his capabilities or, paraphrasing words of Bahá'u'lláh, to tasking a soul beyond its power.[9]

In other words, only the direction of the spiritual growth process is given absolutely: it is towards the (unattainable) ideal of God-like perfection. But the process itself is lived relatively by each individual according to his spiritual and material endowments plus the free will choices he makes in dealing with the particular circumstances of his life. Since only God knows truly what these endowments and circumstances are for any individual, only God can judge the degree of moral responsibility of the individual in any situation.[10]

Here is the way that 'Abdu'l-Bahá explains the essential and intrinsic goodness of all of man's capacities, material or spiritual:

In creation there is no evil; all is good. Certain qualities and natures innate in some men and apparently blameworthy are not so in reality. For example, from the beginning of his life you can see in a nursing child the signs of greed, of anger and of temper. Then, it may be said, good and evil are innate in the reality of man, and this is contrary to the pure goodness of nature and creation. The answer to this is that greed, which is to ask for something more, is a praiseworthy quality provided that it is used suitably. So if a man is greedy to acquire science and knowledge, or to become compassionate, generous and just, it is most praiseworthy. If he exercises his anger and wrath against the bloodthirsty tyrants who are like ferocious beasts, it is very praiseworthy; but if he does not use these qualities in a right way, they are blameworthy.

Then it is evident that in creation and nature evil does not exist at all; but when the natural qualities of man are used in an unlawful way, they are blameworthy.[11]

Thus the main function of the body is to serve as an instrument of the soul during the time when the immortal soul is linked to the mortal body. This period constitutes the first stage of an eternal growth process. The body's capacities, when properly used, contribute to the process of spiritual growth. These material capacities are no more intrinsically bad than the capacities of the soul itself. Both material and spiritual capacities become harmful if they are misused through false or improper development.

However, Bahá'u'lláh and 'Abdu'l-Bahá do stress the fact that the material capacities must be rigorously disciplined (not suppressed) if they are to serve their intended purpose as vehicles for spiritual growth. Since satisfying our physical needs can easily incite us to become aggressive towards others and insensitive to their needs, the individual must engage in a daily struggle with himself to maintain the proper perspective on life and its spiritual meaning.[12]

More will be said later about the nature of this daily spiritual discipline. The main point here is that the tension between the material and the spiritual in man is a creative tension purposely given by God, a tension whose function it is constantly to remind the individual of the necessity of making an effort in the path of spiritual growth. Moreover, the existence of the material body with its needs provides daily opportunities for the individual to dramatize through action the degree of spirituality he has attained and to assess realistically his progress.[13]

If man did not have the spiritual-material duality in his nature, he would be spared the unpleasant tension that often accompanies the struggle to take a step along the path of spiritual growth but he would also be denied the opportunities for growth provided by this very duality.

Metaphysical Considerations

We have seen how the Bahá'í concept of spirituality flows naturally and logically from a coherent concept of the nature of man and of God's purpose for man. It must be admitted, however, that a paradox seems to lie at the heart of this process, or at least of our experience of the process during this earthly life. The paradox is that God has given man immediate and easy access to material reality while denying him such immediate access to spiritual realities. This seems a curious thing for God to have done if, in fact, the most important aspect of reality is the spiritual one and if our basic purpose in life is spiritual. If the spiritual dimension of man's existence is ultimately the most real, then why are we given immediate perception only of the less substantial portion of total reality? Why, in short, are we called upon by God to pursue a spiritual purpose while being immersed in a sea of materiality?

To many people, this basic perception of our human condition is not just a paradox but an outright contradiction. It is impossible, they say, that there could be a world of unseen and unobservable spiritual realities so much less accessible than the world of material reality: the most obvious explanation for the inaccessibility of spiritual reality is that it does not exist. Whether or not the paradox is stated this strongly, it remains the basic stumbling block to atheists, agnostics, materialists and positivists of whatever philosophical stripe in their approach to spiritual questions. For, even if one becomes convinced that there is a significant, nonmaterial dimension to objective reality, the rationale for its having been deliberately hidden from immediate access by a God who nevertheless holds us responsible for relating properly to it remains obscure.

Fortunately for our attempts to grasp the deeper significance of the Bahá'í concept of spirituality, Bahá'u'lláh has explained in clear terms the divine purpose underlying this fundamental feature of the human situation. The explanation lies in the principle of 'separation and distinction' by which God wishes individual moral and spiritual attainment to be the result of the individual's self-responsible and self-directed efforts. Bahá'u'lláh affirms unequivocally that God could certainly have rendered spiritual truth and spiritual reality as irrefutably evident and as immediately accessible to our spiritual senses as is material reality to our physical senses. But, had He done so, all men would have been forever bereft of one important experience: the experience of the state of spiritual deprivation. As the universe is now ordered, everyone can have the experience of moving from a position of relative doubt, insecurity, uncertainty and fear towards a position of relative certitude, security, knowledge and faith.

On this journey, we learn important lessons which would otherwise be denied us. We value true spirituality the more for having experienced, to whatever degree, its lack, and we are grateful for the privilege of having participated in and contributed to the process of its attainment. All of this would not be possible if spiritual knowledge and perfection were simply our natural state of being from the moment of our creation.

Here is one passage in which Bahá'u'lláh explains the principle of separation and distinction:

> The purpose of God in creating man hath been, and will ever be, to enable him to know his Creator and to attain His Presence . . . Whoso hath recognized the Day Spring of Divine guidance and entered His holy court hath drawn nigh unto God and attained His Presence . . . Whoso hath failed to recognize Him will have condemned himself to the misery of remoteness, a remoteness which is naught but utter nothingness and the essence of the

nethermost fire. Such will be his fate, though to outward seeming he may occupy the earth's loftiest seats and be established upon its most exalted throne.

He Who is the Day Spring of Truth is, no doubt, fully capable of rescuing from such remoteness wayward souls and of causing them to draw nigh unto His court and attain His Presence. 'If God had pleased He had surely made all men one people.' His purpose, however, is to enable the pure in spirit and the detached in heart to ascend, by virtue of their own innate powers, unto the shores of the Most Great Ocean, that thereby they who seek the Beauty of the All-Glorious may be distinguished and separated from the wayward and perverse. Thus hath it been ordained by the all-glorious and resplendent Pen . . .

That the Manifestations of Divine justice, the Day Springs of heavenly grace, have when they appeared amongst men always been destitute of all earthly dominion and shorn of the means of worldly ascendancy, should be attributed to this same principle of separation and distinction which animateth the Divine Purpose. Were the Eternal Essence to manifest all that is latent within Him . . . none would be found to question His power or repudiate His truth. Nay, all created things would be so dazzled and thunderstruck by the evidences of His light as to be reduced to utter nothingness.[14]

From this passage, we can understand that the intangibility of spiritual realities is not an accident but rather a deliberate and fundamental aspect of God's purpose for man. Of course, if God had created us with no spiritual inclinations or perceptions whatever, if He had denied us immediate access to any part of reality, material or spiritual, or if He had created us with spiritual and metaphysical longings impossible of genuine fulfillment, we would be unable to succeed in our basic task. By starting the eternal spiritual growth process as spiritual-material hybrids, having immediate access to material reality and being endowed with significant physical and intellectual powers, we are able to learn the subtleties of spiritual development gradually. By experiencing first-hand the order and the lawfulness of the physical creation, we come to understand that the unseen spiritual realm is similarly ordered and governed by lawful, cause-and-effect relationships. At first intuitively, then explicitly and intellectually, and finally through genuine spiritual experience and inner development, we learn to participate consciously in this spiritual order of things. It becomes a day-to-day reality having an immediacy equal to and even greater than the immediacy of physical experience. Indeed, as Bahá'u'lláh explains, if we fulfill our responsibilities and learn our lessons well, we will be ready at the time of our physical death to pass easily into the purely spiritual realm. We will already have become familiar with its basic laws and modes of functioning and will therefore be prepared to take up our lives in that new realm and proceed with our growth process in a harmonious and satisfying manner:

> The Prophets and Messengers of God have been sent down for the sole purpose of guiding mankind to the straight Path of Truth. The purpose underlying their revelation hath been to educate all men, that they may, at the hour of death, ascend, in the utmost purity and sanctity and with absolute detachment, to the throne of the Most High.[15]

The Process of Spiritual Growth

Prerequisites for Spiritual Growth

Spirituality is the process of the proper development of man's innate spiritual capacities. But how does this process start and how is it carried on? What is the relationship between spiritual development and other kinds of development processes (e.g. formal schooling)? Why do there seem to have been so few people who have thus conceived the purpose of their lives and dedicated themselves to the pursuit of spirituality? Answers to these and other similar questions are given in the Bahá'í writings, but we need to proceed systematically to gain perspective.

Clearly the prime condition for embarking on the process of spiritual development is the awareness that the process is useful, necessary and realistically possible: the individual must become fully alert to the objective existence of the spiritual dimension of reality. Since such spiritual realities as God, the soul and the mind are not directly observable, man has no immediate access to them. He has only indirect access through the observable effects that these spiritual realities may produce. The Bahá'í writings acknowledge this situation and affirm that the Manifestation (or Prophet) of God is the most important observable reality which gives man access to intangible reality:

> The door of the knowledge of the Ancient of Days being thus closed in the face of all beings, the Source of infinite grace . . . hath caused those luminous Gems of Holiness to appear out of the realm of the spirit, in the noble form of the human temple, and be made manifest unto all men, that they may impart unto the world the mysteries of the unchangeable Being, and tell of the subtleties of His imperishable Essence. These sanctified Mirrors, these Day-springs of ancient glory are one and all the Exponents on earth of Him Who is the central Orb of the universe, its Essence and ultimate Purpose.[16]

In another passage, 'Abdu'l-Bahá has said:

> The knowledge of the Reality of the Divinity is impossible and unattainable, but the knowledge of the Manifestations of God is the knowledge of God, for the bounties, splendors and divine attributes are apparent in Them. Therefore, if man attains to the knowledge of the Manifestations of God, he will attain to the knowledge of God; and if he be neglectful of the knowledge of the Holy Manifestations, he will be bereft of the knowledge of God.[17]

Thus the Manifestations constitute that part of observable reality which most readily leads man to the knowledge and awareness of the spiritual dimension of existence. Of course, only those living in the lifetime of a Manifestation can observe Him at first hand but His revelation and His writings constitute permanent observable realities which enable us to maintain objective content in our beliefs, concepts and practices:

> Say: The first and foremost testimony establishing His truth is

His own Self. Next to this testimony is His Revelation. For whoso faileth to recognize either the one or the other He hath established the words He hath revealed as proof of His reality and truth.[18]

Elsewhere in the Bahá'í writings it is explained that everything in observable reality, when properly perceived, reveals some aspect of God, its Creator. However, only a conscious, willing, intelligent being such as man can reflect (to whatever limited degree) the higher aspects of God. The Manifestations of God, being the 'most accomplished, the most distinguished, and the most excellent'[19] of men, endowed by God with transhuman spiritual capacities, represent the fullest possible expression of the divine in observable reality.

Thus the first step in the path of spiritual growth is to become as intensely aware as possible of the reality of the spiritual realm of existence. The principal key to such an awareness is knowledge of the Manifestations of God.

Indeed, since the Manifestations constitute such a unique link between man and the unseen world of spiritual reality, knowledge of the Manifestations is the foundation of the whole process of spiritual development.[20] This is not to say that real spiritual progress cannot take place before one recognizes and accepts the Manifestation.[21] However, the Bahá'í writings do affirm that in order to progress beyond a certain level on the path of spirituality, knowledge of the Manifestation is essential. Sooner or later (in this world or the next), knowledge and acceptance of the Manifestation must occur in the life of each individual.

The question naturally arises as to what step or steps follow the recognition of the Manifestation. Here again Bahá'u'lláh is quite clear and emphatic:

> The first duty prescribed by God for His servants is the recognition of Him Who is the Day Spring of His Revelation and the Fountain of His laws, Who representeth the Godhead in both the Kingdom of His Cause and the world of creation. Whoso achieveth this duty hath attained unto all good; and whoso is

deprived thereof, hath gone astray, though he be the author of every righteous deed. It behoveth every one who reacheth this most sublime station, this summit of transcendent glory, to observe every ordinance of Him Who is the Desire of the world. These twin duties are inseparable. Neither is acceptable without the other.[22]

Thus, even though the recognition of the Manifestation of God is described as equal to 'all good', recognition alone is not a sufficient basis for spiritual growth. The effort to conform oneself to the standards of behavior, thought and attitude expressed by the various laws ordained by the Manifestation is also an intrinsic, inseparable part of the process.[23]

The idea that great effort is necessary to the prosecution of the spiritual growth process occurs throughout the Bahá'í writings:

> The incomparable Creator hath created all men from one same substance, and hath exalted their reality above the rest of His creatures. Success or failure, gain or loss, must, therefore, depend upon man's own exertions. The more he striveth, the greater will be his progress.[24]

> Know thou that all men have been created in the nature made by God, the Guardian, the Self-Subsisting. Unto each one hath been prescribed a pre-ordained measure, as decreed in God's mighty and guarded Tablets. All that which ye potentially possess can, however, be manifested only as a result of your own volition.[25]

> He hath entrusted every created thing with a sign of His knowledge, so that none of His creatures may be deprived of its share in expressing, each according to its capacity and rank, this knowledge. This sign is the mirror of His beauty in the world of creation. The greater the effort exerted for the refinement of this sublime and noble mirror, the more faithfully will it be made to reflect the glory of the names and attributes of God, and reveal the wonders of His signs and knowledge . . .
> There can be no doubt whatever that, in consequence of the efforts which every man may consciously exert and as a result of the exertion of his own spiritual faculties, this mirror can be

> so cleansed . . . as to be able to draw nigh unto the meads of eternal holiness and attain the courts of everlasting fellowship.[26]

> Personal effort is indeed a vital prerequisite to the recognition and acceptance of the Cause of God. No matter how strong the measure of Divine grace, unless supplemented by personal, sustained and intelligent effort it cannot become fully effective and be of any real and abiding advantage.[27]

This last statement, from Shoghi Effendi, the Guardian of the Bahá'í Faith from 1921 until his death in 1957, makes clear that recognition of and faith in the Manifestation of God are not simply unidirectional 'gifts' from God to man. Rather, both involve a reciprocal relationship requiring an intelligent and energetic response on the part of the individual. Nor is true faith based on any irrational or psychopathological impulse.[28]

The Nature of the Process

We have seen how the spiritual growth process may begin by acceptance of the Manifestation and obedience to His laws and principles. We need now to gain a measure of understanding of the nature of the process itself.

We have characterized spiritual growth as an educational process of a particular sort for which the individual assumes responsibility and by which he learns to feel, think and act in certain appropriate ways. It is a process through which the individual eventually becomes the truest expression of what he has always potentially been.

Let us consider several further quotations from the Bahá'í writings which confirm this view of the spiritual growth process.

> Whatever duty Thou hast prescribed unto Thy servants of extolling to the utmost Thy majesty and glory is but a token of Thy grace unto them, that they may be enabled to ascend unto the station conferred upon their own inmost being, the station of the knowledge of their own selves.[29]

Here the 'duties' which God has prescribed for man are seen not as ends in themselves but rather as 'tokens', in other words, as symbols for and means towards another, ultimate end. This end is characterized as being a particular kind of knowledge, here called self-knowledge.

In the following, Bahá'u'lláh speaks similarly of self-knowledge:

> O My servants! Could ye apprehend with what wonders of My munificence and bounty I have willed to entrust your souls, ye would, of a truth, rid yourselves of attachment to all created things, and would gain a true knowledge of your own selves – a knowledge which is the same as the comprehension of Mine own Being.[30]

One significant aspect of this passage is that true knowledge of self is identified with knowledge of God. That knowledge of God is identical with the fundamental purpose of life for the individual is clearly stated by Bahá'u'lláh in numerous passages. For example:

> The purpose of God in creating man hath been, and will ever be, to enable him to know his Creator and to attain His Presence. To this most excellent aim, this supreme objective, all the heavenly Books and the divinely-revealed and weighty Scriptures unequivocally bear witness.[31]

Thus while acceptance of the Manifestation of God and obedience to His ordinances is a necessary step which each individual must accomplish at some point in the spiritual growth process, these and other such duties are means to an ultimate end which is described as true self-knowledge. This quality of self-knowledge is equated with knowledge of God and knowledge of God is considered by Bahá'u'lláh as constituting the essential reason for man's existence.

All of this would seem to say that religion, in the final analysis, represents a cognitive discipline of some sort. But what kind of cognitive discipline could involve the full development of all man's spiritual capacities and not just the mind? What kind of knowledge is meant by the true knowledge of self and how can such knowledge be tantamount to knowledge of God?

Bahá'u'lláh gives the key to answering these important questions in an explicit statement clearly describing the highest form of knowledge and development accessible to man:

> Consider the rational faculty with which God hath endowed the essence of man. Examine thine own self, and behold how thy motion and stillness, thy will and purpose, thy sight and hearing, thy sense of smell and power of speech, and whatever else is related to, or transcendeth, thy physical senses or spiritual perceptions, all proceed from, and owe their existence to, this same faculty . . .
>
> Wert thou to ponder in thine heart, from now until the end that hath no end, and with all the concentrated intelligence and understanding which the greatest minds have attained in the past or will attain in the future, this divinely ordained and subtle Reality, this sign of the revelation of the All-Abiding, All-Glorious God, thou wilt fail to comprehend its mystery or to appraise its virtue. Having recognized thy powerlessness to attain to an adequate understanding of that Reality which abideth within thee, thou wilt readily admit the futility of such efforts as may be attempted by thee, or by any of the created things, to fathom the mystery of the Living God, the Day Star of unfading glory, the Ancient of everlasting days. This confession of helplessness which mature contemplation must eventually impel every mind to make is in itself the acme of human understanding, and marketh the culmination of man's development.[32]

This passage seems to indicate that the ultimate form of knowledge available to man is represented by his total awareness of certain limitations which are inherent in his very nature or at least in the fundamental relationship between his nature and the phenomena of existence (including his own being and that of God). In particular, man must assimilate in some profound way the truth that the absolute knowledge of God and even of his own self lie forever beyond his reach. His realization of this truth is consequent to his having made a profound and accurate appraisal of his God-created capacities and potentialities. Thus, in the last analysis, true self-knowledge appears as a deep and mature knowledge of both the limitations and the capacities of the self. Let us recall that attaining to this knowledge is said to require strenuous effort on the part of man and to involve the development of 'all the potential forces with which his inmost true self hath been endowed'.[33]

To gain a broader perspective on this question, let us compare the self-knowledge described here with human knowledge in general, hoping that such a comparison will help us to understand more clearly what is particular to true self-knowledge. In general terms, a 'knowing situation' involves a subjectivity (in this case that of man), some phenomenon which is the object of knowledge, and finally those means and resources which the subject can mobilize in order to obtain the understanding he seeks. If we agree to lump these last aspects of the knowing process under the general term 'method', we arrive at the following schema:

$$\text{knowing subject} \xrightarrow{\text{method}} \text{phenomenon}$$

Quite clearly, the knowledge which is ultimately obtained from this process will depend on all three fundamental aspects of the knowing situation. It will depend on the nature of the phenomenon being studied (e.g. whether it is easily observable and accessible, whether it is complex or simple), on both the capacities and limitations of the knowing subject, and on the method used. In particular, the knowledge which results from this process will necessarily be relative and limited unless the knowing subject possesses some infallible method of knowledge. In this regard, it is important to note that the Bahá'í writings stress repeatedly that human beings (other than the Manifestations) have no such infallible method of knowledge and that human understanding of all things is therefore relative and limited.[34]

For example, in a talk given at Green Acre near Eliot, Maine, in 1912, 'Abdu'l-Bahá discussed the different criteria 'by which the human mind reaches its conclusions'.[35] After a discussion of each criterion, showing why it is fallible and relative, 'Abdu'l-Bahá stated: 'Consequently, it has become evident that the four criteria or standards of judgment by which the human mind reaches its conclusions are faulty and inaccurate.' He then proceeded to explain that the best man can do is to use systematically all of the criteria at his disposal.[36]

In another passage, 'Abdu'l-Bahá affirms:

> Knowledge is of two kinds. One is subjective and the other objective knowledge – that is to say, an intuitive knowledge and a knowledge derived from perception.
>
> The knowledge of things which men universally have is gained by reflection or by evidence – that is to say, either by the power of the mind the conception of an object is formed, or from beholding an object the form is produced in the mirror of the heart. The circle of this knowledge is very limited because it depends upon effort and attainment.[37]

'Abdu'l-Bahá then explains that the first kind of knowledge, that which is subjective and intuitive, is the special consciousness of the Manifestations:

> Since the Sanctified Realities, the supreme Manifestations of God, surround the essence and qualities of the creatures, transcend and contain existing realities and understand all things, therefore, Their knowledge is divine knowledge, and not acquired – that is to say, it is a holy bounty; it is a divine revelation.[38]

Here again we see that 'Abdu'l-Bahá expresses the limited character of all human knowledge (in contrast to the unlimited knowledge of the Manifestations deriving from their special superhuman nature). In yet another passage 'Abdu'l-Bahá puts the matter thus:

> Know that there are two kinds of knowledge: the knowledge of the essence of a thing and the knowledge of its qualities. The essence of a thing is known through its qualities; otherwise, it is unknown and hidden.
>
> As our knowledge of things, even of created and limited

> things, is knowledge of their qualities and not of their essence, how is it possible to comprehend in its essence the Divine Reality, which is unlimited?
>
> ... Knowing God, therefore, means the comprehension and the knowledge of His attributes, and not of His Reality. This knowledge of the attributes is also proportioned to the capacity and power of man; it is not absolute.[39]

It would seem clear from these and other similar passages from the Bahá'í writings that whatever distinctive characteristics the true knowledge of self (or, equivalently, the knowledge of God) may have, it does not differ from other forms of knowledge with regard to degree of certainty. It is not less certain than other forms of knowledge since all human knowledge (including the knowledge of God and of 'created and limited things') is relative and limited. Nor does it differ from these other forms of knowledge by being more certain, as is clear from the passage above and from the passages of Bahá'u'lláh previously cited.[40]

However, if we compare knowledge of God with other forms of knowledge, not from the point of view of degrees of certainty, but rather from the standpoint of the relationship between man as knowing subject on the one hand, and the phenomenon which is the object of study on the other, we can immediately see that there is a tremendous difference. In all sciences and branches of knowledge other than religion, the object of study is a phenomenon which is either inferior to man in complexity and subtlety (in the case of physics and chemistry) or on a level with man (in the case of biology, psychology and sociology). In either case, for each of these sciences the human knower is in a position of relative dominance or superiority which enables him to manipulate to a significant degree the phenomenon being studied. We can successfully use these phenomena as instruments for our purposes. But when we come to knowledge of God, we suddenly find ourselves confronted with a phenomenon which is superior to us and which we cannot manipulate. Many of the reflexes and techniques learned in studying other phenomena no longer apply. Far from learning how to manipulate God, we must learn how to discern expressions of God's Will for us and respond adequately to them. It is we who now must become (consciously acquiescing) instruments for God's purposes.[41]

Viewed in this perspective, the distinctive characteristic of knowing God, as compared with all other forms of (human) knowledge, is that the human knower is in a position of inferiority with respect to the object of knowledge. Rather than encompassing and dominating the phenomenon by aggressive and manipulative techniques, man is now encompassed by a phenomenon more powerful than himself.

Perhaps, then, one of the deep meanings of the true knowledge of self (which is equivalent to the knowledge of God) is that we are here confronted with the task of learning novel, and initially unnatural, patterns of thought, feeling and action. We must retrain ourselves in a wholly new way. We must not only understand our position of dependence on God but also integrate that understanding into our lives until it becomes part of us, and indeed until it becomes us, an expression of what we are.

In other words, the full, harmonious and proper development of our spiritual capacities means developing these capacities so that we may respond ever more adequately, and with increasing sensitivity and nuance, to the Will of God: The process of spiritual growth is the process by which we learn how to conform ourselves to the divine Will on ever deeper levels of our being.[42]

From this viewpoint, conscious dependence upon God and obedience to His Will is not a capitulation of individual responsibility, a sort of helpless 'giving up', but rather an assumption of an even greater degree of responsibility and self-control. We must learn through deep self-knowledge, how to be responsive to the spirit of God.

The ability to respond to God in such a whole-hearted, deeply intelligent and sensitive way is not part of the natural gift of any human being. What is naturally given to us is the capacity, the potential to attain to such a state. Its actual achievement, however, is consequent only to a persistent and strenuous effort on our part. The fact that such effort, and indeed suffering, are necessary to attain this state of spirituality makes life often difficult.[43] But the fact that it is truly possible makes of life a spiritual adventure a hundredfold more exciting than any other physical or romantic adventure could ever possibly be.

George Townshend, a Bahá'í renowned for the spiritual quality of his personal life, has given a description of this state of spiritual-mindedness. One senses that Townshend's statement is based on deep personal experience as well as intelligent contemplation:

> When the veils of illusion which hide a man's own heart from himself are drawn aside, when after purgation he comes to himself and attains self-knowledge and sees himself as he truly is, then at the same moment and by the same act of knowledge he beholds there in his own heart His Father who has patiently awaited His son's return.
>
> Only through this act of self-completion, through this conclusion of the journey which begins in the kingdom of the senses and leads inward through the kingdom of the moral to end in that of the spiritual, does real happiness become possible. Now for the first time a man's whole being can be integrated, and a harmony of all his faculties be established. Through his union with the Divine Spirit he has found the secret of the unifying of his own being. He who is the Breath of Joy becomes the animating principle of his existence. Man knows the Peace of God.[44]

One of Bahá'u'lláh's major works, *The Book of Certitude,* is largely devoted to a detailed explanation of the way in which God has provided for the education of mankind through the periodic appearance in human history of a God-sent Manifestation or Revelator. At one point in His discussion of these questions, Bahá'u'lláh gives a wonderfully explicit description of the steps and stages involved in the individual's progress towards full spiritual development. This portion of *The Book of Certitude* has become popularly known among Bahá'ís as the 'Tablet of the True Seeker', although Bahá'u'lláh does not Himself designate the passage by this or any other such appellation.

In general terms, a 'true seeker' is anyone who has become aware of the objective existence of the spiritual dimension of reality, has realized that spiritual growth and development constitute the basic purpose of existence, and has sincerely and seriously embarked on the enterprise of fostering his spiritual progress. It is quite clear from the context of the passage that Bahá'u'lláh is primarily addressing those who have already reached the stage of accepting the Manifestation of God and obeying his commandments.

Bahá'u'lláh begins by describing in considerable detail the attitudes, thought patterns and behavior patterns that characterize a true seeker. He mentions such things as humility, abstention from backbiting and vicious criticism of others, kindness and helpfulness to those who are poor or otherwise in need, and the regular practice of the discipline of prayer and of meditation. He concludes this description by saying, 'These are among the attributes of the exalted, and constitute the hall-mark of the spiritually-minded . . . When the detached wayfarer and sincere seeker hath fulfilled these essential conditions, then and only then can he be called a true seeker.'[45] He then continues by describing both the quality of effort necessary to the attainment of spirituality and the state of being which this attainment secures to the individual:

> Only when the lamp of search, of earnest striving, of longing desire, of passionate devotion, of fervid love, of rapture, and ecstasy, is kindled within the seeker's heart, and the breeze of His loving-kindness is wafted upon his soul, will the darkness of error be dispelled, the mists of doubts and misgivings be dissipated, and the lights of knowledge and certitude envelop his being. At that hour will the mystic Herald, bearing the joyful tidings of the Spirit, shine forth from the City of God resplendent as the morn, and, through the trumpet-blast of knowledge, will awaken the heart, the soul, and the spirit from the slumber of negligence. Then will the manifold favors and outpouring grace of the holy and everlasting Spirit confer such new life upon the seeker that he will find himself endowed with a new eye, a new ear, a new heart, and a new mind. He will contemplate the manifest signs of the universe, and will penetrate the hidden mysteries of the soul. Gazing with the eye of God, he will perceive within every

atom a door that leadeth him to the stations of absolute certitude. He will discover in all things the mysteries of divine Revelation and the evidences of an everlasting manifestation.[46]

Nor should the achievement of such a degree of spiritual development be considered an ideal, static configuration from which no further change or development is possible, as the following two passages from the writings of 'Abdu'l-Bahá make clear:

> As the divine bounties are endless, so human perfections are endless. If it were possible to reach a limit of perfection, then one of the realities of the beings might reach the condition of being independent of God, and the contingent might attain to the condition of the absolute. But for every being there is a point which it cannot overpass – that is to say, he who is in the condition of servitude, however far he may progress in gaining limitless perfections, will never reach the condition of Deity . . .
> For example, Peter cannot become Christ. All that he can do is, in the condition of servitude, to attain endless perfections . . .[47]

> Both before and after putting off this material form there is progress in perfection but not in state . . . There is no other being higher than a perfect man. But man when he has reached this state can still make progress in perfections but not in state because there is no state higher than that of a perfect man to which he can transfer himself. He only progresses in the state of humanity, for the human perfections are infinite. Thus, however learned a man may be, we can imagine one more learned.
> Hence, as the perfections of humanity are endless, man can also make progress in perfections after leaving this world.[48]

The Dynamics of the Spiritual Growth Process

After contemplating Bahá'u'lláh's description of the state of being resulting from the attainment of true self-knowledge, it would be only natural to wish that this state could be achieved instantaneously, perhaps through some supreme gesture of self-renunciation or whatever. However, the writings of the Bahá'í Faith make it plain that this is not possible. By its very nature, true spirituality is something which can only be achieved as the result of a certain self-aware and self-responsible process of development.

'Abdu'l-Bahá often responded to Bahá'ís who felt overwhelmed by the task of refining their character by stressing the necessity of patience and daily striving. 'Be patient, be as I am,' He would say.[49] Spirituality was to be won 'little by little; day by day'.[50] And again:

> He is a true Bahá'í who strives by day and by night to progress and advance along the path of human endeavor, whose most cherished desire is so to live and act as to enrich and illuminate the world, whose source of inspiration is the essence of Divine virtue, whose aim in life is so to conduct himself as to be the cause of infinite progress. Only when he attains unto such perfect gifts can it be said of him that he is a true Bahá'í.[51]

This last passage in particular would seem to indicate that one of the signs of an individual's maturity is his acceptance of the gradual nature of the process of spiritual growth and of the necessity for daily striving. Indeed, psychology has established that one important measure of maturity is the capacity to delay gratification, i.e. to work for goals whose attainment is not to be had in the short term. Since spirituality is the highest and most important goal anyone can possibly have, it is natural that its achievement should call forth the greatest possible maturity on the part of the individual.[52]

In a similar vein, Shoghi Effendi has said that the Bahá'ís:

> ... should not look at the depraved condition of the society in which they live, nor at the evidences of moral degradation and frivolous conduct which the people around them display. They should not content themselves merely with relative distinction and excellence. Rather they should fix their gaze upon nobler heights by setting the counsels and exhortations of the Pen of Glory as their supreme goal. Then it will be readily realized how numerous are the stages that still remain to be traversed and how far off the desired goal lies – a goal which is none other than exemplifying heavenly morals and virtues.[53]

In describing the experience of the individual as he progresses towards this goal, 'Abdu'l-Bahá has said: 'Know thou, verily, there are many veils in which the Truth is enveloped; gloomy veils; then delicate and transparent veils; then the envelopment of Light, the sight of which dazzles the eyes.'[54] Indeed, one of Bahá'u'lláh's major works, *The Seven Valleys,* describes in poetic and powerfully descriptive language the different stages of spiritual perception through which an individual may pass in his efforts to attain to the goal of spirituality. In the Tablet of Wisdom Bahá'u'lláh says simply: 'Let each morn be better than its eve and each morrow richer than its yesterday.'[55] Elsewhere Bahá'u'lláh has urged man to live in such a way that each day his faith increases over the previous day. All of these passages strongly reinforce the notion that spirituality is to be won only through a gradual process and is not to be attained by any once-and-for-all act of faith.

We want now to understand the dynamics of this process. How do we even take one step forward? Also, we need to understand how a gradual process can produce a change as radical as that described by Bahá'u'lláh in the passage quoted in the previous section.

The answer to this last consideration is that the rate of change produced by the process is not constant. In technical language, the process is exponential and not linear. To say that a growth process is linear means that the *rate* of growth is unchanging. In an exponential process, on the other hand, the rate of growth is very small in the beginning but gradually increases until a sort of saturation point is reached. When this point is passed, the rate of growth becomes virtually infinite, and the mechanism of the process becomes virtually automatic. There is, so to speak, an 'explosion' of progress.[56] As we examine the dynamics of the process of spiritual development we will see precisely how the exponential nature of the process can be concretely understood. Let us turn, then, to an examination of these dynamics.

The main problem is to understand how the various capacities of the individual – mind, heart and will – are to interact in order to produce a definite step forward in the path towards full development. Basic to our understanding of this obviously complex interaction are two important points that Bahá'u'lláh and 'Abdu'l-Bahá both stress regarding the growth process. The first is that no one faculty acting alone is sufficient to produce results.[57] The second point is that there is a hierarchial relationship between these faculties in which knowledge is first, love second and will third. Let us discuss each of these points in turn.

As we have seen in the section on the nature of man, each individual has certain basic, innate spiritual capacities but in a degree and in a proportion which are unique to him. Moreover, the initial development of these innate capacities takes place under conditions over which the individual has very little control (e.g. the conditions of the family into which he is born, the social and physical surroundings to which he is exposed). An important consequence of this universal, existential situation is that each one of us arrives at the threshold of adulthood having developed a more or less spontaneous and unexamined pattern of responses to life situations. This pattern, unique to each individual, is an expression of his basic personality at that stage of his development.[58]

Given the limited and relative nature of our innate spiritual capacities as well as the conditions under which they will have developed up to this point in our lives, our personal response pattern will necessarily involve many imbalances, immaturities and imperfections. Moreover, because of the largely spontaneous and unselfconscious nature of our pattern, we will be unaware of many aspects of it. Thus, our attainment of true self-knowledge will involve our becoming acutely aware of the internal psychic mechanisms of our response pattern. We must take stock of both the strengths and the weaknesses of our pattern and make deliberate efforts to bring it into harmony, balance and full development. We must also begin to correct false or improper development.

This is the beginning of a transformation or growth process for which we assume responsibility. Until this point in our lives, our growth and development has been primarily in the hands of others. Though we have collaborated in the process with some degree of consciousness, nevertheless the major part has been beyond our control and indeed beyond our awareness. We have been the relatively passive recipients of a process to which we have been subjected by others. Now we must become the agents and prime movers of our own growth process. This self-directed process is a continuation of the previously unconscious one but it represents a new and significant stage in our lives.

This new, self-directed growth process is going to take time. Moreover, it is sometimes going to be painful, and in the beginning stages at least, very painful. The new, more balanced functioning for which we begin to strive will appear at first to be unnatural since the spontaneous pattern we will have previously developed is the natural expression of our (relatively undeveloped and immature) selves.

In fact, one of the major problems involved in starting the process of spiritual growth is that we initially feel so comfortable with our spontaneous and unexamined mode of functioning. This is why it often happens that an individual becomes strongly motivated to begin the spiritual growth process only after his spontaneous system of coping has failed in some clear and dramatic way.

The realization that failure has occurred may come in many different forms. Perhaps we are faced with a 'test', a life situation that puts new and unusual strain on our defective response system and thus reveals to us its weakness. We may even temporarily break down, i.e. become unable to function in situations which previously posed no difficulties. This is because we have become so disillusioned by our sudden realization of our weakness that we put the whole framework of our personalities into doubt. Perceiving that things are wrong, but not yet knowing just how or why, we suspend activity until we can gain perspective on what is happening.[59] Or, the perception of the inadequacy of our spontaneous system of functioning may result from our unanticipated failure at some endeavor. We are then led to wonder why we anticipated a success that we were unable to deliver.[60]

The frequency with which the perception of inadequacy and the consequent motivation to change is born through fiery ordeal has led some to build a model of spiritual growth in which such dramatic failures and terrible sufferings are considered to be unavoidable and necessary aspects of the growth process. The Bahá'í writings would appear to take a middle position on this question. On the one hand, they clearly affirm that tests, difficulties and sufferings are inevitable, natural concomitants of the spiritual growth process. Such painful experiences, it is explained, serve to give us deeper understanding of certain spiritual laws upon which our continued growth depends.[61] On the other hand, many instances of human suffering are simply the result of careless living and are therefore potentially avoidable. Bahá'ís are taught to pray to God for preservation from violent or extreme tests. Moreover, the Bahá'í writings strictly forbid asceticism and any other similar philosophies or disciplines which incite the individual actively to seek pain or suffering in the path of spiritual growth. The growth process itself involves enough pain without our seeking more through misguided or thoughtless living. But the deep sufferings and dramatic setbacks are potentially there for everyone who feels inclined to learn the hard way.[62]

Of course, even dramatic failures and sufferings may sometimes not be enough to convince us of our weaknesses and immaturities. We may put up various 'defenses', i.e. we may resist seeing the truth of the matter even when it is plain to everyone but ourselves. We engage in such strategies of self-illusion primarily when, for whatever reason, we find some particular bit of self-revelation unusually hard to take. If we do not learn the lesson from the situation, we may blindly and adamantly persist in the same behavior or thought patterns which continue to produce new and perhaps even more painful situations. We are then in a 'vicious circle' in which our resistance to accepting the truer picture of reality actually increases with each new bit of negative feedback. Regarding such vicious circle situations, 'Abdu'l-Bahá has said:

> Tests are a means by which a soul is measured as to its fitness, and proven out by its own acts. God knows its fitness beforehand, and also its unpreparedness, but man, with an ego, would not believe himself unfit unless some proof were given to him.

Consequently his susceptibility to evil is proven to him when he falls into tests, and the tests are continued until the soul realizes its own unfitness, then remorse and regret tend to root out the weakness.[63]

Let us sum up. We start the process of conscious spiritual development by becoming aware of how we function at our present level of maturity. We assess as realistically as possible the level of intellectual, emotional and behavioral maturity we have attained at present. As we perceive imbalanced development, underdevelopment or improper development, we begin the job of correcting the perceived inadequacies.

It is at this stage, in particular, that the Bahá'í view of the nature of man becomes so important in fostering our spiritual growth and progress.[64] Suppose we perceive, for example, that we have a tendency to be very willful, aggressive and dominant in our relations with others. From the Bahá'í viewpoint, we would not consider the negative features of this pattern as inherently evil or sinful or as arising from some evil part of ourselves, a part which must be despised and suppressed. We are free to recognize the positive potential of this aspect of our character. After examination, we might find that we have not sufficiently developed our feeling capacity and are, therefore, sometimes insensitive to the needs and feelings of others. Or perhaps we often act impulsively and need to develop also our understanding capacity so as to act more reflectively and wisely. Or again, we might find that our mode of relating to others represents an attempt to satisfy in an illegitimate way some need within us (a need for security or self-worth perhaps) that we have not succeeded in meeting legitimately. We will then understand that we have been engaging in an improper (and unproductive) use of will and must, therefore, set about redeploying our psychic forces in a more productive manner. As we gradually succeed in doing this, we will satisfy our inner need legitimately and improve our relationships with others at the same time.[65]

In other words, the model of human spiritual and moral functioning offered by the Bahá'í Faith enables us to respond creatively and constructively once we become aware that change is necessary. We avoid wasting precious energy on guilt, self-hatred or other such unproductive mechanisms. We are able to produce some degree of change almost immediately. This gives us positive feedback, makes us feel better about ourselves and helps generate courage to continue the process of change we have just begun.

We now come to the important question of the mechanism by which we can take a step forward in the path of spiritual progress. What we need to consider is the hierarchical relationship between knowledge, love and action.

Knowledge, Love and Will

A close examination of the psychology of the spiritual growth process as presented in the Bahá'í writings indicates that the proper and harmonious functioning of our basic spiritual capacities depends on recognizing a hierarchical relationship among them. At the apex of this hierarchy is the knowing capacity.

> First and foremost among these favors, which the Almighty hath conferred upon man, is the gift of understanding. His purpose in conferring such a gift is none other except to enable His creature to know and recognize the one true God – exalted be His glory. This gift giveth man the power to discern the truth in all things, leadeth him to that which is right, and helpeth him to discover the secrets of creation. Next in rank, is the power of vision, the chief instrument whereby his understanding can function. The senses of hearing, of the heart, and the like, are similarly to be reckoned among the gifts with which the human body is endowed . . .
>
> These gifts are inherent in man himself. That which is preeminent above all other gifts, is incorruptible in nature, and pertaineth to God Himself, is the gift of Divine Revelation. Every bounty conferred by the Creator upon man, be it material or spiritual, is subservient unto this.[66]

In the last chapter of *Some Answered Questions,* 'Abdu'l-Bahá elaborates even further on this theme. He explains that right actions and moral behavior are not in themselves sufficient for spirituality. Alone, such actions and behavior constitute 'a body of the greatest loveliness, but without spirit'.[67] He then explains 'that which is the cause of everlasting life, eternal honor, universal enlightenment, real salvation and prosperity is, first of all, the knowledge of God'. He continues, affirming: 'Second, comes the love of God, the light of which shines in the lamp of the hearts of those who know God',[68] and 'The third virtue of humanity is the goodwill which is the basis of good actions . . . though a good action is praiseworthy, yet if it is not sustained by the knowledge of God, the love of God, and a sincere intention, it is imperfect.'[69]

In another passage, 'Abdu'l-Bahá expresses the primacy of knowledge with respect to action as follows: 'Although a person of good deeds is acceptable at the Threshold of the Almighty, yet it is first "to know" and then "to do". Although a blind man produceth a most wonderful and exquisite art, yet he is deprived of seeing it . . By faith is meant, first, conscious knowledge, and second, the practice of good deeds.'[70] In yet another passage, 'Abdu'l-Bahá describes the steps towards the attainment of spirituality:

> By what means can man acquire these things? How shall he obtain these merciful gifts and powers? First, through the knowledge of God. Second, through the love of God. Third, through faith. Fourth through philanthropic deeds. Fifth, through self-sacrifice. Sixth, through severance from this world. Seventh, through sanctity and holiness. Unless he acquires these forces and attains to these requirements he will surely be deprived of the life that is eternal.[71]

In the above passages, and in many others not quoted, the hierarchical ordering of spiritual faculties is the same: Knowledge leads to love which generates the courage to act (i.e. faith) which forms the basis of the intention to act (i.e. motive and good will) which in turn leads to action itself (i.e. good deeds). Of course, the knowledge which starts this psycho-spiritual chain reaction is not just any kind of knowledge but the knowledge of God which is equivalent to true self-knowledge.

As we begin to take charge of our own spiritual growth process, one of the main problems we face is that our existing perception of ourselves – of what we are and of what we should be – is bound to be distorted and inadequate in various ways, for this self-perception (or self-image) is the very basis of the spontaneous response pattern we have inherited from our childhood and early youth. Indeed, our mode of functioning at any given stage of our development is largely just a dramatization of our basic self-image; it is the projection of this self-image onto the various life situations we encounter. Thus, our self-image is, in many ways, the key to our personalities.

To say that our self-image is distorted means that it does not correspond to reality, the reality that is within us. Perhaps we have an exaggerated image of ourselves, believing we have talents and abilities we lack in reality. We may, at the same time and in other ways, underestimate ourselves, carrying an unrealistically negative concept of our capacities.

In any case, to the degree that our self-concept is false we will experience unpleasant tensions and difficulties as we become involved in various life situations. The false or unrealistic parts of our self-image will be implicitly judged by our encounter with external reality. We will sense this and begin to perceive, at first vaguely and uncomfortably but then more sharply, that something is wrong. Even though this feedback information from external reality may be from neutral sources and devoid of any value-judgemental quality, we may nevertheless perceive it as a threat or even an attack. If the feedback is not neutral but comes, say, in the form of blatantly negative criticism from others, our sense of being threatened will certainly be much greater.

Moreover, we will perceive the source of these threats as being somewhere outside ourselves. It will not naturally occur to us that the source lies rather within ourselves in the form of an illusory and unrealistic self-concept. Therefore, our instinctive reaction to the negative feedback information will be to resist, to defend our self-image and to strive to maintain it. In defending our self-image, we believe we are defending our selves because we do not view ourselves as a mosaic of true and false, real and unreal. We see only the seamless, undifferentiated whole of 'I' or 'me'. The result is that we begin to bind up more and more of our psychic energies in the defense of our self-image. We confuse egotistic pride, which is our attachment to our limited and distorted self-concept, with self-respect and honor, which are expressions of the deep spiritual truth that we are created in the image of God with an intrinsic value given by Him and without any essentially evil or sinful part.

The 'binding energy' involved in our defense of our self-concept is frequently experienced as various negative emotions like fear, rage, jealousy or aggression. These emotions are all expressions of our attempt to locate the source of our irritation outside ourselves in objective, external reality. We are also liable to experience considerable anxiety as we cling more and more desperately to whatever false part of ourselves we cannot relinquish. Clearly, the greater the pathology of our self-image and the greater our attachment to it, the stronger will be our sense of being threatened and attacked, and the greater will be the amount of psychic energy necessary to maintain and defend the false part of our self-image.

At this point, an increase in self-knowledge will be represented by some insight into ourselves which enables us to discard a false part of our self-image. This act of self-knowledge is the first stage of the mechanism involved in taking a single step forward in the process of spiritual growth. Such an increment in self-knowledge has one immediate consequence: It instantly releases that part of our psychic energy which was previously bound up in defending and maintaining the false self-concept. The release of this binding energy is most usually experienced as an extremely positive emotion, a sense of exhilaration and of liberation. It is love. We have a truer picture of our real (and therefore God-created) selves, and we have a new reservoir of energy which is now freed for its God-intended use in the form of service to others.

Following this release of energy will be an increase in courage. We have more courage partly because we have more knowledge of reality and have therefore succeeded in reducing, however slightly, the vastness of what is unknown and hence potentially threatening to us. We also have more courage because we have more energy to deal with whatever unforeseen difficulties may lie ahead. This new increment of courage is an increase in faith.

Courage generates within us *intentionality,* i.e. the willingness and the desire to act. We want to act because we are anxious to experience the sense of increased mastery that will come from dealing with life situations which previously appeared difficult or impossible but which now seem challenging and interesting. And we are also eager to seek new challenges, to use our new knowledge and energy in circumstances we would have previously avoided. And, most importantly, we have an intense desire to share with others, to serve them and to be an instrument, to whatever possible extent, in the process of their spiritual growth and development.

Finally, this intentionality, this new motivation, expresses itself in concrete action. Until now everything has taken place internally, in the inner recesses of our psyche. No external observer could possibly know that anything significant has taken place. But when we began to act, the reality of this inner process is dramatized. Action, then, is the dramatization of intentionality and therefore of knowledge, faith and love. It is the visible, observable concomitant of the invisible process that has occurred within us.

We have taken a step forward in our spiritual development. We have moved from one level to another. However small the step may be, however minimal the difference between the old level of functioning and the new, a definite transition has taken place.

Whenever we act, we affect not only ourselves but also our physical and social environment. Our action thereby evokes a reaction from others. This reaction is, of course, just a form of the feedback information mentioned above. But the difference is that our action has now been the result of a conscious and deliberate process. We know why we acted the way we did. Thus we will perceive the reaction in a different way, even if it is negative (our good intentions certainly do not guarantee that the reaction will be positive). We will welcome the reaction because it will help us evaluate our actions. In short, the reaction to our actions will give us new knowledge, new self-insight. In this way, the cycle starts again and the process of taking another step along the path of spiritual growth is repeated. We represent this by the following diagram:

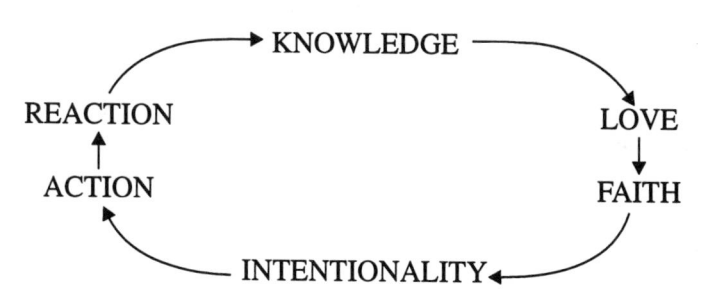

```
           ┌──────→ KNOWLEDGE ──────┐
          /                          \
   REACTION                          LOVE
      ↑                               ↓
   ACTION                           FAITH
          \                          /
           └──── INTENTIONALITY ←───┘
```

As is the case with any new discipline, so it is with learning spiritual growth. Our first steps forward are painfully self-conscious and hesitant. We are acutely aware of each detail, so much so that we wonder whether we will ever be able to make it work. We are elated at our first successes but we tend to linger on the plateaus, becoming sufficiently motivated to take another step only when negative pressures begin to build up intolerably, forcing us to act.

Yet, as we pursue the process, we become more adept at it. Gradually, certain aspects become spontaneous and natural (not unconscious). They become part of us to the point of being reflex actions. The feedback loop resulting from our actions becomes more and more automatic. The rate of progress begins to pick up. The steps merge imperceptibly. Finally, the process becomes almost continuous. In other words, the rate of progress increases as we go along because we are not only making progress but also perfecting our skill at making progress.

'Abdu'l-Bahá has said:

> It is possible to so adjust one's self to the practice of nobility that its atmosphere surrounds and colors all our acts. When these acts are habitually and conscientiously adjusted to noble standards with no thought of the words that might herald them, then nobil-

ity becomes the accent of life. At such a degree of evolution one scarcely needs to try to be good any longer – all our deeds are the distinctive expression of nobility.[72]

A process in which the rate of progress is proportional to the amount of progress made is exponential. Thus an analysis of the mechanism of the spiritual growth process allows us to understand why this process, though remaining a gradual one, is exponential: It is because we perfect the process of growing spiritually as we grow, thereby increasing the rate at which growth occurs.

The above diagram and the detailed analysis of each stage of the mechanism involved in the hierarchical relationship between knowledge, love and will, should not lead us to forget the other fundamental point, namely that all of our spiritual faculties must function together at each stage of the mechanism. In order to gain self-insight, we must will to know the truth about ourselves, and we must be attracted towards the truth. When we act, we must temper our actions with the knowledge and wisdom we have already accumulated at that given point in our development.

Moreover, when we begin the process of conscious, self-directed spiritual growth, we do not start from absolute emptiness but rather from the basis of whatever knowledge, love, faith and will we have developed at that point in our lives. Thus the spiritual growth process is lived and dramatized by each individual in a way which is unique to him even though the basic mechanism of progress and the rules which govern it are universal.

Tools for Spiritual Growth

Our understanding of the process of spiritual growth and its dynamics does not guarantee that we will be successful in our pursuit of spirituality. We stand in need of practical tools to help us at every turn. The Bahá'í writings give a clear indication of a number of such tools. In particular, prayer, meditation on the writings of the Manifestations and active service to mankind are repeatedly mentioned:

When a person becomes a Bahá'í, actually what takes place is that the seed of the spirit starts to grow in the human soul. This seed must be watered by the outpourings of the Holy Spirit. These gifts of the spirit are received through prayer, meditation, study of the Holy Utterances and service to the Cause of God . . . service in the Cause is like the plough which ploughs the physical soil when seeds are sown.[73]

Some of the points mentioned briefly in the above passage are amplified in the following statement by the same writer:

How to attain spirituality is indeed a question to which every young man and woman must sooner or later try to find a satisfactory answer . . .

Indeed the chief reason for the evils now rampant in society is the lack of spirituality. The materialistic civilization of our age has so much absorbed the energy and interest of mankind that people in general do no longer feel the necessity of raising themselves above the forces and conditions of their daily material existence. There is not sufficient demand for things that we call spiritual to differentiate them from the needs and requirements of our physical existence . . .

The universal crisis affecting mankind is, therefore, essentially spiritual in its causes . . . the core of religious faith is that mystic feeling which unites Man with God. This state of spiritual communion can be brought about and maintained by means of meditation and prayer. And this is the reason why Bahá'u'lláh has so much stressed the importance of worship . . . The Bahá'í Faith, like all other Divine Religions, is thus fundamentally mystic in character. Its chief goal is the development of the individual and society, through the acquisition of spiritual virtues and powers. It is the soul of man which has first to be fed. And this spiritual nourishment prayer can best provide.[74]

With regard to meditation, the Bahá'í writings explain that it has no set form and that each individual is free to meditate in the manner he finds most helpful. Statements by 'Abdu'l-Bahá describe meditation as a silent contemplation, a sustained mental concentration or focusing of thought:

Bahá'u'lláh says there is a sign (from God) in every phenomenon: the sign of the intellect is contemplation and the sign of contemplation is silence, because it is impossible for a man to do two things at one time – he cannot both speak and meditate . . .

Meditation is the key for opening the doors of mysteries. In that state man abstracts himself: in that state man withdraws himself from all outside objects; in that subjective mood he is immersed in the ocean of spiritual life and can unfold the secrets of things-in-themselves.[75]

'Abdu'l-Bahá leaves no doubt concerning the importance of meditation as a tool for spiritual growth:

> You cannot apply the name 'man' to any being void of this faculty of meditation; without it he would be a mere animal, lower than the beasts.
> Through the faculty of meditation man attains to eternal life; through it he receives the breath of the Holy Spirit – the bestowal of the Spirit is given in reflection and meditation.[76]

And Bahá'u'lláh has said that 'One hour's reflection is preferable to seventy years of pious worship.'[77]

The Bahá'í writings suggest that the words and teachings of the Manifestations provide a helpful focus for meditation. Also, while giving considerable freedom to the individual concerning prayer, they likewise suggest that the prayers of the Manifestations are especially useful in establishing a spiritual connection between the soul of man and the Divine Spirit. Prayer is defined as conversation or communion with God:

> The wisdom of prayer is this, that it causes a connection between the servant and the True One, because in that state of prayer man with all his heart and soul turns his face towards His Highness the Almighty, seeking His association and desiring His love and compassion. The greatest happiness for a lover is to converse with his beloved, and the greatest gift for a seeker is to become familiar with the object of his longing. That is why the greatest hope of every soul who is attracted to the kingdom of God is to find an opportunity to entreat and supplicate at the ocean of His utterance, goodness and generosity.[78]

'Abdu'l-Bahá has elsewhere explained that the spirit in which one prays is the most important dimension of prayer. A ritualistic mumbling of words or a mindless repetition of syllables is not prayer. Moreover, the Bahá'í writings enjoin the spiritual seeker to make of his whole life, including his professional activities, an act of worship:

> In the Bahá'í Cause arts, sciences and all crafts are counted as worship. The man who makes a piece of notepaper to the best of his ability, conscientiously, concentrating all his forces on perfecting it, is giving praise to God. Briefly, all effort put forth by man from the fullness of his heart is worship, if it is prompted by the highest motives and the will to do service to humanity. This is worship: to serve mankind and to minister to the needs of the people. Service is prayer . . .[79]

Thus it is the spirit and motive of service to others which makes external activity a tool for spiritual progress. In order to pursue the goal of spirituality, one must therefore maintain a persistently high level of motivation. Prayer, meditation and study of the words of the Manifestations are essential in this regard:

> The first thing to do is to acquire a thirst for spirituality, then Live the Life! Live the Life! Live the Life! The way to acquire this thirst is to meditate upon the future life. Study the Holy Words, read your Bible, read the Holy Books, especially study the Holy Utterances of Bahá'u'lláh. Prayer and Meditation, take much time for these two. Then will you know the Great Thirst, and then only can you begin to Live the Life![80]

Thus, while the quality and maturity of one's relationship to others remain the best measure of spiritual progress and growth, acquiring the capacity for such mature relationships depends essentially on an intense inner life and self-development. Moreover, the individual's actions are experienced both by himself and by others, whereas inner life is experienced only by the individual and is thereby more properly 'his'. The sense of 'that mystic feeling which unites Man with God' becomes to the spiritual seeker the most precious of experiences. It is that part of spirituality which lies at the center of his heart and soul.

In this inner dimension, spirituality becomes a sort of dialogue between the human soul and the Divine Spirit as channeled through the Manifestation. It is within this subjective but nevertheless real dimension of inner spirituality that one finds all the passion, the exaltation of spirit, as well as the terrible but somehow precious moments of despair, of utter helplessness and defeat, of shame and repentance. It is here that one learns with the deeply certain knowledge only personal experience can bestow, that the ultimate category of existence, the absolute and transcendent God who guides and oversees our destiny, is an infinitely loving and merciful Being.

The Collective Dimension of Spirituality

The Social Matrix of Individual Growth

Until now in our discussion, we have viewed the process of spiritual growth as being primarily an individual one, a process which effects changes within the individual and in his behavior towards his social and natural environment. However, it is obvious that individual spiritual growth does not and cannot take place in a vacuum. It takes place within the context of a given society that is bound to have a profound influence on the individual in his pursuit of spirituality. Indeed, there are many intricate, subtle and complex interactions between any society and each of the individuals composing it. These interactions produce reciprocal influences that operate on different levels of behavior, life experience and consciousness. It is therefore more accurate to view the spiritual growth process as an organically social one having several identifiable but related components. Some of these are: 1) an individual component, which has been the main focus of our discussion in the previous sections, 2) a collective or global component, involving the evolution of society as a whole, and 3) an interactive component, involving the relationship between the individual and society. In this section, the global and interactive dimensions of the spiritual growth process will be briefly examined.

The Bahá'í writings make clear that, just as the individual has a basically spiritual purpose to his existence, so society also has a spiritual raison d'etre. The spiritual purpose of society is to provide the optimal milieu for the full and adequate spiritual growth and development of the individuals in that society. In the Bahá'í view, all other aspects of social evolution, such as technological innovations, institutional structures, decision-making procedures and the exercise of authority, group interactions and the like, are to be judged positive or negative according to whether they contribute to or detract from the goal of fostering a favorable milieu for spiritual growth.

Such a concept of society and its meaning is certainly a radical departure from the commonly held view that society serves primarily as a vehicle for economic activity to provide for the conditions of material existence. However, the inherent limitations of this common viewpoint become readily apparent when one reflects that nature itself already provides the basic conditions for material existence. Therefore, providing such conditions can hardly be the fundamental purpose of human society, for society then becomes redundant at best and possibly harmful.

Of course, economic activity is an important part of society's function since a certain level of material well-being and stability provides opportunities for spiritual growth. A social milieu in which large segments of the population are starving or living in other such extreme conditions is hardly a milieu which is favorable to the full and adequate spiritual development of its members, although spiritual growth can take place under such conditions. Also, a just, well-organized and efficient economy can serve to free man, at least partially, from boring and excessive labor and thus provide time for higher intellectual and artistic pursuits.

Another spiritual implication of economic activity is that it requires intense human interaction and therefore provides many of the challenges and opportunities necessary to stimulate spiritual growth among its participants. It is in the market place that questions of justice, compassion, honesty, trust and self-sacrifice become living reality and not just abstract philosophy. We therefore cannot safely neglect the 'outer' dimension of society in the name of our basic preoccupation with spiritual growth. Indeed, if the prevailing structures and behavioral norms of society are such as to inhibit or discourage spiritual growth, the individual will be impeded in his personal growth process. The occasional moral hero will succeed in spiritualizing his life against all odds but the vast majority will eventually succumb to the prevailing negative influences.

Also, one of the important characteristics of personal spiritual maturity is a highly developed social conscience. The spiritually minded individual has become intensely aware of the many ways he depends on society and has a keen sense of social obligation. Society thus benefits from the spiritualized individuals within its fold because of the unselfish quality of their service to the collectivity and because their particular talents and capacities are relatively well-developed. At the same time, the individual spiritual seeker's relative dependence on society fosters his humility, and the energy and effort he contributes towards the solution of social problems helps prevent the (necessary) attention he gives to his inner spiritual struggles from leading to an unhealthy degree of self-preoccupation. Bahá'u'lláh has said that the individual in the pursuit of spirituality should be anxiously concerned with the needs of the society in which he lives and that 'All men have been created to carry forward an ever-advancing civilization.'[81]

Unity

In our discussion of the principles governing individual spiritual growth, we have seen that certain attitudes and behavior patterns are conducive to spiritual growth whereas others are not. In the same way, certain social norms and types of social structures are conducive to the spiritual growth process whereas others are not. One of the fundamental features of the Bahá'í Faith is that its teachings include detailed prescriptions regarding social structures and their relationship to spiritual growth. Broadly speaking, Bahá'u'lláh teaches that those social and economic structures which favor cooperation and unity are conducive to the spiritual growth process while those structures based on competition, conflict, power-seeking and dominance-seeking hierarchies are destructive to the growth process. The unity taught by Bahá'u'lláh is not simply a formal juxtaposition of disparate parts but an organic unity based on a spiritual quality of relationship between groups and among individuals working within a given group. Nor is it a uniformity or homogeneity, but a 'unity in diversity', a unity in which the particular qualities of the cooperating components are respected in a way which enables these qualities to contribute to the unity of the whole rather than detracting from it as so often happens in the case of social structures based on competition and dominance-seeking.

The Bahá'í focus on unity and the attention which the Bahá'í writings give to the social and collective dimension of the spiritual growth process probably represent the most original contributions of the Bahá'í Faith to the collective spiritual consciousness of mankind, for the individual dimension of the spiritual growth process has been a part of every revealed religion. Indeed, some revelations, for example those of Jesus and Buddha, have focused almost entirely on the individual. Other revelations, such as those of Moses and Muḥammad, have treated the social dimension to a greater degree, giving laws governing the behavior of groups as well as that of individuals. However, in the case of the Bahá'í Faith, we see for perhaps the first time in religious history the spiritual growth process in its full collective dimension.

Social Evolution: World Order

In the Bahá'í view the whole of mankind constitutes an organic unit which has undergone a collective growth process similar to that of the individual. Just as the individual achieves his maturity in stages, gradually developing his abilities and enlarging the scope of his knowledge and understanding, so mankind has passed through different stages in the as yet unfinished process of achieving its collective maturity. According to Bahá'u'lláh, each occurrence of revelation has enabled mankind to achieve some particular step forward in its growth process. Of course, every revelation has contributed in a general way to mankind's spiritual awareness by restating and elaborating those eternal spiritual truths which are the very basis of human existence. But Bahá'u'lláh affirms that, besides this general and universal function common to all revelations, there is a specific function by which each revelation plays its particular and unique role in the total growth process. Here are some of the ways that these two dimensions of revelation are described in the Bahá'í writings:

> The divine religions embody two kinds of ordinances. First those which constitute essential or spiritual teachings of the Word of God. These are faith in God, the acquirement of the virtues which characterize perfect manhood, praiseworthy moralities, the acquisition of the bestowals and bounties emanating from the divine effulgences; in brief the ordinances which concern the realm of morals and ethics. This is the fundamental aspect of the religion of God and this is of the highest importance because knowledge of God is the fundamental requirement of man . . . This is the essential foundation of all the divine religions, the reality itself, common to all . . .
> Secondly: Laws and ordinances which are temporary and non-essential. These concern human transactions and relations. They are accidental and subject to change according to the exigencies of time and place.[82]

> God's purpose in sending His Prophets unto men is twofold. The first is to liberate the children of men from the darkness of ignorance, and guide them to the light of true understanding. The second is to ensure the peace and tranquillity of mankind, and provide all the means by which they can be established.[83]

> These Manifestations of God have each a twofold station. One is the station of pure abstraction and essential unity . . . If thou wilt observe with discriminating eyes, thou wilt behold Them all abiding in the same tabernacle, soaring in the same heaven, seated upon the same throne, uttering the same speech, and proclaiming the same Faith . . .

The other station is the station of distinction, and pertaineth to the world of creation, and to the limitations thereof. In this respect, each Manifestation of God hath a distinct individuality, a definitely prescribed mission, a predestined revelation, and specially designated limitations. Each one of them is known by a different name, is characterized by a special attribute, fulfills a definite mission, and is entrusted with a particular Revelation.[84]

Bahá'u'lláh associates his 'particular revelation' with the transition from adolescence to adulthood in the collective life of mankind. He affirms that the social history of mankind from its primitive beginnings in the formation of small social groups until the present day represents the stages of the infancy, childhood and adolescence of mankind. Mankind now stands poised on the brink of maturity, and the current turbulence and strife in the world are analogous to the turbulence of the ultimate stages of preadulthood in the life of the individual.

The long ages of infancy and childhood, through which the human race had to pass, have receded into the background. Humanity is now experiencing the commotions invariably associated with the most turbulent stage of its evolution, the stage of adolescence, when the impetuosity of youth and its vehemence reach their climax, and must gradually be superseded by the calmness, the wisdom, and the maturity that characterize the stage of manhood.[85]

The principle of the Oneness of Mankind – the pivot round which all the teachings of Bahá'u'lláh revolve – is no mere outburst of ignorant emotionalism or an expression of vague and pious hope . . . Its message is applicable not only to the individual, but concerns itself primarily with the nature of those essential relationships that must bind all the states and nations as members of one human family . . . It implies an organic change in the structure of present-day society, a change such as the world has not yet experienced . . .

It represents the consummation of human evolution – an evolution that has had its earliest beginnings in the birth of family life, its subsequent development in the achievement of tribal solidarity, leading in turn to the constitution of the city-state, and expanding later into the institution of independent and sovereign nations.

The principle of the Oneness of Mankind, as proclaimed by Bahá'u'lláh, carries with it no more and no less than a solemn assertion that attainment to this final stage in this stupendous evolution is not only necessary but inevitable, that its realization is fast approaching, and that nothing short of a power that is born of God can succeed in establishing it.[86]

Because Bahá'u'lláh conceived His fundamental mission to be that of realizing world unity, His teachings contain detailed proposals for the establishment of institutions and social forms conducive to that end. For example, He proposes the establishment of a world legislature and a world court having final jurisdiction in all disputes between nations. He proposes the adoption of a universal auxiliary language, of universal obligatory education, of the principle of equality of the sexes, and of an economic system which would eliminate the extremes of poverty and wealth. All of these institutions and principles He sees as essential to building a society that encourages and promotes the full spiritual growth of its members.

> The emergence of a world community, the consciousness of world citizenship, the founding of a world civilization and world culture – all of which must synchronize with the initial stages in the unfoldment of the Golden Age of the Bahá'í Era – should, by their very nature, be regarded, as far as this planetary life is concerned, as the furthermost limits in the organization of human society, though man, as an individual, will, nay must indeed as a result of such a consummation, continue indefinitely to progress and develop.[87]

Bahá'u'lláh gave the term 'world order' to the new system He envisaged. Bahá'ís believe that the establishment of this new world order is ultimately the only answer to the quest for spiritual growth. For if the stability, harmony and morally progressive character of human society are not assured, the individual's goal of achieving spiritual development will be frustrated and his basic purpose in life thereby undermined.

The change in focus which results from this global perspective on the spiritual growth process is succinctly and clearly expressed by Shoghi Effendi:

> ... the object of life to a Bahá'í is to promote the oneness of mankind. The whole object of our lives is bound up with the lives of all human beings; not a personal salvation we are seeking, but a universal one ... Our aim is to produce a world civilization which will in turn react on the character of the individual. It is, in a way, the inverse of Christianity which started with the individual unit and through it reached out to the conglomerate life of men.[88]

The Bahá'í Community

The social structures and behavioral norms of present-day society are largely those we have inherited from the past. For the most part they have not been consciously chosen by the collectivity through some deliberate process but rather have evolved in response to various temporary and sometimes contradictory exigencies. They most certainly have not been chosen according to the criterion of fostering spiritual growth.

Especially in the industrialized West, but even in more technologically primitive societies, the currently existing social forms are largely based on competition and on dominance-seeking hierarchies. Such social forms tend to promote disunity, conflict, aggressive behavior, power-seeking behavior and excessive preoccupation with purely material success. The following passage from the writings of Bahá'u'lláh powerfully conveys the destructive effects mankind has suffered as a result of these social forms and behavior patterns:

> And amongst the realms of unity is the unity of rank and station. It redoundeth to the exaltation of the Cause, glorifying it among all peoples. Ever since the seeking of preference and distinction came into play, the world hath been laid waste. It hath become

desolate. Those who have quaffed from the ocean of divine utterance and fixed their gaze upon the Realm of Glory should regard themselves as being on the same level as the others and in the same station. Were this matter to be definitely established and conclusively demonstrated through the power and might of God, the world would become as the Abhá Paradise.

Indeed, man is noble, inasmuch as each one is a repository of the sign of God. Nevertheless, to regard oneself as superior in knowledge, learning or virtue, or to exalt oneself or seek preference, is a grievous transgression. Great is the blessedness of those who are adorned with the ornament of this unity and have been graciously confirmed by God.[89]

Given Bahá'u'lláh's affirmation that unity is the necessary social basis for spiritual growth, it follows that we are now living in a society which is largely indifferent and in many ways detrimental to the spiritual growth process. Indeed, the historical events of the twentieth century and the moral quality of our day to day lives provide powerful confirmations of this hypothesis. The social structures of present-day society are vestiges of past forms which may have been helpful in stimulating certain kinds of growth during previous stages of mankind's spiritual evolution but which have now outlived their usefulness.

This situation obviously poses a deep problem to any individual who is serious in his pursuit of spiritual growth. Even if one accepts Bahá'u'lláh's model of world order and is willing to strive to bring it about as the best hope for mankind, how is one to pursue successfully the spiritual growth process in a milieu that is so unconcerned with it?

The answer the Bahá'í Faith offers to this dilemma is the Bahá'í community. Bahá'u'lláh has not only offered a vision and a hope for the future, He has established a living community which already functions on the basis of the unity principles. This community is conceived as a prototype or an embryo of the future world society. By relating properly to this community and participating in it, the individual finds himself capable of developing his spiritual capacities in a significant way, even if the enveloping society-at-large remains indifferent to the growth process. Bahá'ís view the Bahá'í community established by Bahá'u'lláh as a precious and necessary tool for this transition period from the old to the new social order. At the same time, the growth and development of the Bahá'í community are part of the progressive establishment of the world order itself. Moreover, the Bahá'í community functions as an entity and as a constructive force within the larger community to stimulate the movement of society as a whole towards unity.

The individual's participation in the Bahá'í community is not passive. There is no priesthood, clergy or ecclesiastical hierarchy in the Bahá'í Faith. Spiritual growth is a self-initiated, self-responsible process, and the individual's participation in the Bahá'í community in no way diminishes his responsibility for his personal development.

In order to understand more clearly how participation in the Bahá'í community fosters spiritual development, let us focus for a moment on the spiritually negative features of modern-day society. It is in the contrast between the Bahá'í community, based on unity and cooperation, and the larger society based on competition and dominance-seeking, that we can gain insight into the interactive dimension of the spiritual growth process.

It is the essence of the relationship between an individual and the society to which he belongs that the individual is strongly motivated to succeed according to the prevailing norms of success in the given society. Security, status, material well-being, social acceptance and approval are the main things the individual seeks from society, and success in satisfying societal norms yields these rewards. Society wants the individual's productive effort, his collaboration and support in the realization of collective goals. Society applies both incentives and threats to induce the individual to accept social norms and goals.

To say that an individual accepts the norms and goals of a society means that he uses his understanding capacity to learn the skills necessary for success. He must also cultivate those emotional patterns, attitudes and aspirations which characterize socially successful individuals in the given society. Finally, he must act in a way conducive to success. Such a pattern of behavior will involve producing certain goods or services as well as a certain kind of relationship with other members of the society.

The norms of modern industrialized society largely revolve around material success through competition, dominance-seeking and power-seeking. The goal is usually a high level of economic productivity coupled with a high ranking and status in the social hierarchy. To succeed, the individual must learn those skills and techniques which enable him to best others in competitive struggle and to obtain power over them. He must learn how to manipulate, control and dominate others. The knowledge which is useful to these ends is often diametrically opposed to the kind of knowledge involved in spiritual growth. We have earlier seen that the self-knowledge which is equivalent to the knowledge of God amounts to knowing how to submit to the Will of God: The individual must learn how to be the conscious instrument of a force that is his moral and spiritual superior. Thus, virtually all the skills he develops in the pursuit of social success in a power-oriented society will be useless and, in fact, detrimental to his spiritual growth. The spiritually sensitive individual in modern society is therefore faced with a dilemma. He will either become a split personality, trying to be spiritual part of the time and to manipulate others for the remainder, or else he will ultimately have to choose between the two goals of social success and spiritual progress.[90]

It is not only the development of the knowing capacity that is falsified by the pursuit of success in competition but the heart's feeling capacity as well. One must continually give priority to one's own needs and desires and become increasingly insensitive to the needs of others. Genuine compassion towards and love for other individuals undermines the will to dominate because such empathetic emotions lead one to identify with and to experience the feelings of the dominated other.

The giving and receiving of love is a reciprocal or symmetric relationship. It is a positive and satisfying experience for both parties. Dominance, however, is asymmetrical, yielding positive emotions and a sense of exhilaration for the dominant one but generally negative, depressed, angry and self-deprecating emotions for the one dominated. It is therefore logically and psychologically impossible to seek to dominate someone whom we genuinely love, since the empathetic emotions of love allow us to feel the unpleasant emotions of being dominated and this experience undermines our willingness to become the conscious agent of producing such negative emotions in one we love and respect.

In other words, we cannot be successful in competitive struggle with others without hurting them and we cannot deliberately hurt others if we love them. It is thus easy to see how a person who dedicates himself to success in competitive struggle with others will increasingly become alienated both from himself and from others. His heart will become atrophied and hard. The development of his feeling capacity will be stunted and distorted.

The will capacity is also misused in the pursuit of power and dominance. The force of the will is turned outward towards others and used against them rather than being turned inward towards self-mastery and self-dominance. The will is used to oppose others, to limit their field of action, rather than being applied to develop the internal capacities of the self in the pursuit of spirituality and excellence.

Excellence represents self-development, the flowering of the self's capacities and qualities. It involves comparisons between our performance at different instances and under various circumstances (so-called 'self-competition'). But competition and power-seeking are based on comparisons with the performance of others. Such comparisons usually lead either to mediocrity, arrogance, undeveloped potential and unrealistically low self-expectations or else to depression, jealousy, aggressive behavior and unrealistically high self-expectations, depending on the capacities of those with whom we choose to compare ourselves. Neither of these is conducive to excellence.

In pursuing power, we tend to manipulate others, to use them as means to our ends. This is the very opposite of serving others and of acting towards them in such a way as to contribute to their spiritual advancement – the proper, God-intended expression of the will in action. In fact, unselfish service to society and true self-development go hand in hand, for a high degree of development makes us secure in our identity. It gives us inner peace and self-confidence. Moreover, we have more to give others and our service is therefore more valuable and more effective.

Thus, spirituality and the pursuit of excellence reinforce each other while power struggle and competition are inimical to both. The pursuit of dominance may stimulate some development on the part of the 'winners' but such development is often at the expense of others and of society as a whole. And even for the winners, it frequently produces an unstable, artificial and imbalanced kind of development.

A society based on unity, cooperation and mutual encouragement allows everyone to pursue spirituality and excellence while contributing significantly to the society itself. Just as love is satisfactory to both giver and receiver, so unity is beneficial both to society and to the individual members of the society. Such is the interactive dimension of the spiritual growth process.

Unity, cooperation and mutuality constitute the norms and goals of the Bahá'í community and form the basis of its institutions. Therefore all the spiritual benefits which derive from a society based on unity principles accrue to those who participate in the Bahá'í community. There is, first of all, the association with other people who are also committed to the process of self-aware, self-initiated spiritual growth. Since no two people have exactly the same experiences or have attained an identical level of development in all areas of their lives, the individual participant receives much stimulation and help from others. When facing a spiritual crisis in his personal life, he can usually find those who have already faced a similar crisis and can give helpful advice and loving encouragement. He therefore overcomes many difficulties which, under other circumstances, might have discouraged him to such an extent that he would have abandoned the struggle for spiritual growth. He consequently attains a much higher level of development than would have been the case had he been deprived of such helpful associations and fellowship.

At the same time, the mutuality and reciprocal nature of association based on unity means that the relationship with the community is not unidirectional: The individual is not a passive recipient of spiritual advice from experts but has opportunities to contribute to the growth of others and of the community. His own qualities, experiences and opinions are respected and valued by others. He is constantly being called upon to sacrifice purely selfish interests in the path of service. This acts as a check on pride and arrogance. Since sincerely motivated service to others is the real fruit of the spiritual growth process, the individual is provided almost daily with concrete situations which enable him better to evaluate the level of spiritual development he has attained.

The spiritual seeker in contemplative isolation can easily fall victim to the subtle pitfall of spiritual pride. Preoccupied with his perception of his internal mental processes, he can quickly acquire the self-generated illusion that he has reached a high degree of spiritual development. Constant and vigorous participation in a hard-working community can help to dispel such conceits.

Participation in the Bahá'í community enables one to acquire certain specific skills that cannot be easily acquired elsewhere. For example, the basis of group decision-making in the Bahá'í Faith is *consultation,* a process involving a frank but loving expression of views by those involved on a basis of absolute equality. Consultation represents a subtle and multifaceted spiritual process, and time and effort are required to perfect it. Similarly, the electoral processes in the Bahá'í community involve many unique aspects which will not be discussed in the framework of this paper.

Another important dimension of the Bahá'í community is its diversity and universality. One is called upon to associate intimately with people of all social, cultural and racial backgrounds. In society at large, our associations tend to be based on homogeneity: We associate with people with whom we feel the most comfortable. If most of our associations are on this basis, it will be difficult for us to discover our subtle prejudices and illusory self-concepts. Our friends will be those who are congruent with the false as well as the true aspects of our personality. The immense diversity within the Bahá'í community makes the discovery of prejudice and self-deceit much easier.

Thus, the Bahá'í Faith views the spiritual growth process as both collective and individual. The collective dimension involves the principles by which human society can be properly structured and ordered so as to optimize spiritual and material well-being and to provide a healthy growth milieu for all individuals within it. The individual bears the primary responsibility for prosecuting his own growth process and for working to create a unified and healthy social milieu for everyone. This involves working towards the establishment of world unity. In particular, it involves active participation in the ongoing life of the Bahá'í community which, though forming only a part of society as a whole, already functions on the basis of the unity principles and seeks to implement them progressively in society.

Summary and Conclusion

In the Bahá'í conception, spirituality is the process of the full, adequate, proper and harmonious development of the spiritual capacities of each human being and of the collectivity of human beings. These spiritual capacities are capacities of a nonphysical, indivisible and eternally lasting entity called the soul. The soul of each individual, with its particular characteristics, is formed at the moment of the conception of the physical body. The process of spiritual development is eternal, continuing in other dimensions of existence after the death of the physical body. The body and its physical capacities serve as instruments for this process of spiritual growth during the period of earthly life when the body and soul are linked together.

All of man's initially given capacities, both physical and spiritual, are good and potentially helpful to the spiritual growth process. However, there is a certain tension between the body's physical needs and the metaphysical needs of the soul. Physical needs and desires must therefore be disciplined (not suppressed) if they are to contribute to the process of spiritual development in an effective way. Through the misuse or improper development of his initially given capacities, man can acquire unnatural or inordinate capacities and needs inimical to the spiritual growth process.

Among the basic spiritual capacities to be developed are the understanding or knowing capacity, the heart or feeling capacity, and the will, which represents the capacity to initiate and sustain action. The beginning stage of the process of spiritual development in childhood is one in which the individual is primarily the passive recipient of an educational process initiated by others. As the individual attains the full development of his physical capacities in adolescence, he becomes the active and self-responsible agent of his own growth process.

The goal of the development of the knowing capacity is the attainment of truth, which means that which is in conformity with reality. The ultimate reality to be known is God and the highest form of knowledge is the knowledge of Him. God is the self-aware and intelligent force (Creator) responsible for man and his development. This knowledge of God takes the form of a particular kind of self-knowledge which enables the individual to become a conscious, willing and intelligent instrument for God and for His purposes.

The goal of the development of the heart capacity is love. Love represents the energy necessary to pursue the goal of spiritual development. It is experienced as a strong attraction for and attachment to God and the laws and principles He has established. It also expresses itself as an attraction to others and in particular to the spiritual potential they have as beings like ourselves. Love thereby creates within us the desire to become instruments for the growth process of others.

The goal of the development of the will capacity is service to God, to others and to ourselves. Service is realized by a certain kind of intentionality (good will) which is dramatized through appropriate action (good works). All of these basic capacities must be developed systematically and concomitantly, or else false or improper development (unspirituality) will result.

Our condition during the period of earthly life is one in which we have direct access to material reality but only indirect access to spiritual reality. The proper relationship to God is therefore established by means of recognizing and accepting the Manifestations or prophetic figures who are superhuman beings sent by God for the purpose of educating and instructing mankind. These Manifestations are the link between the visible world of material reality and the invisible, but ultimately more real, world of spiritual reality. Acceptance of the Manifestations and obedience to the laws they reveal are seen to constitute an essential prerequisite for the successful prosecution of the spiritual growth process.

The human race constitutes an organic unit whose fundamental component is the individual. Mankind undergoes a collective spiritual evolution analogous to the individual's own growth process. The periodic appearance of a Manifestation of God is the motive force of this process of social evolution. Human society is currently at the stage of the critical transition from adolescence to adulthood or maturity. The practical expression of this yet-to-be-achieved maturity is a unified world society based on a world government, the elimination of prejudice and war, and the establishment of justice and harmony among the nations and peoples of the world. The particular mission of the revelation of Bahá'u'lláh is to provide the basis for this new world order and the moral impetus to effect this transition in the collective life of mankind. Relating effectively to this present stage of society's evolution is essential to the successful prosecution of the spiritual growth process in our individual lives. Participation in the worldwide Bahá'í community is especially helpful in this regard.

Such, in its barest outlines, is the process of individual and collective spiritual growth as found in the Bahá'í writings. Undoubtedly, what remains to be discovered and understood in the vast revelation of Bahá'u'lláh is infinitely greater than what we can now understand and greater still than what we have been able to discuss in the present article. But the only intelligent response to this perception of our relative ignorance is not to wait passively until such future time as these deeper implications will have become evident but rather to act vigorously and decisively on the basis of our limited understanding. Indeed, without such a response to the revelation of Bahá'u'lláh, we may never arrive at the point where we will be able to penetrate the more subtle and deeper dimensions of the spiritual growth process.

No true knowledge is purely intellectual but spiritual knowledge is unique in the breadth of its experiential dimension: it must be lived to become part of us. Nowhere does this truth appear more clearly than in the succinct and powerful coda to Bahá'u'lláh's *Hidden Words*:

> I bear witness, O friends! that the favor is complete, the argument fulfilled, the proof manifest and the evidence established. Let it now be seen what your endeavors in the path of detachment will reveal.[91]

Bibliography

'Abdu'l-Bahá. *'Abdu'l-Bahá in London*. London: Bahá'í Publishing Trust, 1982.
— *Faith for Every Man*. London: Bahá'í Publishing Trust, 1986.
— *The Foundations of World Unity*. Wilmette, Illinois: Bahá'í Publishing Trust, 1979.
— *Paris Talks*. 11th ed. London: Bahá'í Publishing Trust, 1972.
— *The Promulgation of Universal Peace*. Wilmette, Illinois: Bahá'í Publishing Trust, 1982.
— *Selections from the Writings of 'Abdu'l-Bahá*. Haifa: Bahá'í World Centre, 1978.
— *Some Answered Questions*. Wilmette, Illinois: Bahá'í Publishing Trust, 1981.
— *The Tablets of Abdul-Baha Abbas*. New York: Bahai Publishing Society, 1909-16.
— *Will and Testament of 'Abdu'l-Bahá*. Wilmette, Illinois: Bahá'í Publishing Trust, 1971.
Aquinas, Thomas. *Summa Theologiae*. London, 1964.
Aristotle. *Works*, trans. W. D. Ross. Oxford: Clarendon Press, vol. 2 *Physica*, 1930; vol. 3 *Metaphysica*, 1954.
Avicenna. *Kitab al-Isharat wa-l-Tanbihat*, ed. J. Forget. Leiden, 1892.
— *Livre des directives et remarques*, Beirut, 1951.
— *La métaphysique du Shifa*, trans. G. C. Anawati. Librarie philosophique, Paris, 1985.
— *Najat* (Salvation). Cairo, 1938.
The Báb. *Selections from the Writings of the Báb*. Haifa: Bahá'í World Centre, 1976.
Bahá'í Canada, June-July 1978.
The Bahá'í Magazine, vol. 19, no. 3, 1928.
Bahá'í World Faith. Wilmette, Illinois: Bahá'í Publishing Trust, 1976.
Bahá'u'lláh. *Epistle to the Son of the Wolf*. Wilmette, Illinois: Bahá'í Publishing Trust, 1953.
— *Gleanings from the Writings of Bahá'u'lláh*. Wilmette, Illinois: Bahá'í Publishing Trust, 1976.

— *The Hidden Words of Bahá'u'lláh*. Wilmette, Illinois: Bahá'í Publishing Trust, 1990.
— *Kitáb-i-Aqdas*. Haifa: Bahá'í World Centre, 1992.
— *Kitáb-i-Íqán*. Wilmette, Illinois: Bahá'í Publishing Trust, 1981.
— *Prayers and Meditations by Bahá'u'lláh*. Wilmette, Illinois: Bahá'í Publishing Trust, 1969.
— *Proclamation of Bahá'u'lláh to the Kings and Leaders of the World*. Haifa: Bahá'í World Centre, 1967.
— *Tablets of Bahá'u'lláh revealed after the Kitáb-i-Aqdas*. Haifa: Bahá'í World Centre, 1978.
Balyuzi, H. M. *The Báb: The Herald of the Day of Days*. Oxford: George Ronald, 1975.
— *Bahá'u'lláh: the King of Glory*. Oxford: George Ronald, 1980.
Bible, Revised Standard Version
Compilation of Compilations. Mayborough, Victoria, Australia: Bahá'í Publications Australia, 1991.
Davidson, H. A. 'Avicenna's Proof of the Existence of God as a Necessarily Existent Being', *Islamic Philosophical Theology*, ed. P. Morewedge, SUNY Press, Albany, N.Y., 1979, pp. 165-87.
The Divine Art of Living. ed. Mabel Hyde Paine. Wilmette, Illinois: Bahá'í Publishing Trust, 1960.
Encyclopædia Britannica, Macropedia, 1980, vol. 2.
Hatcher, John S. *The Arc of Ascent*. Oxford: George Ronald, 1994.
Hatcher, William S. 'Foundations of Mathematics', *Encyclopædia Britannica* (forthcoming). Macropedia, 1997.
— *Logic and Logos*. Oxford: George Ronald, 1990.
— *Logical Foundations of Mathematics*. Oxford: Pergamon Press, 1982.
— 'Science of Religion', *Bahá'í Studies*. vol. 2. Ottawa: Association for Bahá'í Studies, 1980.
The Holy Qur'an: Text, Translation and Commentary, trans. Abdu'llah Yusuf Ali.
The Koran. trans. J. M. Rodwell. London: Dent, 1963.
Laurokainen, K. V. 'Quantum Physics, Philosophy, and the Image of God: Insights from Wolfgang Pauli', *Zygon* 25.4 (December 1990), pp. 391-404.
Lecomte du Noüy, Pierre. *L'Homme devant la science*. Paris: Gallimard, 1939.
— *Human Destiny*. New York: Longmans, Green and Co., 1947.
Leibniz, Gottfried. *The Monadology and Other Philosophical Writings*. trans. Robert Latta. London: Oxford University Press, 1925.

BIBLIOGRAPHY

Lights of Guidance. comp. Helen Hornby. 2nd ed. New Delhi: Bahá'í Publishing Trust, 1988.

Maimonides, Moses. *Guide for the Perplexed*, trans. M. Friedlander, New York: Dover Publications, 1956.

Moss, L. S. in *The Bulletin of the American Mathematical Society*, vol. 20, no. 2 (1989), pp. 215-35.

Nabíl. *The Dawn-Breakers*. Wilmette, Illinois: Bahá'í Publishing Trust, 1962.

The Neurosciences: A Study Program. ed. Quarton, Melnechuk and Schmitt. New York: Rockefeller Press, 1967.

The Neurosciences: Second Study Program. ed. F. O. Schmitt. New York: Rockefeller Press, 1970.

The Neurosciences: Third Study Program. ed. Schmitt and Worden. Cambridge: MIT Press, 1974.

The Neurosciences: Fourth Study Program. ed. Schmitt and Worden. Cambridge: MIT Press, 1979.

Prigogine, I. and I. Stengers. *Order Out of Chaos*. London: Fontana Press, 1984.

Quine, Willard V. O. *Word and Object*. Cambridge: MIT Press, 1960.

Russell, Bertrand. *Why I am Not a Christian*. London: Allen and Unwin, 1958.

Schweitz, Martha L. 'The Kitáb-i-Aqdas: Bahá'í Law, Legitimacy, and World Order', *The Journal of Bahá'í Studies*, vol. 6, no. 1, pp. 35-59.

Shoghi Effendi. *The Advent of Divine Justice*. Wilmette, Illinois: Bahá'í Publishing Trust, 1984.

— *Citadel of Faith*. Wilmette, Illinois: Bahá'í Publishing Trust, 1965.

— *Directives from the Guardian*. New Delhi: Bahá'í Publishing Trust, 1973.

— *God Passes By*. Wilmette, Illinois: Bahá'í Publishing Trust, 1974.

— *The Promised Day is Come*. Wilmette, Illinois: Bahá'í Publishing Trust, 1980.

— *Unfolding Destiny*. London: Bahá'í Publishing Trust, 1981.

— *The World Order of Bahá'u'lláh*. Wilmette, Illinois: Bahá'í Publishing Trust, 1955.

Star of the West. Rpt in 8 vols. Oxford: George Ronald, 1984.

Taherzadeh, Adib. *The Revelation of Bahá'u'lláh*, vol. 1. Oxford: George Ronald, 1974.

Townshend, George. *The Mission of Bahá'u'lláh*. Oxford: George Ronald, 1977.

The Universal House of Justice. *Messages from the Universal House of Justice, 1968-1973*. Wilmette, Illinois: Bahá'í Publishing Trust, 1976.

von Neumann, J. 'Eine Axiomatisierung der Mengenlehre', *J. fur Math.*, 154 (1925), pp. 219-40.

Women. Compilation of the Universal House of Justice. London: Bahá'í Publishing Trust, rev. ed. 1990.

REFERENCES AND NOTES

1. 'Abdu'l-Bahá, *Selections*, p. 27.
2. Bahá'u'lláh, *Kitáb-i-Íqán*, p. 198.

Preface (pp. xi-xv)

1. Bahá'u'lláh, *Kitáb-i-Íqán*, p. 211.
2. ibid. 191-2.
3. Both of these individuals had conferred infallibility to render authoritative interpretation of the works of Bahá'u'lláh, and the Universal House of Justice has authority to elucidate Bahá'í scripture.
4. Bahá'u'lláh, *Tablets*, p. 51.
5. Bahá'u'lláh, *Kitáb-i-Íqán*, p. 188.
6. Bahá'u'lláh, *Proclamation*, pp. 79-80.
7. Bahá'u'lláh, *Kitáb-i-Íqán*, pp. 145-6.
8. ibid. p. 15.
9. Bahá'u'lláh, *Gleanings*, p. 198.
10. Bahá'u'lláh, Kitáb-i-Aqdas, note 110.
11. Bahá'u'lláh, *Tablets*, pp. 51-2.
12. 'Abdu'l-Bahá, *Promulgation*, p. 10.
13. Shoghi Effendi, *World Order*, p. 163.

Prologue on Proving God (pp. 1-18)

1. 'Abdu'l-Bahá, *Promulgation*, p. 227.
2. 'Abdu'l-Bahá, in *Bahá'í World Faith*, pp. 383-4.
3. Bahá'u'lláh, *Kitáb-i-Íqán*, p. 192.
4. Bahá'u'lláh, *Gleanings*, p. 194.
5. 'Abdu'l-Bahá, *Promulgation*, p. 29.
6. ibid. p. 50.
7. This latter is the particular logical definition of God we will use in the second of the following two essays.
8. For an elaboration of this point see my article 'The Foundations of Mathematics', *Encyclopædia Britannica*, forthcoming.

9. Intelligence or consciousness would be examples of non-defining attributes of God. Although God is conscious and intelligent, He is not unique in having these attributes.
10. One proof we have not discussed is the so-called ontological proof, which runs something as follows: We humans have a subjective idea of a perfect, all-powerful being. Moreover, ideas, like anything else, have causes. But the actual existence of such a Perfect Being is the more rational explanation or cause of the idea of a perfect being. Thus God exists as the *necessary* cause of our idea of God.

   Most articulations of the ontological proof and its variants make use of *modal logic*, i.e. the logic dealing with the modalities of necessity and possibility. For example, modal logic makes a distinction between simple existence and necessary existence. The problem with the use of modal logic is that, even among experts in logic, there is still today not anything like universal agreement about what should be the rules of modal reasoning.

   However, the rules governing classical, non-modal logic are totally non-controversial, except for an extreme minority of so-called constructivists who refuse, in principle, all pure existence proofs, not only of God but of any abstract or 'unconstructible' entity. Indeed, constructivist restrictions on logic, if rigorously applied, would undermine the hardest of hard science, not just proofs of God's existence. Thus our use of classical logic in proofs of God's existence can be viewed as establishing the existence of God on an equal basis with the existence of photons or gravity.
11. Bahá'u'lláh, *Gleanings*, p. 178.

Causality, Composition and the Origin of Existence (pp. 19-42)

1. See, for example, the article on Avicenna by Seyyed Hossein Nasr in the *Encyclopædia Britannica*, Macropedia, 1980, vol. 2, pp. 540-1.
2. See Aristotle, *Works*, translated under the editorship of W. D. Ross, Oxford: Clarendon Press, vol. 2 *Physica*, 1930, 258b10 ff and vol. 3 *Metaphysica*, 1954, 994a1 ff.
3. See Avicenna, *Najat* (Salvation), Cairo, 1938, pp. 244 ff.; *Kitab al-Isharat wa-l-Tanbihat*, ed. J. Forget, Leiden, 1892, pp. 140 ff., trans. A. Goichon; *Livre des directives et remarques*, Beirut, Paris, 1951, pp. 351 ff; *La métaphysique du Shifa*, Books VI to X, trans. G. C. Anawati, Librarie philosophique, Paris, 1985, pp. 71 ff. Our

exposition of Avicenna's proof also relies heavily on the excellent article H. A. Davidson, 'Avicenna's Proof of the Existence of God as a Necessarily Existent Being', *Islamic Philosophical Theology*, ed. p. Morewedge, SUNY Press, Albany, N.Y., 1979, pp. 165-87. Finally, we also draw on a previous article by the present author, 'From Metaphysics to Logic' in W. S. Hatcher, *Logic and Logos*, pp. 60-80.

4. However, it seems clear that Avicenna did agree with the infinite regression principle, even though his proof makes no use of it. In this connection, see, for example, *La métaphysique du Shifa*, pp. 71-4.

5. A somewhat subtle point should not be overlooked here. By definition, the terms 'simple' and 'composite' are (classical) negations of each other, but this is not the case for the terms 'caused' and 'uncaused'. It is the causality principle that decrees 'caused' and 'uncaused' to be disjoint and exhaustive, i.e. to be negations of each other. Indeed, this is the precise meaning of the causality principle and the reason for assuming it. Philosophically, the underlying idea is that to be uncaused is to be self-sufficient – a positive quality – and not just to be not-caused. Thus there are four logical possibilities only because we assume the causality principle.

6. The *weak contingency principle* (or just the *contingency principle*) is: every composite, each of whose components is caused, is caused. The weak contingency principle is all that is really needed for Avicenna's theorem, as will be clear from our exposition below. Avicenna actually used both the weak and the strong forms of the contingency principle.

7. The intuitive justification of the potency principle is that any entity A which is sufficiently potent to be the cause of entity B must, *a fortiori*, be sufficiently potent to be the cause of any part of B.

8. This fact was already explicitly recognized by Davidson, 'Avicenna's Proof', p. 175.

9. In fact, the situation is slightly more complicated because Avicenna used the term 'necessary' in describing both cases, designating uncaused entities as 'necessary by reason of themselves' and caused entities as 'possible by reason of themselves and necessary by reason of another'. If I have correctly understood him on this point, Avicenna felt that a 'possibly existent' could not actually exist unless brought into being by the necessary

agency of some other actually existent entity. But, whether I am right or wrong in this particular interpretation, the superfluity of the logical modalities 'necessary' and 'possible' to Avicenna's argument stands in any case.

10. See the discussion of this in my *Logical Foundations of Mathematics*, Oxford: Pergamon Press, 1982, pp. 144-6.
11. See note 4 above.
12. Cf. the interesting discussion of this point by L. S. Moss in *The Bulletin of the American Mathematical Society*, vol. 20, no. 2 (1989), pp. 215-35.
13. For further discussion of these logical issues in relation to the theory of sets, see my article 'The Foundations of Mathematics', *Encyclopædia Britannica,* forthcoming.
14. Maimonides, *Guide for the Perplexed*, trans. M. Friedlander, 2nd rev. ed., New York: Dover Publications, 1956.
15. ibid. p. 152.
16. ibid.
17. ibid.
18. ibid.
19. ibid.
20. ibid.
21. ibid. pp. 152-3.
22. ibid. p. 152.
23. For example, in commenting on Thomas Aquinas' version of Avicenna's proof (to be considered in the next section), the Catholic scholar Thomas Gilby says that 'St Thomas owes more to the Arabic philosophers than to [Aristotle] . . . His wording echoes Maimonides, who took the proof from Avicenna'. See Thomas Aquinas, *Summa Theologiae*, Latin and English text, Blackfriars, London, vol. 2, 1964, appendix 8, p. 201.
24. This is, in fact, the explicit teaching of the Bahá'í Faith. The Bahá'í writings affirm that the soul of each individual is an objectively-existing, non-composite, non-physical entity that comes into existence at the moment of the physical conception of the body and that continues to live after the death of the body. 'The soul is not a combination of elements, it is not composed of many atoms, it is of one indivisible substance and therefore eternal. It is entirely out of the order of the physical creation; it is immortal!' 'Abdu'l-Bahá, *Paris Talks*, p. 91.
25. Aquinas, *Summa Theologiae*.
26. ibid. p. 15.

27. See passage quoted above. Henceforth we will not explicitly note references to this passage.
28. Leibniz, 'The Monadology', *The Monadology and Other Philosophical Writings*, trans. Robert Latta, London: Oxford University Press, 1925, p. 242.
29. ibid. pp. 337 ff.
30. See Bertrand Russell, *Why I am Not a Christian*, London: Allen and Unwin, 1958, pp. 145 ff.
31. See J. von Neumann, 'Eine Axiomatisierung der Mengenlehre', *J. fur Math.*, 154 (1925), pp. 219-40. See also article cited in note 13.
32. One further logical point bears mention here. Each of our six axioms is a universal statement, and thus the respective negations of these axioms are existential statements. Since denial of the existence of God necessitates negation of at least one of our axioms, our proof thus establishes conclusively that *any form of atheism depends upon some assertions of existence.* Thus, our proof establishes that an atheist is forced by logic alone to believe in something. Atheism, conceived as the negation of all belief in abstract entities, is logically untenable. Rather, atheism represents a particular choice of belief among several existential possibilities.

In particular, the negation of the contingency principle P.3 asserts the existence of an uncaused phenomenon (which is, however, neither unique, universal nor non-composite). However, since either P.3 or its negation must be true in any case, we have the following further theorem:

If we assume only the axioms S.1-S.3 and P.1-P.2, then an uncaused cause exists.

Thus, the causality and potency principles allow us to prove the existence of an uncaused cause *without any appeal either to the transitivity principle or to the infinite regression principle*, both of which were necessary to Aristotle's proof of the existence of an uncaused cause. In other words, anyone who accepts the set-theoretical principles S.1-S.3 and the philosophical principles of causality and potency is logically committed to belief in the existence of an uncaused cause. The only question for further debate with such a person is whether he wishes to consider his uncaused cause to be universal (P.3 is true) or not (P.3 is false).

A Scientific Proof of the Existence of God (pp. 43-58)

1. 'Abdu'l-Bahá, *Bahá'í World Faith*, pp. 383-4.
2. ibid. pp. 336-48.
3. ibid. pp. 342-3.
4. For example, many of the elements of 'Abdu'l-Bahá's argument can be found in a series of books written by the French scientist and philosopher Pierre Lecomte du Noüy, beginning with *L'Homme devant la science* (1939) and ending with *Human Destiny* (1947). After an analysis somewhat similar to that of the present essay, Lecomte du Noüy concludes boldly that 'an explanation of the evolution of life by chance alone is untenable today' (*Human Destiny*, p. 143). However, for reasons that are too detailed for consideration here, he is much less clear than 'Abdu'l-Bahá in drawing the conclusion that the cause of evolution is an externally acting force. Lecomte du Noüy opts instead for a somewhat unclear and not terribly convincing notion of 'telefinalism' in biology. In fairness to Lecomte du Noüy, it must be recognized that he was dealing with these questions at a time when certain fundamental advances in the science of dynamical systems had not yet occurred. A more recent example of another approach to these issues is K. V. Laurikainen, 'Quantum Physics, Philosophy, and the Image of God' (1990). Though Laurikainen's article is insightful, there are some significant points of difference with the approach I have taken here and previously (see Hatcher, *Logic and Logos,* in particular pp. 49-51). Among other things, I do not agree with Laurikainen's subjectivism and I reject the sharp contrast Laurikainen makes between the methods of quantum mechanics and those of macrophysics and science in general. In other words, I do not feel that quantum mechanics constitutes a methodological exception to general scientific practice. But I do feel that some of the observations Laurikainen makes are accurate and insightful as applied to science in general.
5. In *God Passes By* Shoghi Effendi characterizes 'Abdu'l-Bahá's Tablet to Auguste Forel as 'one of the most weighty the Master ever wrote' (pp. 307-8).
6. The evolution-based argument bears superficial similarity to the classical 'proof from design', which argues that observable reality could not exhibit the order and regularity it does without such structure being the result of a Conscious Designer. However, the evolution-based argument deals with the dynamics of the develop-

ment of complex physical systems, not just the design or structure resulting from such dynamics. This distinctive feature of 'Abdu'l-Bahá's argument sets it quite apart from classical cosmological or design arguments. However, the link between developments in modern physics and the classical design argument has been increasingly recognized. For example, the physicist Laurikainen says: 'The old argument from design has, in fact, gained new strength from the development of modern physics. The trend has been toward increasingly general theories that enable one to deduce an increasing number of facts from a small number of basic principles (axioms). This development, in turn, has clearly brought to light a beautiful logical structure in physical reality – strong evidence of a rational origin of existence that is superior to human intelligence. On the other hand, human intelligence seems to be related to this superior intelligence because we are increasingly able to unveil the beautiful secrets of nature. In religious language, this is expressed in the metaphor that humans are created in the image of God' ('Quantum Physics', p. 402).

7. Quine, *Word and Object*, p. 78.
8. For an expanded discussion of these methodological issues, together with references to the literature on the subject, see Hatcher, *Logic and Logos,* in particular the essay entitled 'Myths, Models and Mysticism', pp. 19-59.
9. This illustration of the entropy principle is based on Hatcher, 'Science', p. 23.
10. Prigogine and Stengers, *Order Out of Chaos.*
11. The various principles discussed in this section constitute a small part of the theory of dynamical systems. This venerable theory has been recently popularized under the name of 'chaos theory', where the word *chaos* is roughly (though not exactly and not always) equivalent to the use here of *randomness* or *disorder.* All of these terms refer to a certain category of states of a system (i.e. 'chaotic' or disordered states). The current popularization of chaos theory is reminiscent of so-called catastrophe theory, which was similarly popularized about 20 years ago. A 'catastrophe' is just an imaginative name given to a certain kind of transition from one state of a dynamical system to another. For a succinct discussion that relates all of these terms to a specific example, see Hatcher, *Logic and Logos*, pp. 128-9.
12. This is why the currently accepted theory of evolution attempts to explain the upward movement (the movement towards greater

order) in evolution as the fortunate coincidence of two random phenomena: the action of *natural selection* (essentially, random environmental impact) on *random mutations* (spontaneous genetic change). In His presentation of His argument, 'Abdu'l-Bahá considers a third logical possibility different from both chance and the hypothesis of an external force. He calls this third alternative *necessity* or *inherent compulsion*. He immediately rejects this possibility, saying that 'the coming together of the various constituent elements of beings . . . cannot be compulsory, for then the formation must be an inherent property of the constituent parts and the inherent property of a thing can in no wise be dissociated from it . . . Thus under such circumstances the decomposition of any formation is impossible, for the inherent properties of a thing cannot be separated from it' *(Bahá'í World Faith,* p. 342). We have not included this part of 'Abdu'l-Bahá's argument in our reformulation because it is generally known and accepted by scientists that the process of evolution is not due to any intrinsic necessity, since the physical elements that make up higher life forms such as the human being may very easily occur in other systems and in other forms. Thus, it would appear that 'Abdu'l-Bahá considers this possibility only to give logical completeness to His argument, not because He considers it a genuine physical possibility.

13. According to the Bahá'í writings, the most effective instrument for attaining the quality of self-knowledge that leads to knowledge of the nature of God is the teachings of the Manifestations of God. For a discussion of the role of these historical figures in this connection, see, for example, Hatcher, 'Concept'.

The Doctrine of the 'Most Great Infallibility' (pp. 59-100)

1. 'Abdu'l-Bahá, *Some Answered Questions*, p. 154.
2. Bahá'u'lláh, *Gleanings*, p. 215.
3. 'In the beginning was the Word, and the Word was with God, and the Word was God. He was in the beginning with God; all things were made through him, and without him was not anything made that was made.' (John 1:1-3). This and all subsequent citations from the Bible are from the Revised Standard Version.
4. 'Abdu'l-Bahá, *Some Answered Questions*, pp. 162-3.
5. Bahá'u'lláh, *Prayers and Meditations*, p. 321.

REFERENCES AND NOTES, pp. 59-100.

6. Letter written on behalf of Shoghi Effendi, quoted in the Kitáb-i-Aqdas, note 188.
7. Bahá'u'lláh, *Kitáb-i-Íqán*, p. 178.
8. John 14:9.
9. Bahá'u'lláh, quoted in *World Order of Bahá'u'lláh*, p. 109.
10. John 12:49.
11. Qur'án 10:16 (Jonah). This and all subsequent citations from the Qur'án are from *The Koran*, translated by J. M. Rodwell.
12. Bahá'u'lláh, *Epistle to the Son of the Wolf*, p. 39.
13. Qur'án 6:101 (Cattle).
14. Qur'án 43:59 (Ornaments of Gold).
15. Qur'án 3:138 (The Family of Imran).
16. John 15:1-3.
17. Bahá'u'lláh, *Epistle*, p. 11-12.
18. 'Abdu'l-Bahá, *Paris Talks*, p. 23.
19. Bahá'u'lláh, *Gleanings*, p. 150.
20. The Báb, *Selections*, p. 98.
21. Bahá'u'lláh vindicates both perspectives when He observes in the *Lawḥ-i-Ḥikmat*: 'As regards thine assertions about the beginning of creation, this is a matter on which conceptions vary by reason of the divergences in men's thoughts and opinions. Wert thou to assert that it hath ever existed and shall continue to exist, it would be true; or wert thou to affirm the same concept as is mentioned in the sacred Scriptures, no doubt would there be about it, for it hath been revealed by God, the Lord of the worlds.' (Bahá'u'lláh, *Tablets*, p. 140).
22. Bahá'u'lláh, *Prayers and Meditations*, pp. 48-9.
23. See Hatcher, *Arc of Ascent* for a full discussion of this concept.
24. Bahá'u'lláh, *Hidden Words*, Arabic no. 3.
25. Bahá'u'lláh, *Gleanings*, p. 65.
26. 'Abdu'l-Bahá, *Some Answered Questions*, p. 203.
27. Bahá'u'lláh, *Prayers and Meditations*, p. 6.
28. Bahá'u'lláh, *Gleanings*, p. 66.
29. ibid. pp. 65-6.
30. 'Abdu'l-Bahá, *Some Answered Questions*, p. 206.
31. ibid. p. 207.
32. ibid.
33. ibid. p. 237.
34. ibid. p. 154.
35. Shoghi Effendi, *World Order*, p. 112.
36. 'Abdu'l-Bahá, *Some Answered Questions*, pp. 171-2.

37. Bahá'u'lláh, *Gleanings*, p. 179.
38. Bahá'u'lláh, *Kitáb-i-Íqán*, pp. 221-2.
39. Thus the wisdom of Christ's metaphor for the returned Prophet as a 'thief in the night' (Matt. 24:43).
40. Bahá'u'lláh, *Kitáb-i-Íqán*, p. 55.
41. ibid. p. 222.
42. Bahá'u'lláh, *Gleanings*, pp. 66-7.
43. The explicit discussion of this twofold nature begins on page 152 and ends on page 181 of the *Kitáb-i-Íqán* but, in effect, the major part of the entire work is devoted to this distinction as it relates to how the Prophets appear and why they have been consistently rejected. In other words, the *Kitáb-i-Íqán* demonstrates the inextricable relationship between the station of essential unity and the station of distinction.
44. Bahá'u'lláh, *Kitáb-i-Íqán*, pp. 152-3.
45. ibid. pp. 153-4.
46. ibid. p. 176.
47. ibid. p. 177.
48. ibid.
49. ibid.
50. ibid. pp. 177-8.
51. ibid. p. 179.
52. ibid. p. 181.
53. Bahá'u'lláh, quoted in *God Passes By*, p. 101.
54. Bahá'u'lláh. *Proclamation*, p. 57.
55. Taherzadeh, *Revelation of Bahá'u'lláh*, vol. 1, p. 23.
56. Bahá'u'lláh, *Prayers and Meditations*, p. 108.
57. Shoghi Effendi, *God Passes By*, p. 213.
58. From a letter written on behalf of Shoghi Effendi to an individual believer, 22 October 1949, *Lights of Guidance*, no. 1633, p. 488.
59. Shoghi Effendi, *God Passes By*, p. 216.
60. Shoghi Effendi, *Promised Day is Come*, p. 124.
61. Luke 2:45-50.
62. Balyuzi, *The Báb*, p. 35.
63. Nabíl, *The Dawn-Breakers*, pp. 32-3.
64. ibid. pp. 32-3.
65. 'Abdu'l-Bahá, *Some Answered Questions*, p. 155.
66. ibid. p. 153.
67. Bahá'u'lláh, *Epistle*, p. 155.
68. From a letter written on behalf of Shoghi Effendi to an individual believer, 5 January 1948, *Lights of Guidance*, no. 1699, p. 504.

69. Bahá'u'lláh, Kitáb-i-Aqdas, para. 177.
70. ibid. para. 47.
71. 'Abdu'l-Bahá, *Some Answered Questions*, p. 173.
72. Shoghi Effendi, *Unfolding Destiny*, p. 449.
73. Bahá'u'lláh, Kitáb-i-Aqdas, para. 131.
74. For a complete account of this episode, see Shoghi Effendi, *God Passes By*, p. 144.
75. ibid. p. 144.
76. Of course, one might assume that, being omniscient, Bahá'u'lláh knew that they could never agree on anything, in which case He was demonstrating mere omniscience and not potential omnipotence.
77. The Báb, *Selections*, p. 59.
78. Bahá'u'lláh, quoted in Shoghi Effendi, *World Order*, pp. 108-9.
79. Matt. 4:1-11.
80. John 16:12.
81. Bahá'u'lláh, *Hidden Words*, Arabic no. 67.
82. Bahá'u'lláh, Kitáb-i-Aqdas, para. 176.
83. Bahá'u'lláh, *Gleanings*, p. 176.
84. Shoghi Effendi, *God Passes By*, p. 138.
85. 'Abdu'l-Bahá, *Some Answered Questions*, p. 153.
86. ibid.
87. ibid.
88. ibid.
89. ibid. p. 85.
90. ibid.
91. ibid. pp. 85-6.
92. ibid. p. 155.
93. From a letter written on behalf of Shoghi Effendi to an individual believer, 30 July 1941, *Lights of Guidance*, no. 1665, p. 496.
94. From a letter written on behalf of Shoghi Effendi to an individual believer, 27 April 1936), ibid. no. 1664, p. 496.
95. Shoghi Effendi, *Advent*, p. 49.
96. The assumption that because event A precedes event B, A is necessarily the cause of event B.
97. 'Abdu'l-Bahá, *Selections*, p. 213.
98. See Shoghi Effendi, *God Passes By*, p. 21.
99. Qur'án 10:16 (Jonah).
100. Sura 12.
101. Bahá'u'lláh, *Tablets*, p. 149.
102. *The Koran*, p. 230, note 1.

Unsealing the Choice Wine (pp. 101-112)

1. Bahá'u'lláh, Kitáb-i-Aqdas, para. 1.
2. See John S. Hatcher, *Arc of Ascent* for a lengthy explication of this theme. In fact, this theme is one of the organizing principles of that study.
3. Bahá'u'lláh, *Prayers and Meditations*, p. 314.
4. Bahá'u'lláh, *Gleanings*, p. 65.
5. 'Abdu'l-Bahá, *Some Answered Questions*, p. 201.
6. 'Abdu'l-Bahá, *Selections*, p. 178.
7. 'Abdu'l-Bahá, *Some Answered Questions*, p. 180.
8. Bahá'u'lláh, *Gleanings*, p. 184.
9. ibid.
10. Bahá'u'lláh, *Hidden Words*, Persian no. 29.
11. In Book VII of Plato's *Republic*, Socrates makes an elaborate conceit commonly known as the 'allegory of the cave' in which he compares the physical world to an inferior expression of the ineffable world of forms and ideas which the physical world reflects. However, one may see in this Socratic doctrine an appreciation for physical reality inasmuch as it provides the images of that spiritual world, and thus the means for our ascent.
12. 'Abdu'l-Bahá, *Tablet to Dr Forel*, p. 14.
13. 'Abdu'l-Bahá, *Promulgation*, p. 10.
14. Bahá'u'lláh, *Gleanings*, p. 215.
15. Bahá'u'lláh, *Kitáb-i-Íqán*, p. 152.
16. ibid. p. 176.
17. Matt. 9:16-17.
18. Shoghi Effendi, *World Order*, p. 5.
19. Shoghi Effendi, *World Order*, p. 163.
20. Shoghi Effendi, *God Passes By*, p. 140.
21. ibid. p. 139. 'Revealed on the eve of the declaration of His Mission, it proffered to mankind the "Choice Sealed Wine", whose seal is of "musk", and broke the "seals" of the "Book" referred to by Daniel, and disclosed the meaning of the "words" destined to remain "closed up" till the "time of the end".'
22. Qur'án 83:17. Citations from the Qur'án are from *The Holy Qur'an: Text, Translation and Commentary*, translated by Abdu'lláh Yusuf Ali.
23. ibid. 83:24-6.
24. Reference to the use of 'wine' in an allegorical sense – such as being the cause of spiritual ecstasy – is found, not only in the

Revelation of Bahá'u'lláh, but in the Bible, in the Qur'án, and in ancient Hindu traditions.

For example, in the Qur'án the righteous are promised that they will be given to drink of the 'choice sealed wine'. In His Tablets, Bahá'u'lláh identifies the 'choice Wine' with His Revelation whose 'musk-laden fragrance' has been wafted 'upon all created things'. He states that He has 'unsealed' this 'Wine', thereby disclosing spiritual truths that were hitherto unknown, and enabling those who quaff thereof to 'discern the splendors of the light of divine unity' and to 'grasp the essential purpose underlying the Scriptures of God'.

In one of His meditations, Bahá'u'lláh entreats God to supply the believers with 'the choice Wine of Thy mercy, that it may cause them to be forgetful of anyone except Thee, and to arise to serve Thy Cause, and to be steadfast in their love for Thee. (Kitáb-i-Aqdas, note 2).

25. Bahá'u'lláh, Kitáb-i-Aqdas, para. 5.
26. Bahá'u'lláh, *Tablets*, p. 105. According to Hasan Balyuzi in *Bahá'u'lláh: the King of Glory*, p. 382, this Tablet belongs to what Shoghi Effendi in *God Passes By*, p. 205, terms one of the three 'distinct categories' of Bahá'u'lláh's writings during this period, the category of Tablets which 'partly enunciate and partly reaffirm the fundamental tenets and principles underlying that Dispensation'.
27. Bahá'u'lláh, *Epistle*, pp. 133-14. See also pp. 44, 83, 88 and 105.
28. Bahá'u'lláh, *Gleanings*, p. 28.
29. 'Abdu'l-Bahá, *Some Answered Questions*, p. 67.
30. ibid. pp. 67-8.
31. Shoghi Effendi, *God Passes By*, p. 213.
32. Shoghi Effendi, *Citadel*, p. 101.
33. Bahá'u'lláh, *Hidden Words*.
34. The term 'learned' and 'rulers' distinguishes between those institutions that are in an advisory capacities and those that have legislative authority; the terms themselves were used by Bahá'u'lláh. See *Letters from the Universal House of Justice, 1968-1973*, pp. 91-5.
35. Bahá'u'lláh, *Prayers and Meditations,* p. 321.
36. 'Abdu'l-Bahá, *Tablets*, p. 120.

REFERENCES AND NOTES, pp. 113-157.

The Kitáb-i-Aqdas: The Causality Principle (pp. 113-157)

1. 'Abdu'l-Bahá, *Some Answered Questions*, p. 3.
2. ibid. p. 4.
3. ibid. p. 3.
4. 'Abdu'l-Bahá, *Paris Talks*, pp. 90-1.
5. ibid, pp. 88-9.
6. ibid. p. 90.
7. 'Abdu'l-Bahá, *Some Answered Questions*, pp. 143-4.
8. See, for example, the four-volume series *The Neurosciences:* [First] Study Program, Rockefeller Press, New York 1967; Second Study Program, Rockefeller Press, New York, 1970; Third Study Program, MIT Press, Cambridge, Mass., 1974; Fourth Study Program, MIT Press, Cambridge, Mass., 1979.
9. 'Abdu'l-Bahá, *Promulgation*, p. 29.
10. ibid. p. 50.
11. 'Abdu'l-Bahá, *Paris Talks*, p. 91.
12. ibid. p. 90.
13. ibid. p. 89.
14. Bahá'u'lláh, *Gleanings*, p. 149.
15. 'Abdu'l-Bahá, *Paris Talks*, p. 90.
16. 'Abdu'l-Bahá, *Some Answered Questions*, pp. 158-9.
17. 'Abdu'l-Bahá, in *Bahá'í World Faith*, pp. 382-3.
18. 'Abdu'l-Bahá, *Some Answered Questions*, pp. 158-9.
19. ibid. pp. 157-8.
20. ibid. p. 230.
21. ibid. p. 237.
22. Bahá'u'lláh, *Gleanings*, pp. 79-80.
23. Shoghi Effendi, *God Passes By*, p. 213.
24. See 'Abdu'l-Bahá, *Selections*, p. 29.
25. Bahá'u'lláh, Kitáb-i-Aqdas, para. 1.
26. ibid. paras. 3 and 4.
27. ibid. para. 5.
28. ibid. para. 119.
29. ibid. para. 125.
30. ibid. p. 6.
31. 'Abdu'l-Bahá, *Will and Testament*, p. 20.
32. It should be noted that local and secondary Houses of Justice are presently known as Spiritual Assemblies.
33. Bahá'u'lláh, Kitáb-i-Aqdas, p. 11.
34. 'Abdu'l-Bahá, *Selections*, p. 27.

REFERENCES AND NOTES, pp.113-157, 158-172.

35. Shoghi Effendi, *Directives from the Guardian*, pp. 86-7.
36. Bahá'u'lláh, Kitáb-i-Aqdas, pp. 100-1.
37. ibid. para. 149.
38. From a letter written on behalf of Shoghi Effendi to an individual believer, 2 February 1925, *Lights of Guidance*, no. 376, p. 111.
39. Bahá'u'lláh, Kitáb-i-Aqdas, para. 19.
40. Bahá'u'lláh, *Gleanings*, p. 106.
41. Bahá'u'lláh, Kitáb-i-Aqdas, para. 36.
42. From the 'Marriage Tablet' of 'Abdu'l-Bahá; see, for example, *Star of the West*, vol. 11, no. 1 (21 March 1920), p. 20.
43. Bahá'u'lláh, Kitáb-i-Aqdas, para. 68.
44. ibid. para. 63.
45. ibid. para. 48.
46. ibid. p. 138.
47. ibid. pp. 138-9.
48. ibid. para. 65.
49. ibid. para. 74-6.
50. Quoted in a letter of the Universal House of Justice published in *Bahá'í Canada*, June-July 1978, p. 3.
51. Bahá'u'lláh, Kitáb-i-Aqdas, para. 33.
52. ibid. para. 97.
53. ibid. para. 146.
54. ibid. para. 20.
55. ibid. p. 127.
56. ibid. note 38, pp. 182-4.
57. 'Abdu'l-Bahá, in *Star of the West*. vol. 9, no. 7 (13 July 1918), p. 87.
58. 'Abdu'l-Bahá, *Promulgation*, p. 281.
59. ibid. p. 135.

Gender Distinction in the Kitáb-i-Aqdas (pp. 158-172)

1. Bahá'u'lláh, in *Women*, no. 58.
2. 'Abdu'l-Bahá, in ibid. no. 13.
3. Bahá'u'lláh, *Gleanings*, p. 176.
4. 'Abdu'l-Bahá, in *Women*, no. 29.
5. 'Abdu'l-Bahá, in ibid. no. 83.
6. ibid. no. 18.
7. ibid. no. 20.
8. ibid. no. 29.
9. ibid. no. 83.

REFERENCES AND NOTES, pp. 158-172.

10. The Universal House of Justice, in *Women*, no. 94.
11. 'Abdu'l-Bahá, in *Women*, no. 47.
12. ibid. no. 50.
13. ibid.
14. The Universal House of Justice, in *Women*, no. 72.
15. 'Abdu'l-Bahá, in ibid. no. 16.
16. The Universal House of Justice, in ibid. no. 38.
17. ibid. no. 78.
18. See the Kitáb-i-Aqdas para. 20. It should be noted that this division of an estate applies only to someone who has not followed the law of Bahá'u'lláh in making a will. In effect, this law attempts to restore financial order to a household that has temporarily become disordered. Bahá'ís are commanded to make a will and in one's will one is free to do as one wishes.
19. The Universal House of Justice, in *Women*, no. 77.
20. 'Abdu'l-Bahá, in ibid. no. 27.
21. ibid. no. 47.
22. The Universal House of Justice, in *Women*, no. 78.
23. ibid.
24. ibid. no. 75.
25. 'Abdu'l-Bahá, in *Bahá'í World Faith*, p. 398.
26. The Universal House of Justice, in *Compilation*, vol. 1, pp. 413-14.
27. From a letter written on behalf of the Universal House of Justice to the National Spiritual Assembly of New Zealand, 28 December 1980, *Lights of Guidance*, no. 730. p. 218.
28. ibid. pp. 218-19.
29. ibid. no. 748, pp. 224-5.
30. Unpublished letter written on half of the Universal House of Justice to an individual believer 16 May 1982.
31. Unpublished letter from the Universal House of Justice to an individual believer, 11 January 1988.
32. 'Abdu'l-Bahá, in *Women*, no. 91.
33. The Universal House of Justice, in ibid. no. 95.
34. 'Abdu'l-Bahá, *Paris Talks*, p. 182.
35. See the Kitáb-i-Aqdas, para. 52 and the explanation discussed in note 80.
36. 'Abdu'l-Bahá, in *Women*, no. 14.
37. ibid. no. 91.
38. ibid. no. 25.
39. ibid. no. 27.

40. ibid. no. 29.
41. ibid. no. 59.
42. The Universal House of Justice, in ibid. no. 125.

The Model of Penology in the Kitáb-i-Aqdas (pp. 173-188)

1. Bahá'u'lláh, Kitáb-i-Aqdas, para. 5.
2. 'The Kitáb-i-Aqdas: Bahá'í Law, Legitimacy, and World Order', *The Journal of Bahá'í Studies*, vol. 6, no. 1, pp. 35-59.
3. In several instances the translators have used the word *refinement* to translate the Arabic word *liṭáfat*, a word that appears frequently in the Kitáb-i-Aqdas and which implies a variety of attributes: 'The original Arabic word "liṭáfat", rendered here as "refinement", has a wide range of meanings with both spiritual and physical implications, such as elegance, gracefulness, cleanliness, civility, politeness, gentleness, delicacy and graciousness, as well as being subtle, refined, sanctified and pure. In accordance with the context of the various passages where it occurs in the Kitáb-i-Aqdas, it has been translated either as "refinement" or "cleanliness".' Kitáb-i-Aqdas, note 74.
4. The Universal House of Justice in ibid. p. 4.
5. ibid. para. 66.
6. ibid. p. 119.
7. ibid. para. 151.
8. ibid. para. 67.
9. ibid. para. 74.
10. ibid. para. 76.
11. ibid. para. 74.
12. The Universal House of Justice, in ibid. pp. 2-3.
13. ibid. p. 4.
14. Bahá'u'lláh, *Tablets*, p. 27.
15. ibid.
16. Bahá'u'lláh uses the word 'adultery', but the notes to the Aqdas quote from interpretations by 'Abdu'l-Bahá which explain that what is intended here is 'sexual intercourse between persons who are unmarried'. He indicates that it remains for the Universal House of Justice to determine the penalty for adultery committed by a married individual. Kitáb-i-Aqdas, note 77.
17. ibid. p. 98.
18. ibid. para. 45.
19. ibid. para. 62.

20. ibid. note 86.
21. 'Abdu'l-Bahá, *Some Answered Questions*, p. 268.
22. ibid. pp. 268-9.
23. This is traditionally a small tear at the corner of the eye, implying a sarcastic disdain for the life they have taken.
24. The Universal House of Justice, in Kitáb-i-Aqdas, note 77.
25. ibid. para. 49.
26. From a letter written on behalf of Shoghi Effendi to an individual believer, 30 September 1949, in *Compilation*, vol. 1, no. 49, p. 57.
27. Bahá'u'lláh, *Epistle*, p. 27.
28. From a letter written on behalf of Shoghi Effendi to an individual believer, 26 July 1946, *Compilation*, vol. 1. no. 685, p. 306.
29. Bahá'u'lláh, Kitáb-i-Aqdas, para. 148.
30. Bahá'u'lláh, *Gleanings*, p. 171.
31. 'Abdu'l-Bahá, *Selections*, p. 179.
32. Bahá'u'lláh, Kitáb-i-Aqdas, para. 45.
33. 'Abdu'l-Bahá, *Some Answered Questions*, p. 270.
34. Bahá'u'lláh states, 'To none is it permitted to seek absolution from another soul; let repentance be between yourselves and God. He, verily, is the Pardoner, the Bounteous, the Gracious, the One Who absolveth the repentant.' (Bahá'u'lláh, Kitáb-i-Aqdas, para. 34).
35. 'Abdu'l-Bahá, *Some Answered Questions*, p. 269.
36. ibid.
37. Bahá'u'lláh, Kitáb-i-Aqdas, para. 148.
38. 'Abdu'l-Bahá, *Some Answered Questions*, p. 270.
39. From a letter written on behalf of Shoghi Effendi to an individual believer, 5 October 1950, in *Compilation*, vol. 2, no. 1329, pp. 22-3.
40. 'Abdu'l-Bahá, *Some Answered Questions*, p. 271. 'Abdu'l-Bahá states: 'So if someone assaults, injures, oppresses and wounds me, I will offer no resistance, and I will forgive him. But if a person wishes to assault Siyyid Manshadí, certainly I will prevent him. Although for the malefactor noninterference is apparently a kindness, it would be an oppression to Manshadí.' All of this should be understood and considered in the light of Bahá'u'lláh's explicit laws in the Kitáb-i-Aqdas prohibiting the individual from striking another (para. 148) and from carrying arms (para. 159).
41. ibid. p. 268.
42. ibid. p. 269.
43. ibid. p. 271.
44. ibid. p. 272.

REFERENCES AND NOTES, pp. 189-250.

The Concept of Spirituality (pp. 189-250)

1. The material contained in this article was developed over a period of several years primarily through courses I have given at the Green Acre Bahá'í School in Eliot, Maine. I am grateful to the many participants in these courses for their insights, comments and criticisms. Special thanks are due to the staff of Green Acre and in particular to the director, Richard Grover, at whose invitation and encouragement these courses were given. This material was also the basis for my contribution to the Conference on Spiritual Education at the Fourth Annual Meeting of the Association for Bahá'í Studies held in Toronto in January, 1979. In preparing this work for publication, I have benefitted from the critical comments of numerous reviewers as well as the editors of *Bahá'í Studies*. I deeply appreciate both the quality of these comments and the generous gift of time and energy they represent.
2. For example, powerful new techniques for manipulating such things as the human genetic endowment raise novel and acute ethical questions concerning their proper and responsible use.
3. 'Abdu'l-Bahá, *Bahá'í World Faith*, p. 240.
4. The present monograph consists in a rather detailed discussion of certain aspects of the Bahá'í conception of these spiritual truths and realities but with little or no attempt to explain the basis upon which such a conception rests. This latter task was the objective of a previous effort by the present writer, published as 'The Science of Religion', *Bahá'í Studies*, vol. 2, rev. ed., 1980.
5. Also, one should not forget that, except for the more historically recent of these systems (such as Islám) we have no direct access to the exact words or the pure form of the original teachings as given by the founder. Moreover, the various interpretations which theologians and thinkers have subsequently attached to those written records that do exist are conditioned and limited by various cultural factors and cannot, therefore, be regarded as surely authentic representations of the thought of the founder.
6. According to the Bahá'í conception, the soul of each individual is eternal while the body, composed as it is of elements, is subject to physical decomposition, i.e. death. Thus the soul is the true source of the individual's consciousness, personality and self. The soul does not depend on the body but rather the body is the instrument of the soul during the period of earthly existence when the soul and the body are linked together. The Bahá'í writings also

make unequivocally clear the Bahá'í belief that each human soul is not preexistent but is 'individualized' at the moment of conception. Bahá'ís do not, therefore, believe in reincarnation – the doctrine that the same individual soul returns in different bodies to live different or successive earthly lives. It is explained rather that the soul's progress after the death of the physical body is towards God and that this progression takes place in other, purely spiritual (i.e. nonmaterial) realms of existence.

Of course, we cannot see the soul since it is not physical but we can deduce its existence from the observable effects it produces. Roughly speaking, we can observe that the physical endowments of the higher apes, and, in particular, their central nervous systems, do not differ substantially from man's. Yet such beings seem incapable of the conscious, self-aware, deliberate intellection which characterizes man. At best, they seem capable only of 'reactive' conditioned response rather than the imaginative, self-initiated thought of man, involving as it does long chains of deduction and anticipation of and adaptation to imagined future events (i.e. hypotheses).

7. 'Abdu'l-Bahá, *Some Answered Questions*, pp. 212-14.
8. Bahá'u'lláh, *Gleanings*, p. 68.
9. ibid. p. 106.
10. This observation explains the time-honored injunction expressed by virtually all religious prophets and thinkers that no man is capable of judging the spiritual or moral worth of any other individual. This has nothing to do with society's right to protect itself against antisocial behavior whether perpetrated deliberately by morally insensitive individuals, or involuntarily by sick or misguided individuals.
11. 'Abdu'l-Bahá, *Some Answered Questions*, p. 216.
12. Also, the Bahá'í writings make totally clear the Bahá'í disbelief in the objective existence of Satan or of any such evil power or force (cf. *Some Answered Questions*, 'The Nonexistence of Evil', pp. 263-4). It is explained that what man perceives as evil within himself is simply the absence of some positive quality (which lack is perhaps perceived in a particularly acute way if the individual suddenly finds himself in a situation where the missing quality would have been very useful). Similarly, strong or irrational urges are not, it is affirmed, the result of the action on us of some extrinsic evil force but rather of subjective desires arising from within ourselves, possibly due either to a prior lack of proper

discipline or to the existence of some deep need which we may have neglected to fulfill in a healthy way (or which has not, in any case, been properly fulfilled). 'Abdu'l-Bahá explains that improper development can pervert our intrinsically good, natural (God-given) capacities into negative and destructive acquired capacities: 'capacity is of two kinds: natural capacity and acquired capacity. The first, which is the creation of God, is purely good ... but the acquired capacity has become the cause of the appearance of evil. For example, God has created all men that they are benefitted by sugar and honey and harmed and destroyed by poison. This nature and constitution is innate, and God has given it equally to all mankind. But man begins little by little to accustom himself to poison by taking a small quantity each day, and gradually increasing it, until he reaches a point that he cannot live without a gram of opium each day. The natural capacities are thus completely perverted. Observe how much the natural capacity and constitution can be changed until by different habits and training they become entirely perverted. One does not criticize vicious people because of their innate capacities and nature, but rather for their acquired capacities and nature.' ibid. pp. 214-15.

13. For example, since everyone knows what the physical sensation of hunger is like, anyone who willingly sacrifices his own physical well-being to help feed others commands a certain respect and communicates a spiritual reality to others in a way which far transcends preaching or philosophical discourse.
14. Bahá'u'lláh, *Gleanings*, pp. 70-2.
15. ibid. pp. 156-7. For a parallel discussion of some of these points see John S. Hatcher, 'The Metaphorical Nature of Physical Reality', *Bahá'í Studies*, vol. 3, 1977.
16. Bahá'u'lláh, *Kitáb-i-Íqán*, pp. 99-100.
17. 'Abdu'l-Bahá, *Some Answered Questions*, p. 222.
18. Bahá'u'lláh, *Gleanings*, p. 105.
19. ibid. p. 179.
20. In this regard, Bahá'u'lláh has said: 'Neither the candle nor the lamp can be lighted through their own unaided efforts, nor can it ever be possible for the mirror to free itself from its dross. It is clear and evident that until a fire is kindled the lamp will never be ignited, and unless the dross is blotted out from the face of the mirror it can never represent the image of the sun nor reflect its light and glory.' *Gleanings*, p. 66. He goes on to point out that

the necessary 'fire' and 'light' are transmitted from God to man through the Manifestations.
21. In one of His works, Bahá'u'lláh describes the stage leading up to the acceptance of the Manifestations as 'the valley of search'. It is a period during which one thinks deeply about the human condition, seeks answers to penetrating questions and sharpens and develops one's capacities in preparation for their full use. It is a period of increasing restlessness and impatience with ignorance and injustice.
22. Bahá'u'lláh, *Gleanings*, pp. 330-1.
23. Bahá'u'lláh and 'Abdu'l-Bahá stress that mankind has undergone a collective process of evolution by which it has now arrived at the threshold of maturity. God now requires more of man, in particular that he assume responsibility for the process of self-development: 'For in this holy Dispensation, the crowning of bygone ages, and cycles, true Faith is no mere acknowledgement of the Unity of God, but the living of a life that will manifest all the perfections implied in such belief.' ('Abdu'l-Bahá in *Divine Art of Living*, p. 25.)
24. Bahá'u'lláh, *Gleanings*, pp. 81-2.
25. ibid. p. 149.
26. ibid. p. 262.
27. Shoghi Effendi, in *The Bahá'í Life*, p. 6.
28. See 'Abdu'l-Bahá, *Bahá'í World Faith,* pp. 382-3, where faith is *defined* to be conscious knowledge: 'By faith is meant, first, conscious knowledge, and second, the practice of good deeds.' Of course, whenever man gains knowledge which contradicts his preconceived notions, he experiences inner conflict and may therefore initially perceive the new knowledge (and thus the new faith) as irrational in that it contradicts what he previously assumed to be true. But this initial perception is gradually overcome as continued experience further confirms the new knowledge, finally leading to an integration of the new with whatever was correct and healthy in the old. However, this model of faith stands in significant contrast to the widely-held view that religious faith is essentially or fundamentally irrational (and blind) in its very nature.
29. Bahá'u'lláh, *Gleanings*, pp. 4-5.
30. ibid. 326-7.
31. ibid. p. 70.
32. ibid. pp. 164-5.

33. ibid. p. 68.
34. It is interesting that modern science and modern scientific philosophy take essentially the same view of human knowledge. I have elsewhere treated this theme at some length (see 'The Science of Religion', *Bahá'í Studies*, vol. 2, 1980), but will not enter into the discussion of such questions here.
35. He explicitly mentioned sense experience, reason, inspiration or intuition, and scriptural authority.
36. 'Abdu'l-Bahá, *Promulgation*, pp. 253-5.
37. 'Abdu'l-Bahá, *Some Answered Questions*, p. 157.
38. ibid. pp. 157-8.
39. ibid. pp. 220-1.
40. Some mystics and religious philosophers have contended that our knowledge of God is absolute and for that reason superior to the relative and limited knowledge obtained by science. Such thinkers offer mysticism as an alternative discipline to science. It is important to realize that the Bahá'í Faith does not lend support to such a view. In particular, concerning the inherent limitations of the individual's intuitive powers, however disciplined or well-developed, Shoghi Effendi has said:

> With regard to your question as to the value of intuition as a source of guidance for the individual; implicit faith in our intuitive powers is unwise, but through daily prayer and sustained effort one can discover, though not always and fully, God's Will intuitively. Under no circumstances, however, can a person be absolutely certain that he is recognizing God's Will, through the exercise of his intuition. It often happens that the latter results in completely misrepresenting the truth, and thus becomes a source of error rather than of guidance . . .

Moreover, the Bahá'í writings clearly recognize that the human mind has a capacity for self-generated illusion which, if not recognized by the individual, can lead him into serious error:

> You yourself must surely know that modern psychology has taught that the capacity of the human mind for believing what it imagines, is almost infinite. Because people think they have a certain type of experience, think they remember something of a previous life, does not mean

they actually had the experience, or existed previously. The power of their mind would be quite sufficient to make them believe firmly such a thing had happened.

This latter passage is also by Shoghi Effendi and both statements are quoted in a letter written by the Universal House of Justice to an individual Bahá'í.

41. In particular, the Manifestations of God represent objective and universally accessible expressions of God's Will. Humanity's interaction with the Manifestations provides an important opportunity to experience concretely a phenomenon which man cannot manipulate or dominate. The Manifestations likewise provide a challenge to each individual's capacity to respond adequately to the divine Will.

42. Another important dimension of spirituality is service to the collectivity. The development of one's spiritual and material capacities makes one a more valuable servant. More will be said about this in a later section.

43. Concerning the necessity of such suffering in the pursuit of spirituality, 'Abdu'l-Bahá has said: 'Everything of importance in this world demands the close attention of its seeker. The one in pursuit of anything must undergo difficulties and hardships until the object in view is attained and the great success is obtained. This is the case of things pertaining to the world. How much higher is that which concerns the Supreme Concourse!' *Divine Art of Living,* p. 92.

44. Townshend, *Mission of Bahá'u'lláh,* pp. 99-100,

45. Bahá'u'lláh, *Kitáb-i-Íqán,* p. 195.

46. ibid. pp. 195-6. Bahá'u'lláh's reference in this passage to 'absolute certitude' might be perceived at first as contradicting the strong statements regarding the limitations on human knowledge which we have earlier quoted. However, this superficial perception is relieved when we reflect that 'certitude' refers to a (psychological) state of being whereas the notion of 'degree of certainty' (and in particular the question of whether knowledge is relative or absolute) is concerned rather with the criteria of verification available to man as knowing subject. Thus Bahá'u'lláh would seem to be saying that man can attain to a sense of absolute certitude even though his criteria of verification, and thus his knowledge, remain limited. Also, it is clear that such phrases as 'the eye of God' should be taken metaphorically and not literally.

This metaphor, together with other such phrases as 'new life' and 'absolute certitude', convey a strong sense of the discontinuity between the respective degrees of understanding possessed by the individual before and after his attainment of true self-knowledge.

47. 'Abdu'l-Bahá, *Some Answered Questions*, pp. 230-1.
48. ibid. p. 237.
49. 'Abdu'l-Bahá, cited in *Dynamic Force of Example*, p. 50.
50. ibid. p. 51.
51. 'Abdu'l-Bahá, *Divine Art of Living*, p. 25.
52. This point of view on spirituality is in sharp contrast with the viewpoint found in many contemporary cults and sects which stress instant gratification and irresponsibility in the name of honesty and spontaneity.
53. Shoghi Effendi, in *Bahá'í Life*, p. 2.
54. 'Abdu'l-Bahá, in *Divine Art of Living*, p. 51.
55. Bahá'u'lláh, *Tablets*, p. 138.
56. In an exponential process, the rate of growth at any given stage of the process is directly proportional to the total growth attained at that stage. Thus, as the process develops and progress is made, the rate of progress increases. An example would be a production process such that the total amount produced at any given stage is double the total amount produced at the previous stage (imagine a reproduction process in which bacteria double each second, starting with one bacterium). Since the double of a large number represents a much greater increase than the double of a small number, doubling is an example of an exponential law of progress.
57. Bahá'u'lláh has stressed that the merit of all deeds is dependent upon God's acceptance (cf. Synopsis and Codification of the Kitáb-i-Aqdas, p. 52), and 'Abdu'l-Bahá has said that 'good actions alone, without the knowledge of God, cannot be the cause of eternal salvation, everlasting success, and prosperity, and entrance into the Kingdom of God.' *Some Answered Questions*, p. 238. On the other hand, knowledge without action is also declared to be unacceptable: 'Mere knowledge of principles is not sufficient. We all know and admit that justice is good but there is need of volition and action to carry out and manifest it.' 'Abdu'l-Bahá, *Foundations of World Unity*, p. 26. At the same time, love and sincere good intentions alone are also insufficient for spiritual progress, for they need to be guided by knowledge and wisdom and expressed through action. Moreover, without true self-knowledge we may sometimes mistake physical attraction or

self-centered emotional need as love and act upon it with negative results.

58. At this point in our development, it is difficult if not impossible to know how much of our mode of functioning is due to our innate qualities and how much is due to the cumulative influence of external conditions. Thus our spontaneous response pattern may be a reasonably authentic expression of our true selves or it may contain significant distortions. It is only by moving on to the next stage of self-aware, self-directed growth that we can gain insight into this question.

59. If a person has been fortunate in the quality of spiritual education he has received during his formative years, his spontaneous system of functioning may be very good indeed compared with others in less fortunate circumstances. If his spiritual education has been especially good, he will have already learned and understood the necessity of assuming the responsibility for his own spiritual growth process (and will have already begun to do so as an adolescent). In such cases as these, the individual will not need any test or dramatic setback in order to awaken him to spiritual realities of which he is already aware. Indeed, the Bahá'í writings explain that the very purpose of the spiritual education of children and youth is to lead them to such an understanding of spiritual realities that, upon reaching adulthood, they will be naturally equipped to take charge of their own lives and spiritual growth processes. Spiritual education of this quality is extremely rare (in fact virtually nonexistent) in our society today, but the Bahá'í writings contain many principles and techniques for the spiritual education of children and affirm that the application of these principles will, in the future, enable the majority of people to attain the age of adulthood with a clear understanding of the dynamics of the spiritual growth process. Though this state of affairs will not eliminate all human suffering (in particular suffering which comes from physical accidents or certain illnesses), it will eliminate that considerable proportion of human suffering which is generated by the sick, distorted and destructive response patterns and modes of functioning so widespread in current society.

60. The answer may be that our expectations were unreasonable to begin with. In this way, failure to obtain some particular external goal can lead to success in gaining valid knowledge and insight into our internal processes, thus fostering spiritual growth. Indeed,

there is very little that happens to us in life that cannot be used to give us new self-insight and hence contribute to fulfilling the basic purpose of prosecuting the spiritual growth process. It sometimes happens that a person whose spontaneous level of functioning is quite weak and defective is soon led to discover this fact while a person whose spontaneous level of functioning is rather high (due to favorable circumstances in early life or to exceptional natural endowments) persists for many years in his spiritually unaware state, making no spiritual progress whatever. In this way, the person whose spontaneous level of functioning is weak may take charge of his growth process much sooner than others and thereby eventually surpass those with more favorable natural endowments or initial life circumstances.

61. Regarding the spiritual meaning and purpose of suffering, 'Abdu'l-Bahá has said: 'Tests are benefits from God, for which we should thank Him. Grief and sorrow do not come to us by chance, they are sent to us by the Divine mercy for our own perfecting . . . The mind and spirit of man advance when he is tried by suffering . . . suffering and tribulation free man from the petty affairs of this worldly life until he arrives at a state of complete detachment. His attitude in this world will be that of divine happiness . . . Through suffering (one) will attain to an eternal happiness which nothing can take from him . . . To attain eternal happiness one must suffer. He who has reached the state of self-sacrifice has true joy. Temporal joy will vanish. 'Abdu'l-Bahá, *Divine Art of Living*, pp. 89-90.

62. Naturally, it is heartening to see examples of murderers, thieves, rapists or drug addicts who turn themselves around and become useful members of society and occasionally morally and intellectually superior human beings. But one can also deplore the fact that people with such potential and talents must waste so many years and cause so much suffering to themselves and others before realizing their potential.

63. Words attributed to 'Abdu'l-Bahá in answer to questions asked by Dr Edward Getsinger. *Star of the West*, vol. 6, no. 6, p. 45.

64. Of course, if our parents and educators have also had the Bahá'í viewpoint of the nature of man, this will have contributed to our development during our formative years. However, our future growth and development will depend on whatever attitudes and viewpoints we personally maintain. Nevertheless, we will continue to be significantly affected by our interactions with others

REFERENCES AND NOTES, pp. 189-250.

and therefore by the attitudes and viewpoints which they have. More will be said about this point in a later section.
65. This hypothetical example serves to stress an important point concerning the Bahá'í view of human nature. To say that human nature, in both its material and spiritual aspects, is good means that all of man's natural needs and urges are God-given. Since Bahá'ís also believe that God's purpose for mankind is positive and beneficial, it follows that there is a legitimate, God-given (and truly satisfactory) way of meeting every natural internal human need. Such a view contrasts sharply with the idea that some of man's basic urges are intrinsically evil and/or inherently socially (and self) destructive. The Bahá'í view of man certainly recognizes that the perversion of a natural capacity or need can lead to virulent social, psychological, moral and spiritual ills, and that dealing with people or groups so afflicted can be extremely difficult. Nevertheless, in effecting a cure even of these terrible spiritual pathologies, it is helpful to realize that the process is based on teaching (and learning) detachment from the false pattern and attachment to the healthy one rather than the purely negative attempt to suppress unacceptable behavior.
66. Bahá'u'lláh, *Gleanings*, pp. 194-5.
67. 'Abdu'l-Bahá, *Some Answered Questions*, p. 300.
68. ibid.
69. ibid. p. 302.
70. 'Abdu'l-Bahá in *Bahá'í World Faith*, pp. 382-3.
71. 'Abdu'l-Bahá, in *Divine Art of Living*, p. 19.
72. 'Abdu'l-Bahá, in *Star of the West*, vol. 17, p. 286.
73. Shoghi Effendi, in *Bahá'í Life, p. 20.*
74. Shoghi Effendi, *Directives*, pp. 86-7.
75. 'Abdu'l-Bahá, *Paris Talks*, pp. 164-5.
76. ibid. p. 175.
77. Bahá'u'lláh, *Kitáb-i-Íqán*, p. 238. These strong statements of Bahá'u'lláh and 'Abdu'l-Bahá concerning meditation should not, however, be taken as implying an absolute faith in man's intuitive powers. See note 40.
78. 'Abdu'l-Bahá, in *Divine Art of Living*, p. 27.
79. ibid. p. 65.
80. 'Abdu'l-Bahá, in *Bahá'í Magazine*, vol. 19, no. 3, 1928.
81. Bahá'u'lláh, *Gleanings*, p. 215.
82. 'Abdu'l-Bahá, *Faith for Every Man*, p. 43.
83. Bahá'u'lláh, *Gleanings*, pp. 79-80.

84. ibid. pp. 50-2.
85. Shoghi Effendi, *World Order*, p. 202.
86. ibid. pp. 42-3.
87. ibid. p. 163.
88. Shoghi Effendi, quoted in *The Spiritual Revolution*, p. 9.
89. Bahá'u'lláh, quoted in a letter from the Universal House of Justice, *Bahá'í Canada*, June-July 1978, p. 3.
90. Success in the pursuit of dominance must be distinguished from success in the pursuit of excellence. Striving for excellence is highly encouraged in the Bahá'í writings. That the two pursuits are different, and that competitive struggle with others is not necessary to attain excellence, are important spiritual and psychological insights.
91. Bahá'u'lláh, *Hidden Words*.

ABOUT THE AUTHORS

JOHN S. HATCHER is Professor of English literature at the University of South Florida in Tampa where he specializes in medieval literature and creative writing. Dr Hatcher has published poetry in a variety of national and international poetry journals and literary periodicals, and a collection of his verse, *A Sense of History*, was published in 1990. His historical novel *Ali's Dream* was published in 1980 and is being translated for publication in French, Greek and Latvian. A second novel, *Conversations*, was published in 1988. He is presently under contract to translate into English the poetry of the nineteenth century Persian poetess Ṭáhirih.

Dr Hatcher's scholarly work spans a variety of fields. He has completed a book-length study of Chaucer's imagery, and *From the Auroral Darkness*, Hatcher's study of the life and poetry of American poet Robert Hayden, was published in 1984 and received praise in such periodicals as *Choice* and *Black American Literature Forum*. His comparative study of theodicy, *The Purpose of Physical Reality: The Kingdom of Names*, published in 1987 is in its third printing and was reviewed in the prestigious *Encyclopédie Philosophique Universelle* vol III, a dictionary of the world's philosophical works published by the Presses Universitaire de France, 1992. Dr Hatcher's sequel to that work, *The Arc of Ascent*, was published in April of 1994. His forthcoming literary analysis of Bahá'u'lláh's works, *The Ocean of His Words: A Literary Guide to the Revelation of Bahá'u'lláh*, is due to be published in 1996.

Raised in the Protestant religion, Dr Hatcher subsequently learned about the Bahá'í Faith from his brother, William S. Hatcher, becoming a member in 1960. Since that time he has served the Bahá'í Faith in various administrative capacities and has lectured extensively in a variety of public forums, at universities, and on radio and television. His course on the Bahá'í Faith at the University of South Florida was the first college credit course to be taught on this religion. Dr Hatcher has four children and two grandchildren. His wife Lucia owns and is principal teacher for Firethorn School of Dance in Temple Terrace, Florida, where she has trained dancers for some of the major dance companies in the United States.

ABOUT THE AUTHORS

WILLIAM S. HATCHER is a mathematician, philosopher and educator. He holds a doctorate in mathematics from the University of Neuchâtel in Switzerland and bachelor's and master's degrees from Vanderbilt University in Nashville, Tennessee. A specialist in the philosophical interpenetration of science and religion, he has, for over thirty years, held university positions in Europe and North America, most recently as Professor of Mathematics at Laval University un Quebec City, Canada.

Dr Hatcher has lectured widely in North America, Europe and Russia. He is the author or co-author of over fifty professional articles, books and monographs in the mathematical sciences, logic and philosophy. Among his best known works are *The Logical Foundations of Mathematics* (Oxford: Pergamon Press, 1982) and *The Bahá'í Faith: The Emerging Global Religion* (San Francisco: Harper & Row, 1985), which he co-authored with J. Douglas Martin and which was designated as a 'Book of the Year' in the field of religious studies by the *Encyclopædia Britannica* in 1986. Dr Hatcher's *Logic and Logos* (Oxford: George Ronald, 1990), a collection of essays on science, religion and philosophy, was reviewed in the highly regarded *Encyclopédie Philosophique Universelle* vol III, a dictionary of the world's philosophical works published by the Presses Universitaire de France, 1992. In this same compendium, Dr Hatcher is one of eight Platonist philosophers listed for the second half of the twentieth century. More recently, he has authored the comprehensive article on 'The Foundations of Mathematics' for the 1997 edition of the *Encyclopædia Britannica*.

Raised in the Protestant religion, Dr Hatcher had determined to enter the ministry upon completing his undergraduate studies and toward that end had received a scholarship to attend Yale Divinity School. However, after having studied the Bahá'í Faith for several years, he became a Bahá'í in 1957 and thus changed his professional orientation to a career in mathematics. Since that time, he has served the Bahá'í community in a wide variety of capacities and is currently a member of the National Spiritual Assembly of the Bahá'ís of the Russian Federation. He and his wife Judith reside and work in St Petersburg, Russia. They have three children and five grandchildren.